MYTH, RI...

RELIGION

VOLUME ONE

MYTH, RITUAL &
RELIGION

VOLUME ONE

ANDREW LANG

SENATE

Myth, Ritual and Religion, Volume One

This impression first published in 1913 by
Longmans, Green and Co., London

This edition published in 1995 by Senate, an imprint of
Studio Editions Ltd, Princess House, 50 Eastcastle
Street, London W1N 7AP, England

Cover design © Studio Editions Ltd 1995

ISBN 1 85958 182 X

Printed and bound in Guernsey by
The Guernsey Press Co. Ltd

In Memoriam.

W. Y. SELLAR.

CONTENTS.

CONTENTS.

CHAPTER III.

CHAPTER IV.

CHAPTER V.

CHAPTER IX.

The Greeks practically civilised when we first meet them in Homer
—Their mythology, however, is full of repulsive features—The
hypothesis that many of these are savage survivals—Are there
other examples of such survival in Greek life and institutions?
—Greek opinion was constant that the race had been savage—
Illustrations of savage survival from Greek law of homicide,
from magic, religion, human sacrifice, religious art, traces of
totemism, and from the mysteries—Conclusion : that savage
survival may also be expected in Greek myths.

CHAPTER X.

Nature of the evidence—Traditions of origin of the world and man
—Homeric, Hesiodic and Orphic myths—Later evidence of
historians, dramatists, commentators—The Homeric story comparatively pure—The story in Hesiod, and its savage analogues
—The explanations of the myth of Cronus, modern and ancient
—The Orphic cosmogony—Phanes and Prajapati—Greek myths
of the origin of man—Their savage analogues.

CHAPTER XI.

The origin of a belief in GOD beyond the ken of history and of
speculation—Sketch of conjectural theories—Two elements in
all beliefs, whether of backward or civilised races—The *Mythical*
and the *Religious*—These may be coeval, or either may be older
than the other—Difficulty of study—The current anthropological
theory—Stated objections to the theory—Gods and spirits—
Suggestion that savage religion is borrowed from Europeans—
Reply to Mr. Tylor's arguments on this head—The morality of
savages.

PREFACE TO NEW IMPRESSION.

WHEN this book first appeared (1886), the philological school of interpretation of religion and myth, being then still powerful in England, was criticised and opposed by the author. In Science, as on the Turkish throne of old, "Amurath to Amurath succeeds"; the philological theories of religion and myth have now yielded to anthropological methods. The centre of the anthropological position was the "ghost theory" of Mr. Herbert Spencer, the "Animistic" theory of Mr. E. R. Tylor, according to whom the propitiation of ancestral and other spirits leads to polytheism, and thence to monotheism. In the second edition (1901) of this work the author argued that the belief in a "relatively supreme being," anthropomorphic was as old as, and might be even older, than animistic religion. This theory he exhibited at greater length, and with a larger collection of evidence, in his *Making of Religion*.

Since 1901, a great deal of fresh testimony as to what Mr. Howitt styles the "All Father" in savage and barbaric religions has accrued. As regards this being in Africa, the reader may consult the volumes

of the New Series of the *Journal of the Anthropological Institute,* which are full of African evidence,
not, as yet, discussed, to my knowledge, by any writer
on the History of Religion.   As late as *Man,* for July,
1906, No. 66, Mr. Parkinson published interesting
Yoruba legends about Oleron, the maker and father
of men, and Oro, the Master of the Bull Roarer.

From Australia, we have Mr. Howitt's account of
the All Father in his *Native Tribes of South-East
Australia,* with the account of the All Father of
the Central Australian tribe, the Kaitish, in *North
Central Tribes of Australia,* by Messrs. Spencer and
Gillen (1904), also *The Euahlayi Tribe,* by Mrs.
Langley Parker (1906).   These masterly books are
indispensable to all students of the subject, while, in
Messrs. Spencer and Gillen's work cited, and in
their earlier *Native Tribes of Central Australia,* we
are introduced to savages who offer an elaborate
animistic theory, and are said to show no traces of
the All Father belief.

The books of Messrs. Spencer and Gillen also present much evidence as to a previously unknown form
of totemism, in which the totem is not hereditary,
and does not regulate marriage.   This prevails
among the Arunta "nation," and the Kaitish tribe.
In the opinion of Mr. Spencer (*Report Australian
Association for Advancement of Science,* 1904) and
of Mr. J. G. Frazer (*Fortnightly Review,* Septem-
ber, 1905), this is the earliest surviving form of
totemism, and Mr. Frazer suggests an animistic
origin for the institution.   I have criticised these
views in *The Secret of the Totem* (1905), and pro-

posed a different solution of the problem. (See also "Primitive and Advanced Totemism" in *Journal of the Anthropological Institute*, July, 1906.) In the works mentioned will be found references to other sources of information as to these questions, which are still *sub judice*. Mrs. Bates, who has been studying the hitherto almost unknown tribes of Western Australia, promises a book on their beliefs and institutions, and Mr. N. W. Thomas is engaged on a volume on Australian institutions. In this place the author can only direct attention to these novel sources, and to the promised third edition of Mr. Frazer's *The Golden Bough*.

A. L.

PREFACE TO NEW EDITION.

THE original edition of *Myth, Ritual and Religion*, published in 1887, has long been out of print. In revising the book I have brought it into line with the ideas expressed in the second part of my *Making of Religion* (1898) and have excised certain passages which, as the book first appeared, were inconsistent with its main thesis. In some cases the original passages are retained in notes, to show the nature of the development of the author's opinions. A fragment or two of controversy has been deleted, and chapters xi. and xii., on the religion of the lowest races, have been entirely rewritten, on the strength of more recent or earlier information lately acquired. The gist of the book as it stands now and as it originally stood is contained in the following lines from the preface of 1887 : "While the attempt is made to show that the wilder features of myth survive from, or were borrowed from, or were imitated from the ideas of people in the savage condition of thought, the existence—even among savages—of comparatively pure, if inarticulate, religious beliefs is insisted on

throughout ". To that opinion I adhere, and I trust
that it is now expressed with more consistency than
in the first edition. I have seen reason, more and
more, to doubt the validity of the " ghost theory,"
or animistic hypothesis, as explanatory of the whole
fabric of religion ; and I present arguments against
Mr. Tylor's contention that the higher conceptions
of savage faith are borrowed from missionaries.[1]
It is very possible, however, that Mr. Tylor has
arguments more powerful than those contained in
his paper of 1892. For our information is not yet
adequate to a scientific theory of the Origin of
Religion, and probably never will be. Behind the
races whom we must regard as " nearest the beginning" are their unknown ancestors from a dateless
past, men as human as ourselves, but men concerning
whose psychical, mental and moral condition we can
only form conjectures. Among them religion arose,
in circumstances of which we are necessarily ignorant.
Thus I only venture on a surmise as to the germ of
a faith in a Maker (if I am not to say " Creator ")
and Judge of men. But, as to whether the higher
religious belief, or the lower mythical stories came
first, we are at least certain that the Christian
conception of God, given pure, was presently en-
tangled, by the popular fancy of Europe, in new *Märchen* about the Deity, the Madonna, her Son, and

---

[1] Tylor, " Limits of Savage Religion." *Journal of the Anthropological
Institute*, vol. xxi.

the Apostles. Here, beyond possibility of denial, pure belief came first. fanciful legend was attached after. I am inclined to surmise that this has always been the case, and, in the pages on the legend of Zeus, I show the processes of degeneration, of mythical accretions on a faith in a Heaven-God, in action. That "the feeling of religious devotion" attests "high faculties" in early man (such as are often denied to men who "cannot count up to seven"), and that "the same high mental faculties . . . would infallibly lead him, as long as his reasoning powers remained poorly developed, to various strange superstitions and customs," was the belief of Mr. Darwin.[1] That is also my view, and I note that the lowest savages are not yet guilty of the very worst practices, "sacrifice of human beings to a blood-loving God," and ordeals by poison and fire, to which Mr. Darwin alludes. "The improvement of our science" has freed us from misdeeds which are unknown to the Andamanese or the Australians. Thus there was, as regards these points in morals, degeneracy from savagery as society advanced, and I believe that there was also degeneration in religion. To say this is not to hint at a theory of supernatural revelation to the earliest men, a theory which I must, *in limine* disclaim.

In vol. ii. p. 19 occurs a reference, in a note, to Mr. Hartland's criticism of my ideas about Australian.

---

[1] *Descent of Man*, p. 68, 1871.

gods as set forth in the *Making of Religion*. Mr.
Hartland, who kindly read the chapters on Australian
religion in this book, does not consider that my note
on p. 19 meets the point of his argument. As to the
Australians, I mean no more than that, *among*
endless low myths, some of them possess a belief in
a "maker of everything," a primal being, still in
existence, watching conduct, punishing breaches of
his laws, and, in some cases, rewarding the good in
a future life. Of course these are the germs of a
sympathetic religion, even if the being thus regarded
is mixed up with immoral or humorous contradictory
myths. My position is not harmed by such myths,
which occur in all old religions, and, in the middle
ages, new myths were attached to the sacred figures
of Christianity in poetry and popular tales.

Thus, if there is nothing "sacred" in a religion
because wild or wicked fables about the gods also
occur, there is nothing "sacred" in almost any
religion on earth.

Mr. Hartland's point, however, seems to be that,
in the *Making of Religion*, I had selected certain
Australian beliefs as especially "sacred" and to be
distinguished from others, because they are inculcated
at the religious Mysteries of some tribes. His aim,
then, is to discover low, wild, immoral myths, inculcated at the Mysteries, and thus to destroy my line
drawn between religion on one hand and myth or
mere folk-lore on the other. Thus there is a being
named Daramulun, of whose rites, among the Coast

Murring, I condensed the account of Mr. Howitt.[1]
From a statement by Mr. Greenway[2] Mr. Hartland
learned that Daramulun's name is said to mean " leg
on one side " or " lame ".   He, therefore, with fine
humour, speaks of Daramulun as " a creator with a
game leg," though when " Baıame " is derived by two
excellent linguists, Mr. Ridley and Mr. Greenway,
from Kamilaroi *baia*, " to make," Mr. Hartland is by
no means so sure of the sense of the name.   It
happens to be inconvenient to him !   Let the names
mean what they may, Mr. Hartland finds, in an
obiter dictum of Mr. Howitt (before he was initiated),
that Daramulun is said to have " died," and that his
spirit is now aloft.   Who says so, and where, we are
not informed,[3] and the question is important.

For the Wiraijuri, *in their mysteries*, tell a myth
of cannibal conduct of Daramulun's, and of deceit and
failure of knowledge in Baiame.[4]   Of this I was
unaware, or neglected it, for I explicitly said that I
followed Mr. Howitt's account, where no such matter
is mentioned.   Mr. Howitt, in fact, described the
Mysteries of the Coast Murring, while the narrator
of the low myths, Mr. Matthews, described those of a
remote tribe, the Wiraijuri, with whom Daramulun
is not the chief, but a subordinate person.   How Mr.
Matthews' friends can at once hold that Daramulun
was " destroyed " by Baiame (their chief deity), and
also that Daramulun's voice is heard at their rites, I

[1] *J. A. I.*, xiii. pp. 440-459.   [2] *Ibid.*, xxi. p. 294.
[3] *Ibid.*, xiii. p. 194.   [4] *Ibid.*, xxv. p. 297.

don't know.[1] Nor do I know why Mr. Hartland
takes the myth of a tribe where Daramulun is " the
evil spirit who rules the night," [2] and introduces it as
an argument against the belief of a distant tribe,
where, by Mr. Howitt's account, Daramulun is not
an evil spirit, but " the master " of all, whose abode
is above the sky, and to whom are attributed powers
of omnipotence and omnipresence, or, at any rate,
the power " to do anything and to go anywhere. . . .
To his direct ordinances are attributed the social and
moral laws of the community." [3] This is not " an
evil spirit " ! When Mr. Hartland goes for scandals
to a remote tribe of a different creed that he may
discredit the creed of the Coast Murring, he might as
well attribute to the Free Kirk " the errors of Rome ".
But Mr. Hartland does it ! [4] Being " cunning of
fence " he may reply that I also spoke loosely
of Wiraijuri and Coast Murring as, indifferently,
Daramulunites. I did, and I was wrong, and my
critic ought not to accept but to expose my error.
The Wiraijuri Daramulun, who was annihilated, yet
who is " an evil spirit that rules the night," is not the
Murring guardian and founder of recognised ethics.

But, in the Wiraijuri mysteries, the master,
Baiame, deceives the women as to the Mysteries!
Shocking to *us*, but to deceive the women as to these
arcana, is, to the Australian mind in general, necessary for the safety of the world. Moreover, we have

[1] *J. A. I.*, May, 1895, p. 419.   [2] *Ibid.*
[3] *Ibid.*, xiii. pp. 458, 459.   [4] *Folk-Lore*, ix., No. iv., p. 299.

heard of a lying spirit sent to deceive prophets in a much higher creed. Finally, in a myth of the Mystery of the Wiraijuri, Baiame is not omniscient. Indeed, even civilised races cannot keep on the level of these religious conceptions, and not to keep on that level is—mythology. Apollo, in the hymn to Hermes, sung on a sacred occasion, needs to ask an old vine-dresser for intelligence. Hyperion "sees all and hears all," but needs to be informed, by his daughters, of the slaughter of his kine. The Lord, in the Book of Job, has to ask Satan, "Whence comest thou?" Now for the sake of dramatic effect, now from pure inability to live on the level of his highest thought, man mythologises and anthropomorphises, in Greece or Israel, as in Australia.

It does not follow that there is "nothing sacred" in his religion. Mr. Hartland offers me a case in point. In Mrs. Langloh Parker's *Australian Legendary Tales* (pp. 11, 94), are myths of low adventures of Baiame. In her *More Australian Legendary Tales* (pp. 84-99), is a very poetical and charming aspect of the Baiame belief. Mr. Hartland says that I will "seek to put" the first set of stories out of court, as "a kind of joke with no sacredness about it". Not I, but the Noongahburrah tribe themselves make this essential distinction. Mrs. Langloh Parker says : [1] "The former series" (with the low Baiame myths) " were all such legends as are told to the black

---

[1] *More Legendary Tales*, p. xv.

picaninnies; among the present are some they would
not be allowed to hear, *touching as they do on sacred
things, taboo to the young*". The blacks draw the
line which I am said to seek to draw.

In yet another case [1] grotesque hunting adventures
of Baiame are told in the mysteries, and illustrated
by the sacred temporary representations in raised
earth. I did not know it; I merely followed Mr.
Howitt. But I do not doubt it. My reply is, that
there was "something sacred" in Greek mysteries,
something purifying, ennobling, consoling. For this
Lobeck has collected (and disparaged) the evidence
of Pindar, Sophocles, Cicero and many others, while
even Aristophanes, as Prof. Campbell remarks, says:
"We only have bright sun and cheerful life who have
been initiated and lived piously in regard to strangers
and to private citizens".[2] Security and peace of
mind, in this world and for the next, were, we know
not how, borne into the hearts of Pindar and
Sophocles in the Mysteries. Yet, if we may at all
trust the Fathers, there were scenes of debauchery,
as at the Mysteries of the Fijians (*Nanga*) there was
buffoonery ("to amuse the boys," Mr. Howitt says
of some Australian rites), the story of Baubo is
only one example, and, in other mysteries than the
Eleusinian, we know of mummeries in which an

---

[1] *J. A. I.*, xxiv. p. 416.

[2] *Religion in Greek Literature*, p. 259. It is to be regretted that the
learned professor gives no references. The Greek Mysteries are treated
later in this volume.

absurd tale of Zeus is related in connection with an oak log. Yet surely there was " something sacred " in the faith of Zeus ! Let us judge the Australians as we judge Greeks. The precepts as to " speaking the straightforward truth," as to unselfishness, avoidance of quarrels, of wrongs to " unprotected women," of unnatural vices, are certainly communicated in the Mysteries of some tribes, with, in another, knowledge of the name and nature of " Our Father," Munganngaur. That a Totemistic dance, or medicine-dance of Emu hunting, is also displayed[1] at certain Mysteries of a given tribe, and that Baiame is spoken of as the hero of this *ballet*, no more deprives the Australian moral and religious teaching (at the Mysteries) of sacred value, than the stupid indecency whereby Baubo made Demeter laugh destroys the sacredness of the Eleusinia, on which Pindar, Sophocles and Cicero eloquently dwell. If the Australian mystæ, at the most solemn moment of their lives, are shown a dull or dirty divine *ballet d'action*, what did Sophocles see, after taking a swim with his pig ? Many things far from edifying, yet the sacred element of religious hope and faith was also represented. So it is in Australia.

These studies ought to be comparative, otherwise they are worthless. As Mr. Hartland calls Daramulun "an eternal Creator with a game leg," who "died," he may call Zeus an " eternal father, who swallowed

---

[1] See *A Picture of Australia*, 1829, p. 264.

his wife, lay with his mother and sister, made love as
a swan, and died, nay, was buried, in Crete ". I
do not think that Mr. Hartland would call Zeus
" a ghost-god " (my own phrase), or think that he
was scoring a point against me, if I spoke of the
sacred and ethical characteristics of the Zeus adored
by Eumæus in the *Odyssey*. He would not be so
humorous about Zeus, nor fall into an *ignoratio
elenchi*. For my point never was that any Australian
tribe had a pure theistic conception unsoiled and un-
obliterated by myth and buffoonery. My argument
was that *among* their ideas is that of a superhuman
being, unceasing (if I may not say eternal), a maker
(if I may not say a Creator), a guardian of certain by
no means despicable ethics, which I never proclaimed
as supernormally inspired ! It is no reply to me to say
that, in or out of Mysteries, low fables about that
being are told, and buffooneries are enacted. For,
though I say that certain high ideas are taught in
Mysteries, I do not think I say that in Mysteries no
low myths are told.

I take this opportunity, as the earliest, to apologise for an error in my *Making of Religion* concerning a passage in the *Primitive Culture* of my friend
Mr. E. B. Tylor. Mr. Tylor quoted [1] a passage from
Captain John Smith's *History of Virginia*, as given
in *Pinkerton*, xiii. pp. 13-39, 1632. In this passage
no mention occurs of a Virginian deity named Ahone

---

[1] *Prim. Cult.*, ii. p. 342.

but "Okee," another and more truculent god, is
named. I observed that, if Mr. Tylor had used
Strachey's *Historie of Travaile* (1612), he would
have found " a slightly varying copy " of Smith's
text of 1632, with Ahone as superior to Okee. I
added in a note (p. 253) : " There is a description of
Virginia, by W. Strachey, including Smith's remarks
published in 1612. Strachey interwove some of this
work with his own MS. in the British Museum."
Here, as presently will be shown, I erred, in company
with Strachey's editor of 1849, and with the writer
on Strachey in the *Dictionary of National Bio-
graphy*. What Mr. Tylor quoted from an edition
of Smith in 1632 had already appeared, in 1612,
in a book (*Map of Virginia, with a description of
the Countrey*) described on the title-page as " written
by Captain Smith," though, in my opinion, Smith
may have had a collaborator. There is no evidence
whatever that Strachey had anything to do with
this book of 1612, in which there is no mention of
Ahone. Mr. Arber dates Strachey's own MS. (in
which Ahone occurs) as of 1610-1615.[1] I myself,
for reasons presently to be alleged, date the MS.
mainly in 1611-1612. If Mr. Arber and I are right,
Strachey must have had access to Smith's MS.
before it was published in 1612, and we shall see
how he used it. My point here is that Strachey
mentioned Ahone (in MS.) before Smith's book of

---

[1] Arber's *Smith*, p. cxxxiii.

1612 was published. This could not be gathered
from the dedication to Bacon prefixed to Strachey's
MS., for that dedication cannot be earlier that 1618.[1]
I now ask leave to discuss the evidence for an early
pre-Christian belief in a primal Creator, held by the
Indian tribes from Plymouth, in New England, to
Roanoke Island, off Southern Virginia.

THE GOD AHONE.

An insertion by a manifest plagiary into the work
of a detected liar is not, usually, good evidence.
Yet this is all the evidence, it may be urged, which
we have for the existence of a belief, in early Virginia,
as to a good Creator, named Ahone. The matter
stands thus : In 1607-1609 the famed Captain John
Smith endured and achieved in Virginia sufferings
and adventures. In 1608 he sent to the Council at
home a MS. map and description of the colony. In
1609 he returned to England (October). In May,
1610, William Strachey, gent., arrived in Virginia,
where he was " secretary of state " to Lord De la
Warr. In 1612 Strachey and Smith were both in
England. In that year Barnes of Oxford published
A Map of Virginia, with a description, etc.,
" written by Captain Smith," according to the title-
page. There was annexed a compilation from various
sources, edited by " W. S.," that is, *not* William
Strachey, but Dr. William Symonds. In the same
year, 1612, or in 1611, William Strachey wrote his

[1] Hakluyt Society, *Strachey*, 1849, pp. xxi., xxii.

Historie of Travaile into Virginia Britannia, at least as far as page 124 of the Hakluyt edition of 1849.[1]

If Strachey, who went out with Lord De la Warr as secretary in 1610, returned with him (as is likely), he sailed for England on 28th March, 1611. In that case, he was in England in 1611, and the passages cited leave it dubious whether he wrote his book in 1611, 1612, or in both years.[2]

Strachey embodies in his work considerable pieces of Smith's *Map of Virginia and Description,* written in 1608, and published in 1612. He continually deserts Smith, however, adding more recent information, reflections and references to the ancient classics, with allusions to his own travels in the Levant. His glossary is much more extensive than Smith's, and he inserts a native song of triumph over the English in the original.[3] Now, when Strachey comes to the religion of the natives [4] he gives eighteen pages (much of it verbiage) to five of Smith's.[5] What Smith (1612) says of their chief

---

[1] For proof see p. 24, third line from foot of page, where 1612 is indi cated. Again, see p. 98, line 5, where "last year" is dated as "1610, about Christmas," which would put Strachey's work at this point as actually of 1611 ; prior, that is, to Smith's publication. Again, p. 124, "this last year, myself being at the Falls" (of the James River), "I found in an Indian house certain clawes . . . which I brought away and into England".

[2] Mr. Arber dates the MS. "1610-1615," and attributes to Strachey *Laws for Virginia,* 1612.

[3] Strachey, pp. 79-80. He may have got the song from Kemps or Machumps, friendly natives.

[4] Pp. 82-100.   [5] Arber, pp. 74-79

god I quote, setting Strachey's version (1611-1612)
beside it.

SMITH (*Published*, 1612).

But their chiefe God
they worship is the Diuell.
Him they call *Oke*, and
serue him more of feare
than loue. They say they
haue conference with him,
and fashion themselues
as neare to his shape as
they can imagine. In
their Temples, they have
his image euile favouredly
carved, and then painted,
and adorned with chaines,
copper, and beades ; and
couered with a skin, in
such manner as the de-
formity may well suit with
such a God. By him is
commonly the sepulcher
of their Kings.

STRACHEY (*Written*, 1611-12).

But their chief god they worship is
no other, indeed, then the divell,
whome they make presentments of,
and shadow under the forme of an
idoll, which they entitle Okeus, and
whome they worship as the Romans
did their hurtful god Vejovis, more for
feare of harme then for hope of any
good ; they saie they have conference
with him, and fashion themselves in
their disguisments as neere to his shape
as they can imagyn. In every territory
of a weroance is a temple and a priest,
peradventure two or thrie ; yet happie
doth that weroance accompt himself
who can detayne with him a Quiyough-
quisock, of the best, grave, lucky, well
instructed in their misteryes, and beloved of their god ; and such a one is
noe lesse honoured then was Dianae's
priest at Ephesus, for whome they
have their more private temples,

with oratories and chauncells therein, according as is the dignity
and reverence of the Quiyough-quisock, which the weroance wilbe
at charge to build upon purpose, sometyme twenty foote broad and
a hundred in length, fashioned arbour wyse after their buylding,
having comonly the dore opening into the east, and at the west end
a spence or chauncell from the body of the temple, with hollow
wyndings and pillers, whereon stand divers black imagies, fashioned
to the shoulders, with their faces looking down the church, and where
within their weroances, upon a kind of biere of reedes, lye buryed ;
and under them, apart, in a vault low in the ground (as a more
secrett thing), vailed with a matt, sitts their Okeus, an image ill-
favouredly carved, all black dressed, with chaynes of perle, the
*presentment and figure of that god (say the priests unto the laity, and
who religiously believe what the priests saie) which doth them all the*

harme they suffer, be yt in their bodies or goods, within doores or
abroad; and true yt is many of them are divers tymes (especyally
offendors) shrewdly scratched as they walke alone in the woods, yt
may well be by the subtyle spirit, the malitious enemy to mankind,
whome, therefore, to pacefie and worke to doe them good (at least no
harme) the priests tell them they must do these and these sacrifices
unto [them] of these and these things, and thus and thus often, by
which meanes not only their owne children, but straungers, are some-
times sacrificed unto him: whilst the great god (the priests tell them)
who governes all the world, and makes the sun to shine, creating the
moone and stars his companyons, great powers, and which dwell with
him, and by whose virtues and influences the under earth is tempered,
and brings forth her fruiets according to her seasons, they calling
Ahone; the good and peaceable god requires no such dutyes, nor
needes be sacrificed unto, for he intendeth all good unto them, and
will doe noe harme, only the displeased Okeus, looking into all men's
accions, and examining the same according to the severe scale of
justice, punisheth them with sicknesse, beats them, and strikes their
ripe corn with blastings, stormes, and thunder clapps, stirrs up warre,
and makes their women falce unto them. Such is the misery and
thraldome under which Sathan hath bound these wretched mis-
creants.

I began by calling Strachey a plagiary. The
reader will now observe that he gives far more than
he takes. For example, his account of the temples
is much more full than that of Smith, and he adds
to Smith's version the character and being of Ahone,
as what "the priests tell them". I submit, therefore, that Strachey's additions, if valid for temples,
are not discredited for Ahone, merely because they
are inserted in the framework of Smith. As far as
I understand the matter, Smith's *Map of Virginia*
(1612) is an amended copy, with additions, by Smith
or another writer of that description, which he sent
home to the Council of Virginia, in November, 1608.[1]

[1] Arber, p. 444.

To the book of 1612 was added a portion of "Relations" by different hands, edited by W. S., namely,
Dr. Symonds. Strachey's editor, in 1849, regarded
W. S. as Strachey, and supposed that Strachey was
the real author of Smith's *Map of Virginia*, so that,
in his *Historie of Travaile*, Strachey merely took
back his own. He did not take back his own; he
made use of Smith's MS., not yet published, if Mr.
Arber and I rightly date Strachey's MS. at 1610-15,
or 1611-12. Why Strachey acted thus it is possible
to conjecture. As a scholar well acquainted with
Virginia, and as Secretary for the Colony, he would
have access to Smith's MS. of 1608 among the
papers of the Council, before its publication.
Smith professes himself "no scholer".[1] On the
other hand, Strachey likes to show off his Latin and
Greek. He has a curious, if inaccurate, knowledge
of esoteric Greek and Roman religious antiquities,
and in writing of religion aims at a comparative
method. Strachey, however, took the trouble to
copy bits of Smith into his own larger work, which
he never gave to the printers.

Now as to Ahone. It suits my argument to suppose
that Strachey's account is no less genuine than his
description of the temples (illustrated by a picture
by John White, who had been in Virginia in 1589),
and the account of the Great Hare of American
mythology.[2] This view of a Virginian Creator, " our

---

[1] Arber, p. 442.   [2] Strachey, p. 98-100.

chief god " "who takes upon him this shape of a hare," was got, says Strachey, "last year, 1610," from a brother of the Potomac King, by a boy named Spilman, who says that Smith "sold" him to Powhattan.[1] In his own brief narrative Spelman (or Spilman) says nothing about the Cosmogonic Legend of the Great Hare. The story came up when Captain Argoll was telling Powhattan's brother the account of creation in Genesis (1610).

Now Strachey's Great Hare is accepted by mythologists, while Ahone is regarded with suspicion. Ahone does not happen to suit anthropological ideas, the Hare suits them rather better. Moreover, and more important, there is abundant corroborative evidence for Oke and for the Hare, Michabo, who, says Dr. Brinton, "was originally the highest divinity recognised by them, powerful and beneficent beyond all others, maker of the heavens and the world," just like Ahone, in fact. And Dr. Brinton instructs us that Michabo originally meant not Great Hare, but "the spirit of light".[2] Thus, originally, the Red Men adored "The Spirit of Light, maker of the heavens and the world". Strachey claims no more than this for Ahone. Now, of course, Dr. Brinton may be right. But I have already expressed my extreme distrust of the philological processes by which he extracts "The Great Light, spirit of light," from Michabo, "beyond a doubt!" In my poor opinion, whatever claims

---

[1] "Spilman's Narrative," Arber, cx.-cxiv.
[2] *Myths of the New World*, p. 178.

Michabo may have as an unique creator of earth and
heaven—"God is Light,"—he owes his mythical
aspect as a Hare to something other than an unconscious pun. In any case, according to Dr. Brinton,
Michabo, regarded as a creator, is equivalent to
Strachey's Ahone. This amount of corroboration,
valeat quantum, I may claim, from the Potomac
Indians, for the belief in Ahone on the James River.
Dr. Brinton is notoriously not a believer in American
" monotheism ".[1]

The opponents of the authenticity of Ahone,
however, will certainly argue : " For Oke, or Oki, as a
redoubted being or spirit, or general name for such
personages, we have plentiful evidence, corroborating
that of Smith. But what evidence as to Ahone
corroborates that of Strachey ? " I must confess that
I have no explicit corroborative evidence for Ahone,
but then I have no accessible library of early books on
Virginia. Now it is clear that if I found and produced evidence for Ahone as late as 1625, I would be
met at once with the retort that, between 1610 and
1625, Christian ideas had contaminated the native
beliefs. Thus if I find Ahone, or a deity of like
attributes, after a very early date, he is of no use for
my purpose. Nor do I much expect to find him.
But do we find Winslow's Massachusetts God,
Kiehtan, named *after* 1622 (" I only ask for information "), and if we don't, does that prevent Mr. Tylor

---

[1] *Myths of the New World*, p. 53.

from citing Kiehtan, with apparent reliance on the evidence?[1]

Again, Ahone, though primal and creative, is, by Strachey's account, a sleeping partner. He has no sacrifice, and no temple or idol is recorded. Therefore the belief in Ahone could only be discovered as a result of inquiry, whereas figures of Oke or Okeus, and his services, were common and conspicuous.[2] As to Oke, I cannot quite understand Mr. Tylor's attitude. Summarising Lafitau, a late writer of 1724, Mr. Tylor writes : " The whole class of spirits or demons, known to the Caribs by the name of *cemi*, in Algonkin as *manitu*, in Huron as *oki*, Lafitau now spells with capital letters, and converts them each into a supreme being".[3] Yet in *Primitive Culture*, ii., 342, 1891, Mr. Tylor had cited Smith's Okee (with a capital letter) as the " chief god " of the Virginians in 1612. How can Lafitau be said to have elevated oki into Oki, and so to have made a god out of " a class of spirits or demons," in 1724, when Mr. Tylor had already cited Smith's Okee, with a capital letter and as a " chief god," in 1612 ? Smith, rebuked for the same by Mr. Tylor, had even identified Okee with the devil. Lafitau certainly did not begin this erroneous view of Oki as a " chief god " among the Virginians. If I cannot to-day

---

[1] *Primitive Culture*, ii. p. 342.

[2] Okee's image, as early as 1607, was borne into battle against Smith, who captured the god (Arber, p. 393). Ahone was not thus *en évidence*.

[3] *Journal of Anthrop. Inst.*, Feb., 1892, pp. 285, 286.

produce corroboration for a god named Ahone, I can
at least show that, from the north of New England
to the south of Virginia, there is early evidence,
cited by Mr. Tylor, for a belief in a primal creative
being, closely analogous to Ahone. And this evidence, I think, distinctly proves that such a being as
Ahone was within the capacity of the Indians in
these latitudes. Mr. Tylor must have thought in
1891 that the natives were competent to a belief in a
supreme deity, for he said, "Another famous native
American name for the supreme deity is Oki".[1] In the
essay of 1892, however, Oki does not appear to exist
as a god's name till 1724. We may now, for earlier
evidence, turn to Master Thomas Heriot, "that
learned mathematician" "who spoke the Indian language," and was with the company which abandoned
Virginia on 18th June, 1586. They ranged 130 miles
north and 130 miles north-west of Roanoke Island,
which brings them into the neighbourhood of Smith's
and Strachey's country. Heriot writes as to the
native creeds : "They believe that there are many
gods which they call Mantoac, but of different sorts
and degrees. *Also that there is one chiefe God that
hath beene from all eternitie*, who, as they say, when
he purposed first to make the world, made first other
gods of a principall order, to be as instruments to be
used in the Creation and Government to follow, and
after the Sunne, Moone and Starres as pettie gods,

---

[1] *Prim. Cult.*, ii. p. 342.

and the instruments of the other order more principall. . . . They thinke that all the gods are of
humane shape," and represent them by anthropomorphic idols. An idol, or image, "Kewasa" (the
plural is "Kewasowok"), is placed in the temples,
" where they worship, pray and make many offerings".
Good souls go to be happy with the gods, the bad
burn in Popogusso, a great pit, "where the sun
sets ". The evidence for this theory of a future
life, as usual, is that of men who died and revived
again, a story found in a score of widely separated
regions, down to our day, when the death, revival
and revelation occurred to the founder of the Ara-
pahoe new religion of the Ghost Dance. The belief
"works for righteousness". "The common sort
. . . have great care to avoyde torment after death,
and to enjoy blesse," also they have "great respect
to their Governors ".

This belief in a chief god "from all eternitie "
(that is, of unexplained origin), may not be convenient to some speculators, but it exactly corroborates Strachey's account of Ahone as creator with
subordinates. The evidence is of 1586 (twenty-six
years before Strachey), and, like Strachey, Heriot
attributes the whole scheme of belief to " the
priestes ". " This is the sum of their religion, which
I learned by having speciall familiaritie with some of
their priests." [1] I see no escape from the conclusion

---

[1] According to Strachey, Heriot could speak the native language.

that the Virginians believed as Heriot says they did,
except the device of alleging that they promptly
borrowed some of Heriot's ideas and maintained
that these ideas had ever been their own. Heriot
certainly did not recognise the identity. " Through
conversing with us they were brought into great
doubts of their owne [religion], and no small admiration of ours ; of which many desired to learne
more than we had the meanes for want of utterance
in their language to expresse." So Heriot could not
be subtle in the native tongue. Heriot did what he
could to convert them : " I did my best to make His
immortall glory knowne ". His efforts were chiefly
successful by virtue of the savage admiration of our
guns, mathematical instruments, and so forth. These
sources of an awakened interest in Christianity would
vanish with the total destruction and discomfiture of
the colony, unless a few captives, later massacred,
taught our religion to the natives.[1]

I shall cite another early example of a New England deity akin to Ahone, with a deputy, a friend of
sorcerers, like Okee. This account is in Smith's
General History of New England, 1606-1624. We
sent out a colony in 1607 ; " they all returned in
the yeere 1608," esteeming the country " a cold,
barren, mountainous rocky desart". I am apt to
believe that they did not plant the fructifying seeds
of grace among the natives in 1607-1608. But the

---

[1] Heriot's *Narrative*, pp. 37-39. Quaritch, London, 1893.

missionary efforts of French traders may, of course, have been blessed; nor can I deny that a yellow-haired man, whose corpse was found in 1620 with some objects of iron, may have converted the natives to such beliefs as they possessed. We are told, however, that these tenets were of ancestral antiquity. I cite E. Winslow, as edited by Smith (1623-24) :—

" Those where is this Plantation [New Plymouth] say Kiehtan [1] made all the other Gods : also one man and one woman, and with them all mankinde, but how they became so dispersed they know not. They say that at first there was no king but Kiehtan, that dwelleth far westerly above the heavens, whither all good men go when they die, and have plentie of all things. The bad go thither also and knock at the door, but [' the door is shut '] he bids them go wander in endless want and misery, for they shall not stay there. They never saw Kiehtan,[2] but they hold it a great charge and dutie that one race teach

---

[1] In 1873 Mr. Tylor regarded Dr. Brinton's etymology of Kiehtan as = Kittanitowit = "Great Living Spirit," as "plausible". In his edition of 1891 he omits this etymology. Personally I entirely distrust the philological theories of the original sense of old divine names as a general rule.

[2] "They never saw Kiehtan." So, about 1854, "The common answer of intelligent black fellows on the Barwon when asked if they know Baiame . . . is this : ' Kamil zaia zummi Baiame, zaia winuzgulda ' ; ' I have not seen Baiame, I have heard or perceived him '. If asked who made the sky, the earth, the animals and man, they always answer ' Baiame '." Daramulun, according to the same authority in Lang's *Queensland*, was the familiar of sorcerers, and appeared as a serpent. This answers, as I show, to Hobamock, the subordinate power to Kiehtan in New England, and to Okee, the familiar of sorcerers in Virginia. (Ridley, *J. A. I.*, 1872, p. 277.)

another; and to him they make feasts and cry and sing for plenty and victory, or anything that is good.

"They have another Power they call Hobamock, which we conceive the Devill, and upon him they call to cure their wounds and diseases; when they are curable he persuades them he sent them, because they have displeased him; but, if they be mortal, then he saith, 'Kiehtan sent them'; which makes them never call on him in their sickness. They say this Hobamock appears to them sometimes like a man, a deer, or an eagle, but most commonly like a snake; not to all but to their Powahs to cure diseases, and Undeses . . . and these are such as conjure in Virginia, and cause the people to do what they list." Winslow (or rather Smith editing Winslow here), had already said, "They believe, as do the Virginians, of many divine powers, yet of one above all the rest, as the Southern Virginians call their chief god Kewassa [an error], and that we now inhabit Oke. . . . The Massachusetts call their great god Kiehtan."[1]

Here, then, in Heriot (1586), Strachey (1611-12) and Winslow (1622), we find fairly harmonious accounts of a polydæmonism with a chief, primal, creative being above and behind it; a being unnamed, and Ahone and Kiehtan.

Is all this invention? Or was all this derived from Europeans before 1586, and, if so, from what Europeans? Mr. Tylor, in 1873, wrote, "After due

---

[1] Arber, pp. 767, 768.

allowance made for misrendering of savage answers, and importation of white men's thoughts, it can hardly be judged that a divine being, whose characteristics are often so unlike what European intercourse would have suggested, and who is heard of by such early explorers among such distant tribes, could be a deity of foreign origin". *Now*, he " can *hardly* be *altogether* a deity of foreign origin ".[1] I agree with Mr. Tylor's earlier statement. In my opinion Ahone —Okeus, Kiehtan—Hobamock, correspond, the first pair to the usually unseen Australian Baiame (a crystal or hypnotic vision of Baiame scarcely counts), while the second pair, Okeus and Hobamock, answer to the Australian familiars of sorcerers, Koin and Brewin; the American "Powers" being those of peoples on a higher level of culture. Like Tharramulun where Baiame is supreme, Hobamock appears as a snake (Asclepius).

For all these reasons I am inclined to accept Strachey's Ahone as a veritable element in Virginian belief. Without temple or service, such a being was not conspicuous, like Okee and other gods which had idols and sacrifices.

As far as I see, Strachey has no theory to serve by inventing Ahone. He asks how any races "if descended from the people of the first creation, should maintain so general and gross a defection from the true knowledge of God". He is reduced to suppose

[1] *Prim. Cult.*, ii. 340, 1873, 1892.

that, as descendants of Ham, they inherit "the ignorance of true godliness." (p. 45). The children of Shem and Japheth alone "retained, until the coming of the Messias, the only knowledge of the eternal and never-changing Trinity". The Virginians, on the other hand, fell heir to the ignorance, and "fearful and superstitious instinct of nature" of Ham (p. 40). Ahone, therefore, is not invented by Strachey to bolster up a theory (held by Strachey), of an inherited revelation, or of a *sensus numinis* which could not go wrong. Unless a proof be given that Strachey had a theory, or any other purpose, to serve by inventing Ahone, I cannot at present come into the opinion that he gratuitously fabled, though he may have unconsciously exaggerated.

What were Strachey's sources? He was for nine months, if not more, in the colony : he had travelled at least 115 miles up the James River, he occasionally suggests modifications of Smith's map, he refers to Smith's adventures, and his glossary is very much larger than Smith's; its accuracy I leave to American linguists. Such a witness, despite his admitted use of Smith's text (if it is really all by Smith throughout) is not to be despised, and he is not despised in America.[1] Strachey, it is true, had not,

---

[1] Arber, cxvii. Strachey mentions that (before his arrival in Virginia) Pocahontas turned cart-wheels, naked, in Jamestown, being then under twelve, and not yet wearing the apron. Smith says she was ten in 1608, but does not mention the cart-wheels. Later, he found it convenient to put her age at twelve or thirteen in 1608. Most American scholars, such as Mr Adams, entirely distrust the romantic later narratives of Smith.

like Smith, been captured by Indians and either treated with perfect kindness and consideration (as Smith reported at the time), or tied to a tree and threatened with arrows, and laid out to have his head knocked in with a stone ; as he alleged sixteen years later ! Strachey, not being captured, did not owe his release (1) to the magnanimity of Powhattan, (2) to his own ingenious lies, (3) to the intercession of Pocahontas, as Smith, and his friends for him, at various dates inconsistently declared. Smith certainly saw more of the natives at home : Strachey brought a more studious mind to what he could learn of their customs and ideas ; and is not a convicted braggart. I conjecture that one of Strachey's sources was a native named Kemps. Smith had seized Kemps and Kinsock in 1609. Unknown authorities (Powell? and Todkill?) represent these two savages as "the most exact villaines in the country ".[1] They were made to labour in fetters, then were set at liberty, but "little desired it ".[2] Some " souldiers " ran away to the liberated Kemps, who brought them back to Smith.[3] Why Kemps and his friend are called " two of the most exact villains in the country " does not appear. Kemps died " of the surveye " (scurvey probably) at Jamestown, in 1610-11. He was much made of by Lord De la Warr, " could speak a pretty deal of our English, and came orderly to church every day to prayers ". He gave Strachey the names

---

[1] *The Proceedings*, etc., by W. S. Arber, p. 151.
[2] *Ibid.*, p. 155. [3] *Ibid.*, p. 157.

of Powhattan's wives, and told him, truly or not, that
Pocahontas was married, about 1610, to an Indian
named Kocoum.[1]   I offer the guess that Kemps and
Machumps, who came and went from Pocahontas,
and recited an Indian prayer which Strachey neglected
to copy out, may have been among Strachey's
authorities. I shall, of course, be told that Kemps
picked up Ahone at church. This did not strike
Strachey as being the fact; he had no opinion of the
creed in which Ahone was a factor, "the misery and
thraldomè under which Sathan has bound these
wretched miscreants". According to Strachey, the
priests, far from borrowing any part of our faith,
"feare and tremble lest the knowledge of God, and
of our Saviour Jesus Christ be taught in these
parts".

Strachey is therefore for putting down the priests,
and, like Smith (indeed here borrowing from Smith),
accuses them of sacrificing children. To Smith's
statement that such a rite was worked at Quiyough-
cohanock, Strachey adds that Sir George Percy (who
was with Smith) "was at, and observed" a similar
mystery at Kecoughtan. It is plain that the rite was
not a sacrifice, but a *Bora*, or initiation, and the
parallel of the Spartan flogging of boys, with the
retreat of the boys and their instructors, is very close,
and, of course, unnoted by classical scholars except
Mr. Frazer. Strachey ends with the critical remark

---

[1] Strachey, pp. 54, 55.

that we shall not know all the certainty of the religion and mysteries till we can capture some of the priests, or Quiyough-quisocks.

Students who have access to a good library of Americana may do more to elucidate Ahone. I regard him as in a line with Kiehtan and the God spoken of by Heriot, and do not believe (1) that Strachey lied; (2) that natives deceived Strachey; (3) that Ahone was borrowed from "the God of Captain Smith".

MYTH, RITUAL, AND RELIGION.

CHAPTER I.

SYSTEMS OF MYTHOLOGY.

Definitions of religion—Contradictory evidence—"Belief in spiritual beings"—Objection to Mr. Tylor's definition—Definition as regards this argument—Problem: the contradiction between religion and myth—Two human moods—Examples—Case of Greece—Ancient mythologists—Criticism by Eusebius—Modern mythological systems—Mr. Max Müller—Mannhardt.

THE word "Religion" may be, and has been, employed in many different senses, and with a perplexing width of significance. No attempt to define the word is likely to be quite satisfactory, but almost any definition may serve the purpose of an argument, if the writer who employs it states his meaning frankly and adheres to it steadily. An example of the confusions which may arise from the use of the term "religion" is familiar to students. Dr. J. D. Lang wrote concerning the native races of Australia: "They have nothing whatever of the character of religion, or of religious observances, to distinguish them from the beasts that perish". Yet in the same book Dr. Lang published evidence assigning to the natives belief

in "Turramullun, the chief of demons, who is the
author of disease, mischief and wisdom".[1] The belief in a superhuman author of "disease, mischief
and wisdom" is certainly a religious belief not con-
spicuously held by "the beasts"; yet all religion was
denied to the Australians by the very author who
prints (in however erroneous a style) an account of
part of their creed. This writer merely inherited the
old missionary habit of speaking about the god of a
non-Christian people as a "demon" or an "evil spirit".

Dr. Lang's negative opinion was contradicted in
testimony published by himself, an appendix by the
Rev. Mr. Ridley, containing evidence of the belief
in Baiame. "Those who have learned that 'God'
is the name by which we speak of the Creator, say
that Baiame is God."[2]

As "a minimum definition of religion," Mr. Tylor
has suggested "the belief in spiritual beings". Against
this it may be urged that, while we have no definite
certainty that any race of men is destitute of belief in
spiritual beings, yet certain moral and creative deities
of low races do not seem to be envisaged as "spiritual"
at all. They are regarded as *existences*, as *beings*,
unconditioned by Time, Space, or Death, and nobody
appears to have put the purely metaphysical question,
"Are these beings spiritual or material?"[3] Now, if
a race were discovered which believed in such beings,
yet had no faith in spirits, that race could not be called
irreligious, as it would have to be called in Mr.

---

[1] See *Primitive Culture*, second edition, i. 419.
[2] Lang's *Queensland*, p. 445, 1861.
[3] See *The Making of Religion*, pp. 201-210.

Tylor's "minimum definition". Almost certainly, no race in this stage of belief in nothing but unconditioned but not expressly spiritual beings is extant. Yet such a belief may conceivably have existed before men had developed the theory of spirits at all, and such a belief, in creative and moral unconditioned beings, not alleged to be spiritual, could not be excluded from a definition of religion.[1]

For these reasons we propose (merely for the purpose of the present work) to define religion as the belief in a primal being, a Maker, undying, usually moral, without denying that the belief in spiritual beings, even if immoral, may be styled religious. Our definition is expressly framed for the purpose of the argument, because that argument endeavours to bring into view the essential conflict between religion and myth. We intend to show that this conflict between the religious and the mythical conception is present, not only (where it has been universally recognised) in the faiths of the ancient civilised peoples, as in Greece, Rome, India and Egypt, but also in the ideas of the lowest known savages.

It may, of course, be argued that the belief in a Creator is itself a myth. However that may be, the attitude of awe, and of moral obedience, in face of

---

[1] "The history of the Jews, nay, the history of our own mind, proves to demonstration that the thought of God is a far easier thought, and a far earlier, than that of a spirit." Father Tyrrell, S.J., *The Month*, October, 1898. As to the Jews, the question is debated. As to our own infancy, we are certainly taught about God before we are likely to be capable of the metaphysical notion of spirit. But we can scarcely reason from children in Christian houses to the infancy of the race.

such a supposed being, is religious in the sense of the Christian religion, whereas the fabrication of fanciful, humorous, and wildly irrational fables about that being, or others, is essentially mythical in the ordinary significance of that word, though not absent from popular Christianity.

Now, the whole *crux* and puzzle of mythology is, "Why, having attained (in whatever way) to a belief in an undying guardian, 'Master of Life,' did mankind set to work to evolve a *chronique scandaleuse* about *Him*? And why is that *chronique* the elaborately absurd set of legends which we find in all mythologies?"

In answering, or trying to answer, these questions, we cannot go behind the beliefs of the races now most immersed in savage ignorance. About the psychology of races yet more undeveloped we can have no historical knowledge. Among the lowest known tribes we usually find, just as in ancient Greece, the belief in a deathless "Father," "Master," "Maker," and also the crowd of humorous, obscene, fanciful myths which are in flagrant contradiction with the religious character of that belief. That belief is what we call rational, and even elevated. The myths, on the other hand, are what we call irrational and debasing. We regard low savages as very irrational and debased characters, consequently the nature of their myths does not surprise us. Their religious conception, however, of a "Father" or "Master of Life" seems out of keeping with the nature of the savage mind as we understand it. Still, there the religious conception actually is, and it seems to follow that we do not

wholly understand the savage mind, or its unknown
antecedents. In any case, there the facts are, as shall be
demonstrated. However the ancestors of Australians,
or Andamanese, or Hurons arrived at their highest
religious conception, they decidedly possess it.[1] The
development of their mythical conceptions is accounted
for by those qualities of their minds which we do
understand, and shall illustrate at length. For the
present, we can only say that the religious conception
uprises from the human intellect in one mood, that
of earnest contemplation and submission: while the
mythical ideas uprise from another mood, that of
playful and erratic fancy. These two moods are
conspicuous even in Christianity. The former, that of
earnest and submissive contemplation, declares itself
in prayers, hymns, and "the dim religious light" of
cathedrals. The second mood, that of playful and
erratic fancy, is conspicuous in the buffoonery of
Miracle Plays, in *Märchen*, these burlesque popular tales
about our Lord and the Apostles, and in the hideous
and grotesque sculptures on sacred edifices. The two
moods are present, and in conflict, through the whole
religious history of the human race. They stand as
near each other, and as far apart, as Love and Lust.

It will later be shown that even some of the most
backward savages make a perhaps half-conscious distinction between their mythology and their religion.
As to the former, they are communicative; as to the
latter, they jealously guard their secret in sacred

---

[1] The hypothesis that the conception was borrowed from European creeds
will be discussed later. See, too, "Are Savage Gods borrowed from
Missionaries?" *Nineteenth Century*, January, 1899.

mysteries. It is improbable that reflective "black
fellows" have been morally shocked by the flagrant
contradictions between their religious conceptions and
their mythical stories of the divine beings. But human
thought could not come into explicit clearness of consciousness without producing the sense of shock and
surprise at these contradictions between the Religion
and the Myth of the same god. Of this we proceed
to give examples.

In Greece, as early as the sixth century B.C., we are
all familiar with Xenophanes' poem [1] complaining that
the gods were credited with the worst crimes of
mortals—in fact, with abominations only known in
the orgies of Nero and Elagabalus. We hear Pindar
refusing to repeat the tale which told him the blessed
were cannibals.[2] In India we read the pious Brahmanic attempts to expound decently the myths which
made Indra the slayer of a Brahman; the sinner, that
is, of the unpardonable sin. In Egypt, too, we study
the priestly or philosophic systems by which the clergy
strove to strip the burden of absurdity and sacrilege
from their own deities. From all these efforts of
civilised and pious believers to explain away the
stories about their own gods we may infer one fact—
the most important to the student of mythology—the
fact that myths were not evolved in times of clear

---

[1] Ritter and Preller, *Hist. Philos.*, Gothæ, 1869, p. 82.

[2] *Olympic Odes*, i., Myers's translation : " To me it is impossible to call
one of the blessed gods a cannibal. . . . Meet it is for a man that concerning the gods he speak honourably, for the reproach is less. Of thee, son of
Tantalus, I will speak contrariwise to them who have gone before me."
In avoiding the story of the cannibal god, however, Pindar tells a tale even
more offensive to our morality.

civilised thought. It is when Greece is just beginning
to free her thought from the bondage of too concrete
language, when she is striving to coin abstract terms,
that her philosophers and poets first find the myths of
Greece a stumbling-block.

All early attempts at an interpretation of mythology are so many efforts to explain the myths on
some principle which shall seem not unreasonable to
men living at the time of the explanation. Therefore
the pious remonstrances and the forced constructions
of early thinkers like Xenophanes, of poets like Pindar,
of all ancient Homeric scholars and Pagan apologists,
from Theagenes of Rhegium (525 B.C.), the early
Homeric commentator, to Porphyry, almost the last
of the heathen philosophers, are so many proofs that
to Greece, as soon as she had a reflective literature,
the myths of Greece seemed impious and *irrational*.
The essays of the native commentators on the Veda,
in the same way, are endeavours to put into myths
felt to be irrational and impious a meaning which
does not offend either piety or reason. We may
therefore conclude that it was not men in an early
stage of philosophic thought (as philosophy is now
understood)—not men like Empedocles and Heraclitus,
nor reasonably devout men like Eumæus, the pious
swineherd of the *Odyssey*—who evolved the blasphemous myths of Greece, of Egypt and of India.
We must look elsewhere for an explanation. We
must try to discover some actual and demonstrable
and widely prevalent condition of the human mind,
in which tales that even to remote and rudimentary
civilisations appeared irrational and unnatural would

seem natural and rational. To discover this intellectual condition has been the aim of all mythologists
who did not believe that myth is a divine tradition
depraved by human weakness, or a distorted version
of historical events.

Before going further, it is desirable to set forth
what our aim is, and to what extent we are seeking
an interpretation of mythology. It is not our purpose
to explain every detail of every ancient legend, either as
a distorted historical fact or as the result of this or that
confusion of thought caused by forgetfulness of the
meanings of language, or in any other way; nay, we
must constantly protest against the excursions of too
venturesome ingenuity. Myth is so ancient, so complex, so full of elements, that it is vain labour to seek
a cause for every phenomenon. We are chiefly occupied with the quest for an historical condition of the
human intellect to which the element in myths, regarded by us as irrational, shall seem rational enough.
If we can prove that such a state of mind widely exists
among men, and has existed, that state of mind may
be provisionally considered as the fount and *origin* of
the myths which have always perplexed men in a
reasonable modern mental condition. Again, if it can
be shown that this mental stage was one through
which all civilised races have passed, the universality
of the mythopœic mental condition will to some extent
explain the universal *diffusion* of the stories.

Now, in all mythologies, whether savage or civilised, and in all religions where myths intrude, there
exist two factors—the factor which we now regard
as rational, and that which we moderns regard as

irrational. The former element needs little explanation ; the latter has demanded explanation ever since human thought became comparatively instructed and abstract.

To take an example ; even in the myths of savages there is much that still seems rational and transparent. If savages tell us that some wise being taught them all the simple arts of life, the use of fire, of the bow and arrow, the barbing of hooks, and so forth, we understand them at once. Nothing can be more natural than that man should believe in an original inventor of the arts, and should tell tales about the imaginary discoverers if the real heroes be forgotten. So far all is plain sailing. But when the savage goes on to say that he who taught the use of fire or who gave the first marriage laws was a rabbit or a crow, or a dog, or a beaver, or a spider, then we are at once face to face with the element in myths which seems to us *irrational*. Again, among civilised peoples we read of the pure all-seeing Varuna in the Vedas, to whom sin is an offence. We read of Indra, the Lord of Thunder, borne in his chariot, the giver of victory, the giver of wealth to the pious ; here once more all seems natural and plain. The notion of a deity who guides the whirlwind and directs the storm, a god of battles, a god who blesses righteousness, is familiar to us and intelligible ; but when we read how Indra drank himself drunk and committed adulteries with Asura women, and got himself born from the same womb as a bull, and changed himself into a quail or a ram, and suffered from the most abject physical terror, and so forth, then we are among myths no longer readily intelligible ; here, we feel, are *irra-tional* stories, of which the original ideas, in their natural sense, can hardly have been conceived by men in a pure and rational early civilisation. Again, in the religions of even the lowest races, such myths as these are in contradiction with the ethical elements of the faith.

If we look at Greek religious tradition, we observe the coexistence of the *rational* and the apparently *irrational* elements. The *rational* myths are those which represent the gods as beautiful and wise beings. The Artemis of the *Odyssey* "taking her pastime in the chase of boars and swift deer, while with her the wild wood-nymphs disport them, and high over them all she rears her brow, and is easily to be known where all are fair," [1] is a perfectly *rational* mythic represen-tation of a divine being. We feel, even now, that the conception of a " queen and goddess, chaste and fair," the abbess, as Paul de Saint-Victor calls her, of the woodlands, is a beautiful and natural fancy, which requires no explanation. On the other hand, the Artemis of Arcadia, who is confused with the nymph Callisto, who, again, is said to have become a she-bear, and later a star ; and the Brauronian Artemis, whose maiden ministers danced a bear-dance,[2] are goddesses whose legend seems unnatural, and needs to be made intelligible. Or, again, there is nothing not explicable and natural in the conception of the Olympian Zeus as represented by the great chryselephantine statue of Zeus at Olympia, or in the Homeric conception of Zeus

---

[1] *Odyssey*, vi. 102.

[2] ἀρκτεύειν ; compare Harpokration on this word.

as a god who "turns everywhere his shining eyes,"
and beholds all things, and protects the righteous, and
deals good or evil fortune to men. But the Zeus
whose grave was shown in Crete, or the Zeus who
played Demeter an obscene trick by the aid of a ram,
or the Zeus who, in the shape of a swan, became the
father of Castor and Pollux, or the Zeus who deceived
Hera by means of a feigned marriage with an inanimate
object, or the Zeus who was afraid of Attes, or the
Zeus who made love to women in the shape of an ant
or a cuckoo, is a being whose myth is felt to be unnatural and bewildering.[1] It is this *irrational* and
unnatural element, as Mr. Max Müller says, "the silly,
senseless, and savage element," that makes mythology
the puzzle which men have so long found it. For,
observe, Greek myth does not represent merely a
humorous play of fancy, dealing with things religiously
sacred as if by way of relief from the strained rever-
ential contemplation of the majesty of Zeus. Many
stories of Greek mythology are such as could not cross,
for the first time, the mind of a civilised Xenophanes
or Theagenes, even in a dream. *This* was the real
puzzle.

We have offered examples—Savage, Indian, and
Greek—of that element in mythology which, as all
civilised races have felt, demands explanation.

[1] These are the features in myth which provoke, for example, the wonder
of Éméric-David. "The lizard, the wolf, the dog, the ass, the frog, and all
the other brutes so common on religious monuments everywhere, do they
not all imply a *thought* which we must divine?" He concludes that these
animals, plants, and monsters of myths are so many "enigmas" and
"symbols" veiling some deep, sacred idea, allegories of some esoteric
religious creed. *Jupiter*, Paris, 1832, p. lxxvii.

To be still more explicit, we may draw up a brief list of the chief problems in the legendary stories attached to the old religions of the world—the problems which it is our special purpose to notice. First we have, in the myths of all races, the most grotesque conceptions of the character of gods when mythically envisaged. Beings who, in religion, leave little to be desired, and are spoken of as holy, immortal, omniscient, and kindly, are, in myth, represented as fashioned in the likeness not only of man, but of the beasts ; as subject to death, as ignorant and impious.

Most pre-Christian religions had their " zoomorphic " or partially zoomorphic idols, gods in the shape of the lower animals, or with the heads and necks of the lower animals.   In the same way all mythologies represent the gods as fond of appearing in animal forms. Under these disguises they conduct many amours, even with the daughters of men, and Greek houses were proud of their descent from Zeus in the shape of an eagle or ant, a serpent or a swan ; while Cronus and the Vedic Tvashtri and Poseidon made love as horses, and Apollo as a dog. Not less wild are the legends about the births of gods from the thigh, or the head, or feet, or armpits of some parent ; while tales describing and pictures representing unspeakable divine obscenities were frequent in the mythology and in the temples of Greece.   Once more, the gods were said to possess and exercise the power of turning men and women into birds, beasts, fishes, trees, and stones, so that there was scarcely a familiar natural object in the Greek world which had not once (according to legend) been a man or a woman.   The myths of the origin of

the world and man, again, were in the last degree
childish and disgusting. The Bushmen and Australians
have, perhaps, no story of the origin of species quite
so barbarous in style as the anecdotes about Phanes
and Prajapati which are preserved in the Orphic hymns
and in the Brahmanas. The conduct of the earlier
dynasties of classical gods towards each other was as
notoriously cruel and loathsome as their behaviour
towards mortals was tricksy and capricious. The
classical gods, with all their immortal might, are, by
a mythical contradiction of the religious conception,
regarded as capable of fear and pain, and are led into
scrapes as ludicrous as those of Brer Wolf or Brer
Terrapin in the tales of the Negroes of the Southern
States of America. The stars, again, in mythology,
are mixed up with beasts, planets and men in the
same embroglio of fantastic opinion. The dead and
the living, men, beasts and gods, trees and stars, and
rivers, and sun, and moon, dance through the region
of myths in a burlesque *ballet* of Priapus, where
everything may be anything, where nature has no
laws and imagination no limits.

Such are the irrational characteristics of myths,
classic or Indian, European or American, African or
Asiatic, Australian or Maori. Such is one element we
find all the world over among civilised and savage
people, *quod semper, quod ubique, quod ab omnibus.*
It is no wonder that pious and reflective men have,
in so many ages and in so many ways, tried to account
to themselves for their possession of beliefs closely
connected with religion which yet seemed ruinous to
religion and morality.

The explanations which men have given of their own
sacred stories, the apologies for their own gods which
they have been constrained to offer to themselves, were
the earliest babblings of a science of mythology. That
science was, in its dim beginnings, intended to satisfy
a moral need. Man found that his gods, when mythically envisaged, were not made in his own moral image
at its best, but in the image sometimes of the beasts,
sometimes of his own moral nature at its very worst :
in the likeness of robbers, wizards, sorcerers, and
adulterers. Now, it is impossible here to examine
minutely all systems of mythological interpretation.
Every key has been tried in this difficult lock ; every
cause of confusion has been taken up and tested, deemed
adequate, and finally rejected or assigned a subordinate
place. Probably the first attempts to shake off the
burden of religious horror at mythical impiety were
made by way of silent omission. Thus most of the
foulest myths of early India are absent, and presumably were left out, in the Rig-Veda. " The religious
sentiment of the hymns, already so elevated, has
discarded most of the tales which offended it, but
has not succeeded in discarding them all." [1] Just as
the poets of the Rig-Veda prefer to avoid the more
offensive traditions about Indra and Tvashtri, so
Homer succeeds in avoiding the more grotesque and
puerile tales about his own gods.[2] The period of actual

[1] *Les Religions de l'Inde*, Barth, p. 14. See also *postea*, "Indian
Myths ".

[2] The reasons for Homer's reticence are probably different in different
passages. Perhaps in some cases he had heard a purer version of myth
than what reached Hesiod ; perhaps he sometimes purposely (like Pindar)
purified a myth ; usually he must have selected, in conformity with the

apology comes later. Pindar declines, as we have seen, to accuse a god of cannibalism. The Satapatha Brahmana invents a new story about the slaying of Visvarupa. Not Indra, but Trita, says the Brahmana apologetically, slew the three-headed son of Tvashtri. "Indra assuredly was free from that sin, for he is a god," says the Indian apologist.[1] Yet sins which to us appear far more monstrous than the peccadillo of killing a three-headed Brahman are attributed freely to Indra.

While poets could but omit a blasphemous tale or sketch an apology in passing, it became the business of philosophers and of antiquarian writers deliberately to " whitewash " the gods of popular religion. Systematic explanations of the sacred stories, whether as preserved in poetry or as told by priests, had to be provided. India had her etymological and her legendary school of mythology.[2] Thus, while the hymn *seemed* to tell how the Maruts were gods, " born together with the spotted deer," the etymological interpreters explained that the word for deer only meant the many-coloured lines of clouds.[3] In the armoury of apologetics etymology has been the most serviceable weapon. It is easy to see that by

noble humanity and purity of his taste, the tales that best conformed to his ideal. He makes his deities reluctant to drag out in dispute old scandals of their early unheroic adventures, some of which, however, he gives, as the kicking of Hephæstus out of heaven, and the imprisonment of Ares in a vessel of bronze. Compare Professor Jebb's *Homer*, p. 83 : "Whatever the instinct of the great artist has tolerated, at least it has purged these things away," that is, divine amours in bestial form.

[1] *Satapatha Brahmana*, Oxford, 1882, vol. i. p. 47.

[2] *Rig-Veda Sanhita*, Max Müller, p. 59.

[3] *Postea*, " Indian Divine Myths".

aid of etymology the most repulsive legend may be
compelled to yield a pure or harmless sense, and may
be explained as an innocent blunder, caused by mere
verbal misunderstanding.   Brahmans, Greeks, and
Germans have equally found comfort in this hypothesis. In the *Cratylus* of Plato, Socrates speaks of
the notion of explaining myths by etymological
guesses at the meaning of divine names as " a philosophy which came to him all in an instant ".   Thus
we find Socrates shocked by the irreverence which
styled Zeus the son of Cronus, "who is a proverb
for stupidity ".   But on examining philologically the
name Kronos, Socrates decides that it must really
mean Koros, "not in the sense of a youth, but
signifying the pure and garnished mind".   Therefore,
when people first called Zeus the son of Cronus, they
meant nothing irreverent, but only that Zeus is the
child of the pure mind or pure reason.   Not only is
this etymological system most pious and consolatory,
but it is, as Socrates adds, of universal application.
" For now I bethink me of a very new and ingenious
notion, . . . that we may put in and pull out letters
at pleasure, and alter the accents." [1]

Socrates, of course, speaks more than half in irony,
but there is a certain truth in his account of etymological analysis and its dependence on individual
tastes and preconceived theory.

The ancient classical schools of mythological interpretation, though unscientific and unsuccessful,
are not without interest.   We find philosophers
and grammarians looking, just as we ourselves are

----
[1] Jowett's *Plato*, vol. i. pp. 632, 670.

looking, for some condition of the human intellect out of which the absurd element in myths might conceivably have sprung. Very naturally the philosophers supposed that the human beings in whose brain and speech myths had their origin must have been philosophers like themselves—intelligent, educated persons. But such persons, they argued, could never have meant to tell stories about the gods so full of nonsense and blasphemy.

Therefore the nonsense and blasphemy must originally have had some harmless, or even praiseworthy, sense. What could that sense have been? This question each ancient mythologist answered in accordance with his own taste and prejudices, and above all, and like all other and later speculators, in harmony with the general tendency of his own studies. If he lived when physical speculation was coming into fashion, as in the age of Empedocles, he thought that the Homeric poems must contain a veiled account of physical philosophy. This was the opinion of Theagenes of Rhegium, who wrote at a period when a crude physicism was disengaging itself from the earlier religious and mythical cosmogonic systems of Greece. Theagenes was shocked by the Homeric description of the battle in which the gods fought as allies of the Achæans and Trojans. He therefore explained away the affair as a veiled account of the strife of the elements. Such "strife" was familiar to readers of the physical speculations of Empedocles and of Heraclitus, who blamed Homer for his prayer against Strife.[1]

[1] *Is. et Osir.*, 48.

It did not occur to Theagenes to ask whether any evidence existed to show that the pre-Homeric Greeks were Empedoclean or Heraclitean philosophers. He readily proved to himself that Apollo, Helios, and Hephæstus were allegorical representations, like what such philosophers would feign,—of fire, that Hera was air, Poseidon water, Artemis the moon, and the rest he disposed of in the same fashion.[1]

Metrodorus, again, turned not only the gods, but the Homeric heroes into " elemental combinations and physical agencies "; for there is nothing new in the mythological philosophy recently popular, which saw the sun, and the cloud, and the wind in Achilles, Athene, and Hermes.[2]

In the *Bacchæ* (291-297), Euripides puts another of the mythological systems of his own time into the mouth of Cadmus, the Theban king, who advances a philological explanation of the story that Dionysus was sewn up in the thigh of Zeus. The most famous of the later theories was that of Euhemerus (316 B.C.). In a kind of philosophical romance, Euhemerus declared that he had sailed to some No-man's-land, Panchæa, where he found the verity about mythical times engraved on pillars of bronze. This truth he published in the *Sacra Historia,* where he rationalised the fables, averring that the gods had been men, and that the myths were exaggerated and distorted records of facts. (See Eusebius, *Præp. E.,* ii. 55.) The Abbé Banier

---

[1] Scholia on *Iliad,* xx. 67. Dindorf (1877), vol. iv. p. 231. "This manner of apologetics is as old as Theagenes of Rhegium. Homer offers theological doctrine in the guise of physical allegory."

[2] Grote, *Hist. of Greece,* ed. 1869, i. p. 404.

(*La Mythologie expliquée par l'Histoire*, Paris, 1738, vol. ii. p. 218) attempts the defence of Euhemerus, whom most of the ancients regarded as an atheist. There was an element of truth in his romantic hypothesis.[1]

Sometimes the old stories were said to conceal a moral, sometimes a physical, sometimes a mystical or Neo-platonic sort of meaning. As every apologist interpreted the legends in his own fashion, the interpretations usually disagreed and killed each other. Just as one modern mythologist sees the wind in Æetes and the dawn in Medea, while another of the same school believes, on equally good evidence, that both Æetes and Medea are the moon, so writers like Porphyry (270 A.D.) and Plutarch (60 A.D.) made the ancient deities types of their own favourite doctrines, whatever these might happen to be.

When Christianity became powerful, the Christian writers naturally attacked heathen religion where it was most vulnerable, on the side of the myths, and of the mysteries which were dramatic representations of the myths. "Pretty gods you worship," said the Fathers, in effect, "homicides, adulterers, bulls, bears, mice, ants, and what not." The heathen apologists for the old religion were thus driven in the early ages of Christianity to various methods of explaining away the myths of their discredited religion.

The early Christian writers very easily, and with considerable argumentative power, disposed of the apologies for the myths advanced by Porphyry and Plutarch. Thus Eusebius in the *Præparatio Evangelica* first attacks the Egyptian interpretations of

[1] See Block, *Euhémère et sa Doctrine*, Mons, 1876.

their own bestial or semi-bestial gods. He shows that
the various interpretations destroy each other, and
goes on to point out that Greek myth is in essence
only a veneered and varnished version of the faith of
Egypt. He ridicules, with a good deal of humour,
the old theories which resolved so many mythical
heroes into the sun ; he shows that while one system
is contented to regard Zeus as mere fire and air,
another system recognises in him the higher reason,
while Heracles, Dionysus, Apollo, and Asclepius,
father and child, are all indifferently the sun.

Granting that the myth-makers were only con-
structing physical allegories, why did they wrap them
up, asks Eusebius, in what *we* consider abominable
fictions ? In what state were the people who could
not look at the pure processes of Nature without being
reminded of the most hideous and unnatural offences ?
Once more : "The physical interpreters do not even
agree in their physical interpretations". All these
are equally facile, equally plausible, and equally
incapable of proof. Again, Eusebius argues, the interpreters take for granted in the makers of the myths
an amount of physical knowledge which they certainly
did not possess. For example, if Leto were only
another name for Hera, the character of Zeus would
be cleared as far as his amour with Leto is concerned.
Now, the ancient believers in the "physical phenomena theory " of myths made out that Hera, the wife
of Zeus, was really the same person under another
name as Leto, his mistress. "For Hera is the earth "
(they said at other times that Hera was the air), "and
Leto is the night; but night is only the shadow of the

earth, and therefore Leto is only the shadow of Hera."
It was easy, however, to prove that this scientific view
of night as the shadow of earth was not likely to be
known to myth-makers, who regarded " swift Night "
as an actual person. Plutarch, too, had an abstruse
theory to explain the legend about the dummy wife,
—a log of oak-wood, which Zeus pretended to marry
when at variance with Hera.[1]

This quarrel, he said, was merely the confusion and
strife of elements. Zeus was heat, Hera was cold (she
had already been explained as earth and air), the
dummy wife of oak-wood was a tree that emerged
after a flood, and so forth. Of course, there was no
evidence that mythopœic men held Plutarchian
theories of heat and cold and the conflict of the elements ; besides, as Eusebius pointed out, Hera had
already been defined once as an allegory of wedded
life, and once as the earth, and again as the air, and
it was rather too late to assert that she was also the
cold and watery element in the world. As for his own
explanation of the myths, Eusebius holds that they
descend from a period when men in their lawless
barbarism knew no better than to tell such tales.
"Ancient folk, in the exceeding savagery of their
lives, made no account of God, the universal Creator
[here Eusebius is probably wrong] . . . but betook
them to all manner of abominations. For the laws of
decent existence were not yet established, nor was any
settled and peaceful state ordained among men, but
only a loose and savage fashion of wandering life,
while, as beasts irrational, they cared for no more

[1] Pausanias, ix. 31.

than to fill their bellies, being in a manner without
God in the world." Growing a little more civilised
men, according to Eusebius, sought after something
divine, which they found in the heavenly bodies.
Later, they fell to worshipping living persons, especially "medicine men" and conjurors, and continued to
worship them even after their decease, so that Greek
temples are really tombs of the dead.[1] Finally, the
civilised ancients, with a conservative reluctance to
abandon their old myths (κινεῖν τὰ πάτρια τολμῶντος
οὐδενὸς), invented for them moral or physical explanations, like those of Plutarch and others, earlier and
later.[2]

As Eusebius, like Clemens of Alexandria, Arnobius,
and the other early Christian disputants, had no prejudice in favour of Hellenic mythology, and no senti-
mental reason for wishing to suppose that the origin
of its impurities was pure, he found his way almost
to the theory of the irrational element in mythology
which we propose to offer.

Even to sketch the history of mythological hypothesis
in modern times would require a book to itself. It
must suffice here to indicate the various lines which
speculation as to mythology has pursued.

All interpretations of myth have been formed in
accordance with the ideas prevalent in the time of the
interpreters. The early Greek physicists thought that
mythopœic men had been physicists. Aristotle hints
that they were (like himself) political philosophers.[3]
Neo-platonists sought in the myths for Neo-platonism;
most Christians (unlike Eusebius) either sided with

---

[1] *Præp. E.*, ii. 5.   [2] *Ibid.*, 6, 19.   [3] *Met.*, xi. 8, 19.

Euhemerus, or found in myth the inventions of devils, or a tarnished and distorted memory of the Biblical revelation.

This was the theory, for example, of good old Jacob Bryant, who saw everywhere memories of the Noachian deluge and proofs of the correctness of Old Testament ethnology.[1]

Much the same attempt to find the Biblical truth at the bottom of savage and ancient fable has been recently made by the late M. Lenormant, a Catholic scholar.[2]

In the beginning of the present century Germany turned her attention to mythology. As usual, men's ideas were biassed by the general nature of their opinions. In a pious kind of spirit, Friedrich Creuzer sought to find *symbols* of some pure, early, and Oriental theosophy in the myths and mysteries of Greece. Certainly the Greeks of the philosophical period explained their own myths as symbols of higher things, but the explanation was an after-thought.[3] The great Lobeck, in his *Aglaophamus* (1829), brought back common sense, and made it the guide of his vast, his unequalled learning. In a gentler and more genial spirit, C Otfried Müller laid the foundation of a truly scientific and historical mythology.[4] Neither of these writers had, like Alfred Maury,[5] much knowledge of the

---

[1] Bryant, *A New System, wherein an Attempt is made to Divest Tradition of Fable*, 1774.

[2] *Les Origines de l'Histoire d'après le Bible*, 1880-1884.

[3] Creuzer, *Symbolik und Mythologie*, 2d edit., Leipzig, 1836-43.

[4] *Introduction to a Scientific System of Mythology*, English trans., London, 1844.

[5] *Histoire des Religions de la Grèce Antique*, Paris, 1857.

myths and faiths of the lower races, but they often seem on the point of anticipating the ethnological method.

When philological science in our own century came to maturity, in philology, as of old in physics and later in symbols, was sought the key of myths. While physical allegory, religious and esoteric symbolism, verbal confusion, historical legend, and an original divine tradition, perverted in ages of darkness, have been the most popular keys in other ages, the scientific nineteenth century has had a philological key of its own. The methods of Kuhn, Bréal, Max Müller, and generally the philological method, cannot be examined here at full length.[1] Briefly speaking, the modern philological method is intended for a scientific application of the old etymological interpretations. Cadmus in the *Bacchæ* of Euripides, Socrates in the *Cratylus* of Plato, dismiss unpalatable myths as the results of verbal confusion. People had originally said something quite sensible—so the hypothesis runs—but when their descendants forgot the meaning of their remarks, a new and absurd meaning followed from a series of unconscious puns.[2] This view was supported in ancient times by purely conjectural and impossible etymologies. Thus the myth that Dionysus was sewn up in the *thigh* of Zeus (ὁ μηρὸς) was explained by Euripides as the result of a confusion of words. People had origin-

---

[1] See *Mythology* in *Encyclop. Brit.* and in *La Mythologie* (A.L.), Paris, 1886, where Mr. Max Müller's system is criticised. See also *Custom and Myth* and *Modern Mythology.*

[2] That a considerable number of myths, chiefly myths of place names, arise from popular etymologies is certain; what is objected to is the vast proportion given to this element in myths.

ally said that Zeus gave a pledge (ὅμηρος) to Hera.
The modern philological school relies for explanations
of untoward and other myths on similar confusions.
Thus Daphne is said to have been originally not a girl
of romance, but the dawn (Sanskirt, *dahanâ : ahanâ*)
pursued by the rising sun.   But as the original Aryan
sense of *Dahanâ* or *Ahanâ* was lost, and as Daphne
came to mean the laurel—the wood which burns easily
—the fable arose that the tree had been a girl called
Daphne.[1]

This system chiefly rests on comparison between
the Sanskrit names in the Rig-Veda and the mythic
names in Greek, German, Slavonic, and other Aryan
legends.   The attempt is made to prove that, in the
common speech of the undivided Aryan race, many
words for splendid or glowing natural phenomena
existed, and that natural processes were described in
a figurative style.   As the various Aryan families
separated, the sense of the old words and names
became dim, the *nomina* developed into *numina*, the
names into gods, the descriptions of elemental processes into myths.   As this system has already been
criticised by us elsewhere with minute attention, a
reference to these reviews must suffice in this place.
Briefly, it may be stated that the various masters of
the school—Kuhn, Max Müller, Roth, Schwartz, and

---

[1] Max Müller, *Nineteenth Century*, December, 1885; "Solar Myths,"
January, 1886 ; *Myths and Mythologists* (A. L.).   Whitney, Mannhardt,
Bergaigne, and others dispute the etymology.   *Or. and Ling. Studies*,
1874, p. 160; Mannhardt, *Antike Wald und Feld Kultus* (Berlin, 1877),
p. xx. ; Bergaigne, *La Religion Védique*, iii. 293 ; nor does Curtius like it
much, *Principles of Greek Etymology*, English trans., ii. 92, 93 ; *Modern
Mythology* (A. L.), 1897.

the rest—rarely agree where agreement is essential,
that is, in the philological foundations of their building.
They differ in very many of the etymological analyses
of mythical names. They also differ in the interpretations they put on the names, Kuhn almost invariably
seeing fire, storm, cloud, or lightning where Mr. Max
Müller sees the chaste Dawn.   Thus Mannhardt, after
having been a disciple, is obliged to say that comparative Indo-Germanic mythology has not borne the fruit
expected, and that "the *certain* gains of the system
reduce themselves to the scantiest list of parallels,
such as Dyaus = Zeus = Tius, Parjanya = Perkunas,
Bhaga = Bog, Varuna = Uranos" (a position much
disputed), etc.   Mannhardt adds his belief that a
number of other "equations"—such as Sâramêya =
Hermeias, Saranyus = Demeter Erinnys, Kentauros
=Gandharva, and many others—will not stand criticism, and he fears that these ingenious guesses will
prove mere *jeux d'esprit* rather than actual facts.[1]
Many examples of the precarious and contradictory
character of the results of philological mythology,
many instances of "dubious etymologies," false logic,
leaps at foregone conclusions, and attempts to make
what is peculiarly Indian in thought into matter of
universal application, will meet us in the chapters on
Indian and Greek divine legends.[2]   "The method in
its practical working shows a fundamental lack of the

---

[1] *Baum und Feld Kultus*, p. xvii.   Kuhn's "epoch-making" book
is *Die Herabkunft des Feuers*, Berlin, 1859.   By way of example of the
disputes as to the original meaning of a name like Prometheus, compare
Mémoires de la Société de Linguistique de Paris, t. iv. p. 336.

[2] See especially Mannhardt's note on Kuhn's theories of Poseidon and
Hermes, *B. u. F. K.*, pp. xviii., xix., note 1.

historical sense," says Mannhardt. Examples are torn
from their contexts, he observes; historical evolution
is neglected; passages of the Veda, themselves totally
obscure, are dragged forward to account for obscure
Greek mythical phenomena. Such are the accusations
brought by the regretted Mannhardt against the
school to which he originally belonged, and which was
popular and all-powerful even in the maturity of his
own more clear-sighted genius. Proofs of the correctness of his criticism will be offered abundantly in the
course of this work. It will become evident that,
great as are the acquisitions of Philology, her least
certain discoveries have been too hastily applied in
alien "matter," that is, in the region of myth. Not
that philology is wholly without place or part in the
investigation of myth, when there is agreement among
philologists as to the meaning of a divine name. In
that case a certain amount of light is thrown on the
legend of the bearer of the name, and on its origin
and first home, Aryan, Greek, Semitic, or the like.
But how rare is agreement among philologists!

"The philological method," says Professor Tiele,[1]
"is inadequate and misleading, when it is a question
of discovering the *origin* of a myth, or the physical
explanation of the oldest myths, or of accounting for
the rude and obscene element in the divine legends of
civilised races. But these are not the only problems
of mythology. There is, for example, the question of
the *genealogical* relations of myths, where we have
to determine whether the myths of peoples whose
speech is of the same family are special modifications

[1] *Rev. de l'Hist. des Rel.*, xii. 3, 260, Nov., Dec., 1885.

of a mythology once common to the race whence these peoples have sprung. The philological method alone can answer here." But this will seem a very limited province when we find that almost all races, however remote and unconnected in speech, have practically much the same myths.

CHAPTER II.

NEW SYSTEM PROPOSED.

Chapter I. recapitulated—Proposal of a new method: Science of comparative or historical study of man—Anticipated in part by Eusebius, Fontenelle, De Brosses, Spencer (of C.C.C., Cambridge), and Mannhardt—Science of Tylor—Object of inquiry: to find condition of human intellect in which marvels of myth are parts of practical everyday belief—This is the savage state—Savages described—The wild element of myth a survival from the savage state—Advantages of this method—Partly accounts for wide *diffusion* as well as *origin* of myths —Connected with general theory of evolution—Puzzling example of myth of the water-swallower—Professor Tiele's criticism of the method —Objections to method, and answer to these—See Appendix B.

THE past systems of mythological interpretation have been briefly sketched. It has been shown that the practical need for a reconciliation between *religion* and *morality* on one side, and the *myths* about the gods on the other, produced the hypotheses of Theagenes and Metrodorus, of Socrates and Euemerus, of Aristotle and Plutarch. It has been shown that in each case the reconcilers argued on the basis of their own ideas and of the philosophies of their time. The early physicist thought that myth concealed a physical philosophy; the early etymologist saw in it a confusion of language; the early political speculator supposed that myth was an invention of legislators; the literary Euhemerus found the secret of myths in the course of an imaginary voyage to a fabled island.

Then came the moment of the Christian attacks, and
Pagan philosophers, touched with Oriental pantheism,
recognised in myths certain pantheistic symbols and
a cryptic revelation of their own Neo-platonism.
When the gods were dead and their altars fallen,
then antiquaries brought their curiosity to the problem
of explaining myth. Christians recognised in it a
depraved version of the Jewish sacred writings, and
found the ark on every mountain-top of Greece.
The critical nineteenth century brought in, with
Otfried Müller and Lobeck, a closer analysis; and
finally, in the sudden rise of comparative philology,
it chanced that philologists annexed the domain of
myths. Each of these systems had its own amount
of truth, but each certainly failed to unravel the
whole web of tradition and of foolish faith.

Meantime a new science has come into existence,
the science which studies man in the sum of all his
works and thoughts, as evolved through the whole
process of his development. This science, Comparative Anthropology, examines the development of law
out of custom; the development of weapons from the
stick or stone to the latest repeating rifle; the development of society from the horde to the nation.
It is a study which does not despise the most backward nor degraded tribe, nor neglect the most civilised,
and it frequently finds in Australians or Nootkas
the germ of ideas and institutions which Greeks
or Romans brought to perfection, or retained, little
altered from their early rudeness, in the midst of
civilisation.

It is inevitable that this science should also try its

hand on mythology. Our purpose is to employ the anthropological method—the study of the evolution of ideas, from the savage to the barbarous, and thence to the civilised stage—in the province of myth, ritual, and religion. It has been shown that the light of this method had dawned on Eusebius in his polemic with the heathen apologists. Spencer, the head of Corpus, Cambridge (1630-93), had really no other scheme in his mind in his erudite work on Hebrew Ritual.[1] Spencer was a student of man's religions generally, and he came to the conclusion that Hebrew ritual was but an expurgated, and, so to speak, divinely "licensed" adaptation of heathen customs at large. We do but follow his guidance on less perilous ground when we seek for the original forms of classical rite and myth in the parallel usages and legends of the most backward races.

Fontenelle, in the last century, stated, with all the clearness of the French intellect, the system which is partially worked out in this essay—the system which explains the irrational element in myth as inherited from savagery. Fontenelle's paper (*Sur l'Origine des Fables*) is brief, sensible, and witty, and requires little but copious evidence to make it adequate. But he merely threw out the idea, and left it to be neglected.[2]

Among other founders of the anthropological or historical school of mythology, De Brosses should not be forgotten. In his *Dieux Fétiches* (1760) he follows the path which Eusebius indicated—the path

---

[1] *De Legibus Hebræorum Ritualibus*, Tubingæ, 1732.
[2] See Appendix A., Fontenelle's *Origine des Fables*.

of Spencer and Fontenelle—now the beaten road of
Tylor and M'Lennan and Mannhardt.

In anthropology, in the science of Waitz, Tylor,
and M'Lennan, in the examination of man's faith in
the light of his social, legal, and historical conditions
generally, we find, with Mannhardt, some of the keys
of myth. This science " makes it manifest that the
different stages through which humanity has passed
in its intellectual evolution have still their living
representatives among various existing races. The
study of these lower races is an invaluable instrument
for the interpretation of the survivals from earlier
stages, which we meet in the full civilisation of cultivated peoples, but whose origins were in the remotest
fetichism and savagery." [1]

It is by following this road, and by the aid of
anthropology and of human history, that we propose
to seek for a demonstrably actual condition of the
human intellect, whereof the puzzling qualities of
myth would be the natural and inevitable fruit. In
all the earlier theories which we have sketched,
inquirers took it for granted that the myth-makers
were men with philosophic and moral ideas like their
own—ideas which, from some reason of religion or
state, they expressed in *bizarre* terms of allegory.
We shall attempt, on the other hand, to prove that
the human mind has passed through a condition
quite unlike that of civilised men—a condition in
which things seemed natural and rational that now
appear unnatural and devoid of reason, and in which,
therefore, if myths were evolved, they would, if they

---

[1] Mannhardt, *op. cit.*. p. xxiii.

survived into civilisation, be such as civilised men find strange and perplexing.

Our first question will be, Is there a stage of human society and of the human intellect in which facts that appear to us to be monstrous and irrational—facts corresponding to the wilder incidents of myth—are accepted as ordinary occurrences of everyday life? In the region of romantic rather than of mythical invention we know that there is such a state. Mr. Lane, in his preface to the *Arabian Nights*, says that the Arabs have an advantage over us as story-tellers. They can introduce such incidents as the change of a man into a horse, or of a woman into a dog, or the intervention of an Afreet without any more scruple than our own novelists feel in describing a duel or the concealment of a will. Among the Arabs the agencies of magic and of spirits are regarded as at least as probable and common as duels and concealments of wills seem to be thought by European novelists. It is obvious that we need look no farther for the explanation of the supernatural events in Arab romances. Now, let us apply this system to mythology. It is admitted that Greeks, Romans, Aryans of India in the age of the Sanskrit commentators, and Egyptians of the Ptolemaic and earlier ages, were as much puzzled as we are by the mythical adventures of their gods. But is there any known stage of the human intellect in which similar adventures, and the metamorphoses of men into animals, trees, stars, and all else that puzzles us in the civilised mythologies, are regarded as possible incidents of daily human life? Our answer is, that everything in the civilised mythologies which we

regard as irrational seems only part of the accepted
and natural order of things to contemporary savages,
and in the past seemed equally rational and natural to
savages concerning whom we have historical information.[1] Our theory is, therefore, that the savage and
senseless element in mythology is, for the most part,
a legacy from the fancy of ancestors of the civilised
races who were once in an intellectual state not higher,
but probably lower, than that of Australians, Bush-

---

[1] We have been asked to *define* a savage. He cannot be defined in an
epigram, but by way of choice of a type :—

1. In material equipment the perfect savage is he who employs tools of
stone and wood, not of metal ; who is nomadic rather than settled ; who is
acquainted (if at all) only with the rudest forms of the arts of potting,
weaving, fire-making, etc. ; and who derives more of his food from the
chase and from wild roots and plants than from any kind of agriculture or
from the flesh of domesticated animals.

2. In psychology the savage is he who (extending unconsciously to the
universe his own implicit consciousness of personality) regards all natural
objects as animated and intelligent beings, and, drawing no hard and fast
line between himself and the things in the world, is readily persuaded that
men may be metamorphosed into plants, beasts and stars ; that winds and
clouds, sun and dawn, are persons with |human passions and parts ; and
that the lower animals especially may be creatures more powerful than
himself, and, in a sense, divine and creative.

3. In religion the savage is he who (while often, in certain moods, conscious of a far higher moral faith) believes also in ancestral ghosts or spirits
of woods and wells that were never ancestral ; prays frequently by dint of
magic ; and sometimes adores inanimate objects, or even appeals to the
beasts as supernatural protectors.

4. In society the savage is he who (as a rule) bases his laws on the well-
defined lines of totemism—that is, claims descent from or other close
relation to natural objects, and derives from the sacredness of those objects
the sanction of his marriage prohibitions and blood-feuds, while he makes
skill in magic a claim to distinguished rank.

Such, for our purpose, is the savage, and we propose to explain the more
"senseless" factors in civilised mythology as "survivals" of these ideas
and customs preserved by conservatism and local tradition, or, less probably,
borrowed from races which were, or had been, savage.

men, Red Indians, the lower races of South America, and other worse than barbaric peoples. As the ancestors of the Greeks, Aryans of India, Egyptians and others advanced in civilisation, their religious thought was shocked and surprised by myths (originally dating from the period of savagery, and natural in that period, though even then often in contradiction to morals and religion) which were preserved down to the time of Pausanias by local priesthoods, or which were stereotyped in the ancient poems of Hesiod and Homer, or in the Brahmanas and Vedas of India, or were retained in the popular religion of Egypt. This theory recommended itself to Lobeck. "We may believe that ancient and early tribes framed gods like unto themselves in action and in experience, and that the allegorical softening down of myths is the explanation added later by descendants who had attained to purer ideas of divinity, yet dared not reject the religion of their ancestors."[1] The senseless element in the myths would, by this theory, be for the most part a "survival"; and the age and condition of human thought whence it survived would be one in which our most ordinary ideas about the nature of things and the limits of possibility did not yet exist, when all things were conceived of in quite other fashion; the age, that is, of savagery.

It is universally admitted that "survivals" of this kind do account for many anomalies in our institu-

---

[1] *Aglaoph.*, i. 153. Had Lobeck gone a step farther and examined the mental condition of *veteres et priscæ gentes*, this book would have been superfluous. Nor did he know that the purer ideas were also existing among certain low savages.

tions, in law, politics, society, even in dress and
manners. If isolated fragments of earlier ages abide
in these, it is still more probable that other fragments
will survive in anything so closely connected as is
mythology with the conservative religious sentiment
and tradition. Our object, then, is to prove that the
" silly, savage, and irrational " element in the myths
of civilised peoples is, as a rule, either a survival from
the period of savagery, or has been borrowed from
savage neighbours by a cultivated people, or, lastly,
is an imitation by later poets of old savage *data*.[1]
For example, to explain the constellations as metamorphosed men, animals, or other objects of terrestrial
life is the habit of savages,[2]—a natural habit among
people who regard all things as on one level of personal life and intelligence. When the stars, among
civilised Greeks or Aryans of India, are also popularly
regarded as transformed and transfigured men, animals
and the like, this belief may be either a survival from
the age when the ancestors of Greeks and Indians
were in the intellectual condition of the Australian
Murri ; or the star-name and star-myth may have been
borrowed from savages, or from cultivated peoples
once savage or apt to copy savages ; or, as in the case
of the *Coma Berenices*, a poet of a late age may have
invented a new artificial myth on the old lines of
savage fancy.

[1] We may be asked why do savages entertain the irrational ideas which
survive in myth ? One might as well ask why they eat each other, or use
stones instead of metal. Their intellectual powers are not fully developed,
and hasty analogy from their own unreasoned consciousness is their chief
guide. Myth, in Mr. Darwin's phrase, is one of the "miserable and in-
direct consequences of our highest faculties". *Descent of Man*, p. 69.

[2] See *Custom and Myth*, "Star-Myths".

This method of interpreting a certain element in mythology is, we must repeat, no new thing, though, to judge from the protests of several mythologists, it is new to many inquirers. We have seen that Eusebius threw out proposals in this direction; that Spencer, De Brosses, and Fontenelle unconsciously followed him; and we have quoted from Lobeck a statement of a similar opinion. The whole matter has been stated as clearly as possible by Mr. E. B. Tylor :—

"Savages have been for untold ages, and still are, living in the myth-making stage of the human mind. It was through sheer ignorance and neglect of this direct knowledge how and by what manner of men myths are really made that their simple philosophy has come to be buried under masses of commentator's rubbish. . . ." [1] Mr. Tylor goes on thus (and his words contain the gist of our argument): "The general thesis maintained is that myth arose in the savage condition prevalent in remote ages among the whole human race; that it remains comparatively unchanged among the rude modern tribes who have departed least from these primitive conditions, while higher and later civilisations, partly by retaining its actual principles, and partly by carrying on its inherited results in the form of ancestral tradition, continued it not merely in toleration, but in honour ".[2] Elsewhere Mr. Tylor points out that by this method of interpretation we may study myths in various stages of evolution, from the rude guess of the savage at an explanation of natural phenomena, through the systems of the higher barbarisms, or lower civilisations (as in ancient Mexico),

---

[1] *Primitive Culture*, 2nd edit., i. p. 283.　　[2] *Op. cit.*, p. 275.

and the sacerdotage of India, till myth reaches its
most human form in Greece. Yet even in Greek myth
the beast is not wholly cast out, and Hellas by no
means "let the ape and tiger die". That Mr. Tylor
does not exclude the Aryan race from his general
theory is plain enough.[1] "What is the Aryan conception of the Thunder-god but a poetic elaboration of
thoughts inherited from the savage stage through
which the primitive Aryans had passed?"[2]

The advantages of our hypothesis (if its legitimacy
be admitted) are obvious. In the first place, we have
to deal with an actual demonstrable condition of the
human intellect. The existence of the savage state in
all its various degrees, and of the common intellectual
habits and conditions which are shared by the backward peoples, and again the survival of many of these
in civilisation, are indubitable facts. We are not
obliged to fall back upon some fanciful and unsup-
ported theory of what "primitive man" did, and said,
and thought. Nay, more ; we escape all the fallacies
connected with the terms "primitive man". We are
not compelled (as will be shown later)[3] to prove that
the first men of all were like modern savages, nor that
savages represent primitive man. It may be that the
lowest extant savages are the nearest of existing
peoples to the type of the first human beings. But
on this point it is unnecessary for us to dogmatise.
If we can show that, whether men began their career

[1] *Primitive Culture*, 2nd edit., ii. 265.
[2] Pretty much the same view seems to be taken by Mr. Max Müller
(*Nineteenth Century*, January, 1882) when he calls Tsui Goab (whom the
Hottentots believe to be a defunct conjuror) "a Hottentot Indra or Zeus".
[3] Appendix B.

as savages or not, they have at least passed through
the savage *status* or have borrowed the ideas of races
in the savage *status*, that is all we need. We escape
from all the snares of theories (incapable of historical
proof) about the really primeval and original condition
of the human family.

Once more, our theory naturally attaches itself to
the general system of Evolution. We are enabled to
examine mythology as a thing of gradual development
and of slow and manifold modifications, corresponding
in some degree to the various changes in the general
progress of society. Thus we shall watch the barbaric
conditions of thought which produce barbaric myths,
while these in their turn are retained, or perhaps
purified, or perhaps explained away, by more advanced
civilisations. Further, we shall be able to detect the
survival of the savage ideas with least modification,
and the persistence of the savage myths with least
change, among the classes of a civilised population
which have shared least in the general advance.
These classes are, first, the rustic peoples, dwelling
far from cities and schools, on heaths or by the sea;
second, the conservative local priesthoods, who retain
the more crude and ancient myths of the local gods
and heroes after these have been modified or rejected
by the purer sense of philosophers and national poets.
Thus much of ancient myth is a woven warp and woof
of three threads: the savage *donnée*, the civilised and
poetic modification of the savage *donnée*, the version
of the original fable which survives in popular tales
and in the "sacred chapters" of local priesthoods. A
critical study of these three stages in myth is in

accordance with the recognised practice of science. Indeed, the whole system is only an application to this particular province, mythology, of the method by which the development either of organisms or of human institutions is traced. As the anomalies and apparently useless and accidental features in the human or in other animal organisms may be explained as stunted or rudimentary survivals of organs useful in a previous stage of life, so the anomalous and irrational myths of civilised races may be explained as survivals of stories which, in an earlier state of thought and knowledge, seemed natural enough. The persistence of the myths is accounted for by the well-known conservatism of the religious sentiment—a conservatism noticed even by Eusebius. "In later days, when they became ashamed of the religious beliefs of their ancestors, they invented private and respectful interpretations, each to suit himself. For no one dared to shake the ancestral ‚beliefs, as they honoured at a very high rate the sacredness and antiquity of old associations, and of the teaching they had received in childhood." [1]

Thus the method which we propose to employ is in harmony both with modern scientific procedure and with the views of a clear-sighted Father of the Church. Consequently no system could well be less "heretical" and "unorthodox".

The last advantage of our hypothesis which need here be mentioned is that it helps to explain the *diffusion* no less than the *origin* of the wild and crazy element in myth. We seek for the origin of

[1] *Præp. E.*, ii. 6, 19.

the savage factor of myth in one aspect of the intellectual condition of savages. We say "in one aspect"
expressly; to guard against the suggestion that the
savage intellect has no aspect but this, and no saner
ideas than those of myth. The *diffusion* of stories
practically identical in every quarter of the globe
may be (provisionally) regarded as the result of the
prevalence in every quarter, at one time or another,
of similar mental habits and ideas. This explanation
must not be pressed too hard nor too far. If we find
all over the world a belief that men can change themselves and their neighbours into beasts, that belief
will account for the appearance of metamorphosis in
myth. If we find a belief that inanimate objects are
really much on a level with man, the opinion will
account for incidents of myth such as that in which
the wooden figure-head of the Argo speaks with a
human voice. Again, a widespread belief in the
separability of the soul or the life from the body
will account for the incident in nursery tales and
myths of the "giant who had no heart in his body,"
but kept his heart and life elsewhere. An ancient
identity of mental status and the working of similar
mental forces at the attempt to explain the same
phenomena will account, without any theory of borrowing, or transmission of myth, or of original unity
of race, for the world-wide diffusion of many mythical
conceptions.

But this theory of the original similarity of the
savage mind everywhere and in all races will scarcely
account for the world-wide distribution of long and
intricate mythical *plots*, of consecutive series of adroitly

interwoven situations. In presence of these long
romances, found among so many widely severed
peoples, conjecture is, at present, almost idle. We do
not know, in many instances, whether such stories
were independently developed, or carried from a
common centre, or borrowed by one race from another,
and so handed on round the world.

This chapter may conclude with an example of a
tale whose *diffusion* may be explained in divers ways,
though its *origin* seems undoubtedly savage. If we
turn to the Algonkins, a stock of Red Indians, we come
on a popular tradition which really does give pause
to the mythologist.   Could this story, he asks himself,
have been separately invented in widely different
places, or could the Iroquois have borrowed from the
Australian blacks or the Andaman Islanders ? It is
a common thing in most mythologies to find everything
of value to man—fire, sun, water—in the keeping of
some hostile power. The fire, or the sun, or the water
is then stolen, or in other ways rescued from the enemy
and restored to humanity. The Huron story (as far
as water is concerned) is told by Father Paul Le Jeune,
a Jesuit missionary, who lived among the Hurons about
1636. The myth begins with the usual opposition between two brothers, the Cain and Abel of savage legend.
One of the brothers, named Ioskeha, slew the other, and
became the father of mankind (as known to the Red
Indians) and the guardian of the Iroquois. The earth
was at first arid and sterile, but Ioskeha destroyed the
gigantic frog which had swallowed all the waters, and
guided the torrents into smooth streams and lakes.[1]

1 *Relations de la Nouvelle France*, 1636, p. 103 (Paris, Cramoisy, 1637).

Now where, outside of North America, do we find this frog who swallowed all the water? We find him in Australia.

"The aborigines of Lake Tyers," remarks Mr. Brough Smyth, "say that at one time there was no water anywhere on the face of the earth. All the waters were contained in the body of a huge frog, and men and women could get none of them. A council was held, and . . . it was agreed that the frog should be made to laugh, when the waters would run out of his mouth, and there would be plenty in all parts."

To make a long story short, all the animals played the jester before the gigantic solemn frog, who sat as grave as Louis XV. "I do not like buffoons who don't make me laugh," said that majestical monarch. At last the eel danced on the tip of his tail, and the gravity of the prodigious Batrachian gave way. He laughed till he literally split his sides, and the imprisoned waters came with a rush. Indeed, many persons were drowned, though this is not the only Australian version of the Deluge.

The Andaman Islanders dwell at a very considerable distance from Australia and from the Iroquois, and, in the present condition of the natives of Australia and Andaman, neither could possibly visit the other. The frog in the Andaman version is called a toad, and he came to swallow the waters in the following way: One day a woodpecker was eating honey high up in the boughs of a tree. Far below, the toad was a witness of the feast, and asked for some honey. "Well, come up here, and you shall have some," said the woodpecker. "But how am I to climb?" "Take hold of that

creeper, and I will draw you up," said the woodpecker ;
but all the while he was bent on a practical joke. So
the toad got into a bucket he happened to possess, and
fastened the bucket to the creeper. " Now, pull ! "
Then the woodpecker raised the toad slowly to the
level of the bough where the honey was, and presently
let him down with a run, not only disappointing the
poor toad, but shaking him severely. The toad went
away in a rage and looked about him for revenge. A
happy thought occurred to him, and he drank up all
the water of the rivers and lakes. Birds and beasts
were perishing, woodpeckers among them, of thirst.
The toad, overjoyed at his success, wished to add insult
to the injury, and, very thoughtlessly, began to dance
in an irritating manner at his foes. But then the
stolen waters gushed out of his mouth in full volume,
and the drought soon ended. One of the most curious
points in this myth is the origin of the quarrel between
the woodpecker and the toad. The same beginning—
the tale of an insult put on an animal by hauling up
and letting him down with a run—occurs in an African
Märchen.[1]

Now this strangely diffused story of the slaying of
the frog which had swallowed all the water seems to
be a savage myth of which the more heroic conflict of
Indra with Vrittra (the dragon which had swallowed all
the waters) is an epic and sublimer version.[2] " The

---

[1] Brough Smyth, *Aborigines of Victoria*, i. 429, 430 ; Brinton, *American
Hero Myths*, i. 55. *Cf.* also *Relations de la Nouvelle France*, 1636, 1640,
1671 ; [Sagard, *Hist. du Canada*, 1636, p. 451 ;] *Journal Anthrop. Inst.*,
1881.

[2] Ludwig, *Der Rig-Veda*, iii. p. 337. See *postea*, " Divine Myths of
India ".

heavenly water, which Vrittra withholds from the world, is usually the prize of the contest."

The serpent of Vedic myth is, perhaps, rather the robber-guardian than the swallower of the waters, but Indra is still, like the Iroquois Ioskeha, "he who wounds the full one".[1] This example of the wide distribution of a myth shows how the question of diffusion, though connected with, is yet distinct from that of origin. The advantage of our method will prove to be, that it discovers an historical and demonstrable state of mind as the origin of the wild element in myth. Again, the wide prevalence in the earliest times of this mental condition will, to a certain extent, explain the *distribution* of myth. Room must be left, of course, for processes of borrowing and transmission, but how Andamanese, Australians and Hurons could borrow from each other is an unsolved problem.

Finally, our hypothesis is not involved in dubious theories of race. To us, myths appear to be affected (in their origins) much less by the race than by the stage of culture attained by the people who cherish them. A fight for the waters between a monstrous dragon like Vrittra and a heroic god like Indra is a nobler affair than a quarrel for the waters between a woodpecker and a toad. But the improvement and transfiguration, so to speak, of a myth at bottom the same is due to the superior culture, not to the peculiar race, of the Vedic poets, except so far as culture itself depends on race. How far the purer

---

[1] Gubernatis, *Zoological Myth*, ii. 395, note 2. "When Indra kills the serpent he opens the torrent of the waters" (p. 393). See also *Aitareya Brahmana*, translated by Haug, ii. 483.

culture was attained to by the original superiority of
the Aryan over the Andaman breed, it is not necessary
for our purpose to inquire. Thus, on the whole, we
may claim for our system a certain demonstrable
character, which helps to simplify the problems of
mythology, and to remove them from the realm of
fanciful guesses and conflicting etymological conjectures into that of sober science. That these
pretensions are not unacknowledged even by mythologists trained in other schools is proved by the
remarks of Dr. Tiele.[1]

Dr. Tiele writes: "If I were obliged to choose
between this method" (the system here advocated)
"and that of comparative philology, it is the former
that I would adopt without the slightest hesitation.
This method alone enables us to explain the fact,
which has so often provoked amazement, that people
so refined as the Greeks, . . . or so rude, but morally
pure, as the Germans, . . . managed to attribute to
their gods all manner of cowardly, cruel and disorderly
conduct. This method alone explains the why and
wherefore of all those strange metamorphoses of gods
into beasts and plants, and even stones, which scanda-
lised philosophers, and which the witty Ovid played
on for the diversion of his contemporaries. In short,
this method teaches us to recognise in all those strange
stories the survivals of a barbaric age, long passed
away, but enduring to later times in the form of
religious traditions, of all traditions the most per-

---

[1] *Rev. de l' Hist. des Rel.*, " Le Mythe de Cronos," January, 1886. Dr.
Tiele is not, it must be noted, a thorough adherent of our theory. See
Modern Mythology : " The Question of Allies".

sistent. . . . Finally, this method alone enables us to explain the origin of myths, because it endeavours to study them in their rudest and most primitive shape, thus allowing their true significance to be much more clearly apparent than it can be in the myths (so often touched, retouched, augmented and humanised) which are current among races arrived at a certain degree of culture."

The method is to this extent applauded by a most competent authority, and it has been warmly accepted by a distinguished French school of students, represented by M. Gaidoz. But it is obvious that the method rests on a double hypothesis : first, that satisfactory evidence as to the mental conditions of the lower and backward races is obtainable ; second, that the civilised races (however they began) either passed through the savage state of thought and practice, or borrowed very freely from people in that condition. These hypotheses have been attacked by opponents ; the trustworthiness of our evidence, especially, has been assailed. By way of facilitating the course of the exposition and of lessening the disturbing element of controversy, a reply to the objections and a defence of the evidence has been relegated to an Appendix.[1] Meanwhile we go on to examine the peculiar characteristics of the mental condition of savages and of peoples in the lower and upper barbarisms.

[1] Appendix B.

CHAPTER III.

THE MENTAL CONDITION OF SAVAGES—CON-FUSION WITH NATURE—TOTEMISM.

The mental condition of savages the basis of the irrational element in myth
—Characteristics of that condition : (1) Confusion of all things in an
equality of presumed animation and intelligence; (2) Belief in sorcery;
(3) Spiritualism ; (4) Curiosity; (5) Easy credulity and mental indolence—The curiosity is satisfied, thanks to the credulity, by myths
in answer to all inquiries—Evidence for this—Mr. Tylor's opinion—
Mr. Im Thurn—Jesuit missionaries' *Relations*—Examples of confusion
between men, plants, beasts and other natural objects—Reports of
travellers—Evidence from institution of totemism—Definition of
totemism—Totemism in Australia, Africa, America, the Oceanic
Islands, India, North Asia—Conclusions : Totemism being found so
widely distributed, is a proof of the existence of that savage mental
condition in which no line is drawn between men and the other things
in the world. This confusion is one of the characteristics of myth in
all races.

WE set out to discover a stage of human intellectual
development which would necessarily produce the
essential elements of myth. We think we have found
that stage in the condition of savagery. We now
proceed to array the evidence for the mental processes
of savages. We intend to demonstrate the existence
in practical savage life of the ideas which most surprise
us when we find them in civilised sacred legends.

For the purposes of this inquiry, it is enough to
select a few special peculiarities of savage thought.

1. First we have that nebulous and confused frame

of mind to which all things, animate or inanimate, human, animal, vegetable, or inorganic, seem on the same level of life, passion and reason. The savage, at all events when myth-making, draws no hard and fast line between himself and the things in the world. He regards himself as literally akin to animals and plants and heavenly bodies; he attributes sex and procreative powers even to stones and rocks, and he assigns human speech and human feelings to sun and moon and stars and wind, no less than to beasts, birds and fishes.[1]

2. The second point to note in savage opinion is the belief in magic and sorcery. The world and all the things in it being vaguely conceived of as sensible and rational, obey the commands of certain members of the tribe, chiefs, jugglers, conjurors, or what you will. Rocks open at their order, rivers dry up, animals are their servants and hold converse with them. These magicians cause or heal diseases, and can command even the weather, bringing rain or thunder or sunshine at their will.[2] There are few supernatural attributes of "cloud-compelling Zeus" or of Apollo that are not freely assigned to the tribal conjuror. By virtue, doubtless, of the community of nature between man and the things in the world, the conjuror (like Zeus or Indra) can assume at will the shape of any animal, or can metamorphose his neighbours or enemies into animal forms.

[1] "So fasst auch das Alterthum ihren Unterschied von den Menschen ganz anders als die spätere Zeit."—*Grimm*, quoted by Liebrecht, *Zur Volkskunde*, p. 17.

[2] See Roth in *North-West Central Queensland Aborigines*, chapter xii., 1897.

3. Another peculiarity of savage belief naturally connects itself with that which has just been described. The savage has very strong ideas about the persistent existence of the souls of the dead. They retain much of their old nature, but are often more malignant after death than they had been during life. They are frequently at the beck and call of the conjuror, whom they aid with their advice and with their magical power. By virtue of the close connection already spoken of between man and the animals, the souls of the dead are not rarely supposed to migrate into the bodies of beasts, or to revert to the condition of that species of creatures with which each tribe supposes itself to be related by ties of kinship or friendship. With the usual inconsistency of mythical belief, the souls of the dead are spoken of, at other times, as if they inhabited a spiritual world, sometimes a paradise of flowers, sometimes a gloomy place, which mortal men may visit, but whence no one can escape who has tasted of the food of the ghosts.

4. In connection with spirits a far-reaching savage philosophy prevails. It is not unusual to assign a ghost to all objects, animate or inanimate, and the spirit or strength of a man is frequently regarded as something separable, capable of being located in an external object, or something with a definite locality in the body. A man's strength and spirit may reside in his kidney fat, in his heart, in a lock of his hair, or may even be stored by him in some separate receptacle. Very frequently a man is held capable of detaching his soul from his body, and

letting it roam about on his business, sometimes in the form of a bird or other animal.

5. Many minor savage beliefs might be named, such as the common faith in friendly or protecting animals, and the notion that " natural deaths " (as we call them) are always *unnatural*, that death is always caused by some hostile spirit or conjuror. From this opinion comes the myth that man is naturally not subject to death : that death was somehow introduced into the world by a mistake or misdeed is a corollary. (See " Myths of the Origin of Death " in *Modern Mythology*.)

6. One more mental peculiarity of the savage mind remains to be considered in this brief summary. The savage, like the civilised man, is curious. The first faint impulses of the scientific spirit are at work in his brain ; he is anxious to give himself an account of the world in which he finds himself. But he is not more curious than he is, on occasion, credulous. His intellect is eager to ask questions, as is the habit of children, but his intellect is also lazy, and he is content with the first answer that comes to hand. " Ils s'arrêtent aux premières notions qu'ils en ont," says Père Hierome Lalemant.[1] " Nothing," says School-craft, " is too capacious (*sic*) for Indian belief." [2] The replies to his questions he receives from tradition or (when a new problem arises) evolves an answer for himself in the shape of *stories*. Just as Socrates, in the Platonic dialogues, recalls or invents a myth in the despair of reason, so the savage has a story for

---

[1] *Relations de la Nouvelle France*, 1648, p. 70.
[2] *Algic Researches*, i. 41.

answer to almost every question that he can ask
himself. These stories are in a sense scientific, because they attempt a solution of the riddles of the
world. They are in a sense religious, because there
is usually a supernatural power, a *deus ex machina*,
of some sort to cut the knot of the problem. Such
stories, then, are the science, and to a certain extent
the religious tradition, of savages.[1]

Now these tales are necessarily cast in the mould
of the savage ideas of which a sketch has been given
The changes of the heavenly bodies, the processes of
day and night, the existence of the stars, the invention
of the arts, the origin of the world (as far as known
to the savage), of the tribe, of the various animals
and plants, the origin of death itself, the origin of the
perplexing traditional tribal customs, are all accounted
for in stories. At the same time, an actual divine
Maker is sometimes postulated. The stories, again,
are fashioned in accordance with the beliefs already
named : the belief in human connection with and kinship with beasts and plants ; the belief in magic ; the
belief in the perpetual possibility of metamorphosis or
" shape shifting " ; the belief in the permanence and
power of the ghosts of the dead ; the belief in the
personal and animated character of all the things in
the world, and so forth.

No more need be said to explain the wild and (as
it seems to us moderns) the irrational character of
savage myth. It is a jungle of foolish fancies, a

[1] " The Indians (Algonkins) conveyed instruction—moral, mechanical
and religious—through traditionary fictions and tales."—Schoolcraft, *Algic
Researches*, i. 12.

walpurgis nacht of gods and beasts and men and
stars and ghosts, all moving madly on a level of
common personality and animation, and all changing
shapes at random, as partners are changed in some
fantastic witches' revel. Such is savage mythology,
and how could it be otherwise when we consider the
elements of thought and belief out of which it is
mainly composed ? We shall see that part of the
mythology of the Greeks or the Aryans of India is
but a similar *walpurgis nacht*, in which an incestuous
or amorous god may become a beast, and the object of
his pursuit, once a woman, may also become a beast,
and then shift shapes to a tree or a bird or a star.
But in the civilised races the genius of the people
tends to suppress, exclude and refine away the wild
element, which, however, is never wholly eliminated.
The Erinyes soon stop the mouth of the horse of
Achilles when he begins, like the horse in Grimm's
Goose Girl, to hold a sustained conversation.[1] But
the ancient, cruel, and grotesque savage element, nearly
overcome by Homer and greatly reduced by the Vedic
poets, breaks out again in Hesiod, in temple legends
and Brahmanic glosses, and finally proves so strong
that it can only be subdued by Christianity, or rather
by that break between the educated classes and the
traditional past of religion which has resulted from
Christianity. Even so, myth lingers in the folk-lore
of the non-progressive classes of Europe, and, as in
Roumania, invades religion.

We have now to demonstrate the existence in the
savage intellect of the various ideas and habits which

[1] *Iliad*, xix. 418.

we have described, and out of which mythology
springs. First, we have to show that "a nebulous
and confused state of mind, to which all things,
animate or inanimate, human, animal, vegetable or
inorganic, seem on the same level of life, passion and
reason," does really exist.[1] The existence of this
condition of the intellect will be demonstrated first on
the evidence of the statements of civilised observers,
next on the evidence of the savage institutions in
which it is embodied.

The opinion of Mr. Tylor is naturally of great
value, as it is formed on as wide an acquaintance
with the views of the lower races as any inquirers can
hope to possess. Mr. Tylor observes : "We have to
inform ourselves of the savage man's idea, which is
very different from the civilised man's, of the nature
of the lower animals. . . . The sense of an absolute
psychical distinction between man and beast, so prevalent in the civilised world, is hardly to be found
among the lower races."[2] The universal attribution of
"souls" to all things—the theory known as "Animism"
—is another proof that the savage draws no hard
and fast line between man and the other things
in the world. The notion of the Italian country-
people, that cruelty to an animal does not matter
because it is not a "Christian," has no parallel in the
philosophy of the savage, to whom all objects seem to
have souls, just as men have. Mr. Im Thurn found
the absence of any sense of a difference between man
and nature a characteristic of his native companions

[1] Creuzer and Guigniaut, vol. i. p. 111.
[2] *Primitive Culture*, i. 167-169.

in Guiana. "The very phrase, 'Men and other
animals,' or even, as it is often expressed, 'Men
and animals,' based as it is on the superiority which
civilised man feels over other animals, expresses a
dichotomy which is in no way recognised by the
Indian. . . . It is therefore most important to realise
how comparatively small really is the difference between men in a state of savagery and other animals,
and how completely even such difference as exists
escapes the notice of savage men. . . . It is not,
therefore, too much to say that, according to the
view of the Indians, other animals differ from men
only in bodily form and in their various degrees of
strength ; in spirit they do not differ at all."[1] The
Indian's notion of the life of plants and stones is on
the same level of unreason, as we moderns reckon
reason. He believes in the spirits of rocks and stones,
undeterred by the absence of motion in these objects.
"Not only many rocks, but also many waterfalls,
streams, and indeed material objects of every sort, are
supposed each to consist of a body and a spirit, as
does man."[2] It is not our business to ask here how
men came by the belief in universal animation. That
belief is gradually withdrawn, distinctions are gradually introduced, as civilisation and knowledge advance.
It is enough for us if the failure to draw a hard and
fast line between man and beasts, stones and plants,
qe practically universal among savages, and if it
gradually disappears before the fuller knowledge of
civilisation. The report which Mr. Im Thurn brings

[1] *Among the Indians of Guiana* (1883), p. 350.
[2] *Op. cit.*, 355,

from the Indians of Guiana is confirmed by what
Schoolcraft says of the Algonkin races of the northern
part of the continent. "The belief of the narrators
and listeners in every wild and improbable thing told
helps wonderfully, in the original stories, in joining
all parts together. The Indian believes that the whole
visible and invisible creation is animated. . . . To
make the matter worse, these tribes believe that
animals of the lowest as well as highest class in the
chain of creation are alike endowed with reasoning
powers and faculties. As a natural conclusion they
endow birds, beasts and all other animals with souls." [1]
As an example of the ease with which the savage
recognises consciousness and voluntary motion even
in stones, may be cited Kohl's account of the beliefs
of the Objibeways. [2] Nearly every Indian has discovered, he says, an object in which he places special
confidence, and to which he sacrifices more zealously
than to the Great Spirit. The "hope" of Otamigan
(a companion of the traveller) was a rock, which once
advanced to meet him, swayed, bowed and went back
again. Another Indian revered a Canadian larch,
"because he once heard a very remarkable rustling
in its branches". It thus appears that while the
savage has a general kind of sense that inanimate
things are animated, he is a good deal impressed by
their conduct when he thinks that they actually
display their animation. In the same way a devout
modern spiritualist probably regards with more rever-

[1] Schoolcraft, *Algic Researches*, i. 41.

[2] Kohl, *Wanderings Round Lake Superior*, pp. 58, 59 ; Müller, *Ameri
kan Urrelig.*, pp. 62-67.

ence a table which he has seen dancing and heard
rapping than a table at which he has only dined.
Another general statement of failure to draw the line
between men and the irrational creation is found in
the old Jesuit missionary Le Jeune's *Relations de la
Nouvelle France*.[1] "Les sauvages se persuadent que
non seulement les hommes et les autres animaux,
mais aussi que toutes les autres choses sont animées."
Again : " Ils tiennent les poissons raisonnables, comme
aussi les cerfs ". In the Solomon Islands, Mr. Romilly
sailed with an old chief who used violent language to
the waves when they threatened to dash over the
boat, and "old Takki's exhortations were successful ".[2]
Waitz[3] discovers the same attitude towards the
animals among the negroes. Man, in their opinion, is
by no means a separate sort of person on the summit
of nature and high above the beasts ; these he rather
regards as dark and enigmatic beings, whose life is
full of mystery, and which he therefore considers now
as his inferiors, now as his superiors. A collection
of evidence as to the savage failure to discriminate
between human and non-human, animate and inanimate, has been brought together by Sir John Lubbock.[4]

To a race accustomed like ourselves to arrange and
classify, to people familiar from childhood and its
games with "vegetable, animal and mineral," a
condition of mind in which no such distinctions are
drawn, any more than they are drawn in Greek or

---

[1] 1636, p. 109.   [2] *Western Pacific*, p. 84.

[3] *Anthropologie der Natur-Völker*, ii. 177.

[4] *Origin of Civilisation*, p. 33. A number of examples of this mental
attitude among the Bushmen will be found in chap. v., *postea*.

Brahmanic myths, must naturally seem like what
Mr. Max Müller calls "temporary insanity". The
imagination of the savage has been defined by Mr.
Tylor as "midway between the conditions of a healthy,
prosaic, modern citizen, and of a raving fanatic, or of
a patient in a fever-ward". If any relics of such
imagination survive in civilised mythology, they will
very closely resemble the productions of a once universal "temporary insanity". Let it be granted, then,
that "to the lower tribes of man, sun and stars, trees
and rivers, winds and clouds, become personal, animate
creatures, leading lives conformed to human or animal
analogies, and performing their special functions in
the universe with the aid of limbs like beasts, or of
artificial instruments like men; or that what men's
eyes behold is but the instrument to be used or the
material to be shaped, while behind it there stands
some prodigious but yet half-human creature, who
grasps it with his hands or blows it with his breath.
The basis on which such ideas as these are built is not
to be narrowed down to poetic fancy and transformed
metaphor. They rest upon a broad philosophy of
nature ; early and crude, indeed, but thoughtful,
consistent, and quite really and seriously meant." [1]

For the sake of illustration, some minor examples
must next be given of this confusion between man
and other things in the world, which will presently
be illustrated by the testimony of a powerful and
long diffused set of institutions.

The Christian Quiches of Guatemala believe that
each of them has a beast as his friend and protector,

---

[1] *Primitive Culture*, i. 285.

just as in the Highlands "the dog is the friend of the Maclaines". When the Finns, in their epic poem the *Kalewala,* have killed a bear, they implore the animal to forgive them. "Oh, Ot-so," chant the singers, " be not angry that we come near thee. The bear, the honey-footed bear, was born in lands between sun and moon, and he died, not by men's hands, but of his own will." [1] The Red Men of North America [2] have a tradition showing how it is that the bear does not die, but, like Herodotus with the sacred stories of the Egyptian priests, Mr. Schoolcraft "cannot induce himself to write it out". [3] It is a most curious fact that the natives of Australia tell a similar tale of *their* "native bear". "He did not die" when attacked by men. [4] In parts of Australia it is a great offence to skin the native bear, just as on a part of the west coast of Ireland, where seals are superstitiously regarded, the people cannot be bribed to skin them. In New Caledonia, when a child tries to kill a lizard, the men warn him to "beware of killing his own ancestor". [5] The Zulus spare to destroy a certain species of serpents, believed to be the spirits of kinsmen, as the great snake which appeared when Æneas did sacrifice was held to be the ghost of Anchises. Mexican women [6]

[1] *Kalewala,* in *La Finlande,* Leouzon Le Duc (1845), vol. ii. p. 100; *cf.* also the Introduction.

[2] Schoolcraft, v. 420.

[3] See similar ceremonies propitiatory of the bear in Jewett's *Adventures among the Nootkas,* Edinburgh, 1824.

[4] Brough Smyth, i. 449.   [5] J. J. Atkinson's MS.

[6] Sahagun, ii. viii. 250; Bancroft, iii. 111. Compare stories of women who give birth to animals in *Mélusine,* 1886, August-November. The Batavians believe that women, when delivered of a child, are frequently delivered at the same time of a young crocodile as a twin. Hawkesworth's *Voyages,* iii. 756. Liebrecht, *Zur Volkskunde,* p. 17 *et seq.*

believed that children born during an eclipse turn into
mice. In Australia the natives believe that the wild
dog has the power of speech; whoever listens to him
is petrified; and a certain spot is shown where " the
wild dog spoke and turned the men into stone ";[1]
and the blacks run for their lives as soon as the dog
begins to speak. What it said was " Bones ".

These are minor examples of a form of opinion which
is so strong that it is actually the chief constituent in
savage society. That society, whether in Ashantee or
Australia, in North America or South Africa, or North
Asia or India, or among the wilder tribes of ancient
Peru, is based on an institution generally called
"totemism". This very extraordinary institution,
whatever its origin, cannot have arisen except among
men capable of conceiving kinship and all human
relationships as existing between themselves and all
animate and inanimate things. It is the rule, and
not the exception, that savage societies are founded
upon this belief. The political and social conduct of
the backward races is regulated in such matters as
blood-feud and marriage by theories of the actual
kindred and connection by descent, or by old friendship, which men have in common with beasts, plants,
the sun and moon, the stars, and even the wind and
the rain. Now, in whatever way this belief in such
relations to beasts and plants may have arisen, it
undoubtedly testifies to a condition of mind in which
no hard and fast line was drawn between man and
animate and inanimate nature. The discovery of the
wide distribution of the social arrangements based on

[1] Brough Smyth, *Aborigines of Victoria*, i. 497.

this belief is entirely due to Mr. J. F. M'Lennan, the
author of *Primitive Marriage*. Mr. M'Lennan's essays
("The Worship of Plants and Animals," "Totems
and Totemism") were published in the *Fortnightly
Review*, 1869-71. Any follower in the footsteps of
Mr. M'Lennan has it in his power to add a little evidence to that originally set forth, and perhaps to sift
the somewhat uncritical authorities adduced.[1]

The name "Totemism" or "Totamism" was first
applied at the end of the last century by Long[2] to the
Red Indian custom which acknowledges human kinship with animals. This institution had already been
recognised among the Iroquois by Lafitau,[3] and by
other observers. As to the word "totem," Mr. Max
Müller[4] quotes an opinion that the interpreters,
missionaries, Government inspectors, and others who
apply the name *totem* to the Indian "family mark"
must have been ignorant of the Indian languages, for
there is in them no such word as *totem*. The right
word, it appears, is *otem ;* but as "totemism" has the
advantage of possessing the ground, we prefer to say
"totemism" rather than "otemism". The facts are
the same, whatever name we give them. As Mr.
Müller says himself,[5] "every warrior has his crest,
which is called his *totem*" ;[6] and he goes on to describe
a totem of an Indian who died about 1793. We may
now return to the consideration of "otemism" or

---

[1] See also Mr. Frazer's *Totemism*, and *Golden Bough*, with chapter on
Totemism in *Modern Mythology*.
[2] *Voyages and Travels*, 1791.   [3] *Mœurs des Sauvages* (1724), p. 461.
[4] *Academy*, December 15, 1883.   [5] *Selected Essays* (1881), ii. 376.
[6] Compare Mr. Max Müller's *Contributions to the Science of Mythology*.

totemism. We approach it rather as a fact in the
science of mythology than as a stage in the evolution
of the modern family system. For us totemism is
interesting because it proves the existence of that
savage mental attitude which assumes kindred and
alliance between man and the things in the world.
As will afterwards be seen, totemism has also left
its mark on the mythologies of the civilised races.
We shall examine the institution first as it is found in
Australia, because the Australian form of totemism
shows in the highest known degree the savage habit
of confusing in a community of kinship men, stars,
plants, beasts, the heavenly bodies, and the forces of
Nature. When this has once been elucidated, a shorter
notice of other totemistic races will serve our purpose.

The society of the Murri or black fellows of
Australia is divided into *local* tribes, each of which
possesses, or used to possess, and hunt over a considerable tract of country. These *local* tribes are united
by contiguity, and by common *local* interests, but not
necessarily by *blood kinship*. For example, the Port
Mackay tribe, the Mount Gambier tribe, the Ballarat
tribe, all take their names from their district. In the
same way we might speak of the people of Strathclyde
or of Northumbria in early English history. Now, all
these *local* tribes contain an indefinite number of
stocks of *kindred*, of men believing themselves to be
related by the ties of blood and common descent. That
descent the groups agree in tracing, not from some
real or idealised human parent, but from some animal,
plant, or other natural object, as the kangaroo, the
emu, the iguana, the pelican, and so forth. Persons

of the pelican stock in the north of Queensland regard themselves as relations of people of the same stock in the most southern parts of Australia. The creature from which each tribe claims descent is called "of the same flesh," while persons of another stock are "fresh flesh". A native may not marry a woman of "his own flesh"; it is only a woman of "fresh" or "strange" flesh he may marry. A man may not eat an animal of "his own flesh"; he may only eat "strange flesh". Only under great stress of need will an Australian eat the animal which is the flesh-and-blood cousin and protector of his stock.[1] (These rules of marriage and blood, however, do not apply among the Arunta of Central Australia, whose Totems (if Totems they should be called) have been developed on very different lines.[2]) Clearer evidence of the confusion between man and beast, of the claiming of kin between man and beast, could hardly be.

But the Australian philosophy of the intercommunion of Nature goes still farther than this. Besides the *local* divisions and the *kindred* stocks which trace their descent from animals, there exist among many Australian tribes divisions of a kind still unexplained. For example, every man of the Mount Gambier *local* tribe is by birth either a Kumite or a Kroki. This classification applies to the whole of the sensible universe. Thus smoke and honeysuckle trees belong to the division Kumite, and are akin to the fishhawk stock of men. On the other hand, the kangaroo,

---

[1] Dawson, *Aborigines*, pp. 26, 27 ; Howitt and Fison, *Kamilaroi and Kurnai*, p. 169.

[2] Spencer and Gillen, *Native Tribes of Central Australia.*

summer, autumn, the wind and the shevak tree belong
to the division Kroki, and are akin to the black
cockatoo stock of men. Any human member of the
Kroki division has thus for his brothers the sun, the
wind, the kangaroo, and the rest ; while any man of
the Kumite division and the crow surname is the
brother of the rain, the thunder, and the winter.
This extraordinary belief is not a mere idle fancy—
it influences conduct. " A man does not kill or use
as food any of the animals of the same subdivision
(Kroki or Kumite) with himself, excepting when
hunger compels, and then they express sorrow for
having to eat their *wingong* (friends) or *tumanang*
(their flesh). When using the last word they touch
their breasts, to indicate the close relationship, meaning almost a portion of themselves. To illustrate :
One day one of the blacks killed a crow. Three or
four days afterwards a Boortwa (a man of the crow
surname and stock), named Larry, died. He had
been ailing for some days, but the killing of his
wingong (totem) hastened his death." [1] Commenting
on this statement, Mr. Fison observes : " The South
Australian savage looks upon the universe as the
'Great Tribe, to one of whose divisions he himself
belongs ; and all things, animate and inanimate, which
belong to his class are parts of the body corporate
whereof he himself is part ". This account of the
Australian beliefs and customs is borne out, to a
certain extent, by the evidence of Sir George Grey,[2]
and of the late Mr. Gideon Scott Lang.[3] These two

[1] *Kamilaroi and Kurnai*, p. 169.   [2] *Travels*, ii. 225.
[3] Lang, *Lecture on Natives of Australia*, p. 10.

writers take no account of the singular "dichotomous" divisions, as of Kumite and Kroki, but they draw attention to the groups of kindred which derive their surnames from animals, plants, and the like. "The origin of these family names," says Sir George Grey, "is attributed by the natives to different causes. . . . One origin frequently assigned by the natives is, that they were derived from some vegetable or animal being very common in the district which the family inhabited." We have seen from the evidence of Messrs. Fison and Howitt that a more common native explanation is based on kinship with the vegetable or plant which bestows the family surname. Sir George Gray mentions that the families use their plant or animal as a crest or *kobong* (totem), and he adds that natives never willingly kill animals of their *kobong*, holding that some one of that species is their nearest friend. The consequences of eating forbidden animals vary considerably. Sometimes the *Boyl-yas* (that is, ghosts) avenge the crime. Thus when Sir George Grey ate some mussels (which, after all, are not the crest of the Greys), a storm followed, and one of his black fellow improvised this stave :—

> Oh, wherefore did he eat the mussels?
> Now the Boyl-yas storms and thunders make ;
> Oh, wherefore would he eat the mussels?

There are two points in the arrangements of these stocks of kindred named from plants and animals which we shall find to possess a high importance. No member of any such kindred may marry a woman of the same name and descended from the same

object.[1]   Thus no man of the Emu stock may marry an
Emu woman; no Blacksnake may marry a Blacksnake
woman, and so forth.   This point is very strongly put
by Mr. Dawson, who has had much experience of the
blacks.   "So strictly are the laws of marriage carried
out, that, should any sign of courtship or affection be
observed between those 'of one flesh,' the brothers or
male relatives of the woman beat her severely."   If
the incestuous pair (though not in the least related
according to our ideas) run away together, they are
"half-killed"; and if the woman dies in consequence
of her punishment, her partner in iniquity is beaten
again.   No "eric" or blood-fine of any kind is paid
for her death, which carries no blood-feud.   "Her
punishment is legal."[2]   This account fully corroborates
that of Sir George Grey.[3]

Our conclusion is that the belief in "one flesh" (a
kinship shared with the animals) must be a thoroughly
binding idea, as the notion is sanctioned by capital
punishment.

Another important feature in Australian totemism
strengthens our position.   The idea of the animal
kinship must be an ancient one in the race, because
the family surname, Emu, Bandicoot, or what not, and
the crest, *kobong,* or protecting and kindred animal,
are inherited *through the mother's side* in the majority

[1] Taplin, *The Narrinyeri*, p. 2.   "Every tribe, regarded by them as a
family, has its *ngaitge,* or tutelary genius or tribal symbol, in the shape of
some bird, beast, fish, reptile, insect, or substance.   Between individuals
of the same tribe no marriage can take place."   Among the Narrinyeri
kindred is reckoned (p. 10) on the father's side.   See also (p. 46) *ngaitge* =
Samoan *aitu.*   "No man or woman will kill their *ngaitge,*" except with
precautions, for food.

[2] *Op. cit.,* p. 28.   [3] *Ibid.,* ii. 220.

of stocks. This custom, therefore, belongs to that early period of human society in which the woman is the permanent and recognised factor in the family while male parentage is uncertain.[1] One other feature of Australian totemism must be mentioned before we leave the subject. There is some evidence that in certain tribes the *wingong* or totem of each man is indicated by a tattooed representation of it upon his flesh. The natives are very licentious, but men would shrink from an amour with a woman who neither belonged to their own district nor spoke their language, but who, in spite of that, was of their totem. To avoid mistakes, it seems that some tribes mark the totem on the flesh with incised lines.[2] The natives frequently design figures of some kind on the trees growing near the graves of deceased warriors. Some observers have fancied that in these designs they recognised the totem of the dead men; but on this subject evidence is by no means clear. We shall see that this primitive sort of heraldry, this carving or painting of hereditary blazons, is common among the Red Men of America.[3]

Though a large amount of evidence might be added to that already put forward, we may now sum up the inferences to be drawn from the study of totemism in Australia. It has been shown (1) that the natives

[1] *Cf.* Bachofen, *Das Mutterrecht;* M'Lennan, *Primitive Marriage, passim; Encycl. Brit.* s. v. *Family.*

[2] Fison, *op. cit.*, p. 66.

[3] Among other recent sources see Howitt in "Organisation of Australian Tribes" (*Transactions of Royal Society of Victoria*, 1889), and Spencer and Gillen, *Natives of Central Australia.* In Central Australia there is a marked difference in the form of Totemism.

think themselves actually akin to animals, plants, the sun, and the wind, and things in general; (2) that those ideas influence their conduct, and even regulate their social arrangements, because (3) men and women of the kinship of the same animal or plant may not intermarry, while men are obliged to defend, and in case of murder to avenge, persons of the stock of the family or plant from which they themselves derive their family name. Thus, on the evidence of institutions, it is plain that the Australians are (or before the influence of the Europeans became prevalent were) in a state of mind which draws no hard and fast line between man and the things in the world. If, therefore, we find that in Australian myth, men, gods, beasts, and things all shift shapes incessantly, and figure in a *coroboree* dance of confusion, there will be nothing to astonish us in the discovery. The myths of men in the Australian intellectual condition, of men who hold long conversations with the little "native bear," and ask him for oracles, will naturally and inevitably be grotesque and confused.[1]

It is "a far cry" from Australia to the West Coast of Africa, and it is scarcely to be supposed that the Australians have borrowed ideas and institutions from Ashantee, or that the people of Ashantee have derived their conceptions of the universe from the Murri of Australia. We find, however, on the West African. Coast, just as we do in Australia, that there exist large *local* divisions of the natives. These divisions are spoken of by Mr. Bowditch (who visited the country on a mission in 1817) as nations, and they are much

---

[1] Brough Smyth, i. 447, on MS. authority of W. Thomas.

more populous and powerful (as the people are more civilised) than the local tribes of Australia. Yet, just as among the local tribes of Australia, the nations of the West African Coast are divided into stocks of kindred, each *stock* having its representatives in each *nation*. Thus an Ashantee or a Fantee may belong to the same stock of kindred as a member of the Assin or Akini nation. When an Ashantee of the Annona stock of kindred meets a Warsaw man of the same stock they salute and acknowledge each other as brothers. In the same way a Ballarat man of the Kangaroo stock in Australia recognises a relative in a Mount Gambier man who is also a Kangaroo. Now, with one exception, all the names of the twelve stocks of West African kindreds, or at least all of them which Mr. Bowditch could get the native interpreters to translate, are derived from animals, plants and other natural objects, just as in Australia.[1] Thus Quonna is a buffalo, Abrootoo is a cornstalk, Abbradi a plantain. Other names are, in English, the parrot, the wild cat, red earth, panther and dog. Thus all the natives of this part of Africa are parrots, dogs, buffaloes, panthers, and so forth, just as the Australians are emus, iguanas, black cockatoos, kangaroos, and the rest. It is remarkable that there is an Incra stock, or clan of ants, in Ashantee, just as there was a race of Myrmidons, believed to be descended from or otherwise connected

---

[1] The evidence of native interpreters may be viewed with suspicion. It is improbable, however, that in 1817 the interpreters were acquainted with the totemistic theory of mythologists, and deliberately mistranslated the names of the stocks, so as to make them harmonise with Indian, Australian, and Red Indian totem kindreds. This, indeed, is an example where the criterion of "recurrence" or "coincidence" seems to be valuable. Bowditch's *Mission to Ashantee* (1873), p. 181.

with ants, in ancient Greece. Though Bowditch's
account of these West African family divisions is brief,
the arrangement tallies closely with that of Australia.
It is no great stretch of imagination to infer that the
African tribes do, or once did, believe themselves to be
of the kindred of the animals whose names they bear.[1]
It is more or less confirmatory of this hypothesis that
no family is permitted to use as food the animal from
which it derives its name. We have seen that a similar
rule prevails, as far as hunger and scarcity of victuals
permit it to be obeyed, among the natives of Australia.
The Intchwa stock in Ashantee and Fantee is particularly unlucky, because its members may not eat the
dog, "much relished by native epicures, and therefore
a serious privation". Equally to be pitied were the
ancient Egyptians, who, if they belonged to the district
of the sheep, might not eat mutton, which their neighbours, the Lycopolitæ, devoured at pleasure. These
restrictions appear to be connected with the almost
universal dislike of cannibals to eat persons of their
own kindred except as a pious duty. This law of the
game in cannibalism has not yet been thoroughly examined, though we often hear of wars waged expressly
for the purpose of securing food (human meat), while
some South American tribes actually bred from captive women by way of securing constant supplies of
permitted flesh.[2] When we find stocks, then, which

[1] This view, however, does not prevail among the totemistic tribes of
British Columbia, for example.

[2] Cieza de Leon (Hakluyt Society), p. 50. This amazing tale is supported
by the statement that kinship went by the female side (p. 49); the father
was thus not of the kin of his child by the alien woman. Cieza was with
Validillo in 1538.

derive their names from animals and decline to eat
these animals, we may at least *suspect* that they once
claimed kinship with the name-giving beasts. The
refusal to eat them raises a presumption of such faith.
Old Bosman [1] had noticed the same practices. "One
eats no mutton, another no goat's flesh, another no
beef, swine's flesh, wild fowl, cocks with white feathers,
and they say their ancestors did so from the beginning
of the world."

While in the case of the Ashantee tribes, we can
only infer the existence of a belief in kinship with the
animals from the presence of the other features of
fully developed totemism (especially from the refusal
to eat the name-giving animal), we have direct evidence
for the opinion in another part of Africa, among the
Bechuanas.[2] Casalis, who passed twenty-three years
as a missionary in South Africa, thus describes the
institution : " While the united communities usually
bear the name of their chief or of the district which
they inhabit " (local tribes, as in Australia), " each stock
(*tribu*) derives its title from an animal or a vegetable·
All the Bechuanas are subdivided thus into *Bakuenas*
(crocodile-men), *Batlapis* (men of the fish), *Banarer*
(of the buffalo), *Banukus* (porcupines), *Bamoraras*
(wild vines), and so forth. *The Bakuenas call the
crocodile their father*, sing about him in their feasts,
swear by him, and mark the ears of their cattle with
an incision which resembles the open jaws of the
creature." This custom of marking the cattle with
the crest, as it were, of the stock, takes among some
races the shape of deforming themselves, so as the

---

[1] In Pinkerton, xvi. 400.   [2] E. Casalis, *Les Bassoutos*, 1859.

more to resemble the animal from which they claim
descent. "The chief of the family which holds the
chief rank in the stock is called 'The Great Man
of the Crocodile'. Precisely in the same way the
Duchess of Sutherland is styled in Gaelic 'The Great
Lady of the Cat,'" though totemism is probably *not*
the origin of this title.

Casalis proceeds : "No one would dare to eat the
flesh or wear the skin of the animal whose name he
bears. If the animal be dangerous—the lion, for
example—people only kill him after offering every
apology and asking his pardon. Purification must
follow such a sacrifice." Casalis was much struck
with the resemblance between these practices and the
similar customs of North American races. Livingstone's account [1] on the whole corroborates that of
Casalis, though he says the Batau (tribe of the lion)
no longer exists. "They use the word *bina* 'to dance,'
in reference to the custom of thus naming themselves,
so that when you wish to ascertain what tribe they
belong to, you say, 'What do you dance ?' It would
seem as if this had been part of the worship of old."
The mythological and religious knowledge of the
Bushmen is still imparted in dances; and when a
man is ignorant of some myth he will say, "I do not
dance that dance," meaning that he does not belong to
the guild which preserves that particular "sacred
chapter".[2]

Casalis noticed the similarity between South African
and Red Indian opinion about kinship with vegetables

---

[1] *Missionary Travels* (1857), p. 13.
[2] Orpen, *Cape Monthly Magazine*, 1872.

and beasts. The difficulty in treating the Red Indian
belief is chiefly found in the abundance of the evidence.
Perhaps the first person who ever used the word
"totemism," or, as he spells it, "totamism," was (as we
said) Mr. Long, an interpreter among the Chippeways,
who published his *Voyages* in 1791. Long was not
wholly ignorant of the languages, as it was his business
to speak them, and he was an adopted Indian. The
ceremony of adoption was painful, beginning with a
feast of dog's flesh, followed by a Turkish bath and a
prolonged process of tattooing.[1] According to Long,[2]
"The totam, they conceive, assumes the form of some
beast or other, and therefore they never kill, hurt,
or eat the animal whose form they think this totam
bears". One man was filled with religious apprehen-
sions, and gave himself up to the gloomy belief of
Bunyan and Cowper, that he had committed the
unpardonable sin, because he dreamed he had killed
his totem, a bear.[3] This is only one example, like the
refusal of the Osages to kill the beavers, with which
they count cousins,[4] that the Red Man's belief is an
actual creed, and does influence his conduct.

As in Australia, the belief in common kin with
beasts is most clearly proved by the construction of
Red Indian society. The "totemistic" stage of thought
and manners prevails. Thus Charlevoix says,[5] "Plu-
sieurs nations ont chacune trois familles ou tribus
principales, *aussi anciennes, à ce qu'il paroit, que
leur origine.* Chaque tribu porte le nom d'un animal,
et la nation entière a aussi le sien, dont elle prend le

---

[1] Long, pp. 46-49.   [2] *Ibid.*, p. 86.   [3] *Ibid.*, p. 87.
[4] Schoolcraft, i. 319.   [5] *Histoire de la France-Nouvelle*, iii. 266.

nom, et dont la figure est sa marque, ou, se l'on veut, ses armoiries, on ne signe point autrement les traités qu'en traceant ces figures." Among the animal totems Charlevoix notices porcupine, bear, wolf and turtle. The *armoiries*, the totemistic heraldry of the peoples of Virginia, greatly interested a heraldic ancestor of Gibbon the historian,[1] who settled in the colony. According to Schoolcraft,[2] the totem or family badge of a dead warrior is drawn in a reverse position on his grave-post. In the same way the leopards of England are drawn reversed on the shield of an English king opposite the mention of his death in old monkish chronicles. As a general rule,[3] persons bearing the same totem in America cannot intermarry. "The union must be between various totems." Moreover, as in the case of the Australians, "the descent of the chief is in the female line". We thus find among the Red Men precisely the same totemistic regulations as among the Aborigines of Australia. Like the Australians, the Red Men " never " (perhaps we should read " hardly ever ") eat their totems. Totemists, in short, spare the beasts that are their own kith and kin. To avoid multiplying details which all corroborate each other, it may suffice to refer to Schoolcraft for totemism among the Iowas[4] and the Pueblos;[5] for the Iroquois, to Lafitau, a missionary of the early part of the eighteenth century. Lafitau was perhaps the first writer who ever

---

[1] *Introductio ad Latinam Blasoniam*, by John Gibbon, Blue Mantle, London, 1682. "The dancers, were painted some *party per pale, gul* and *sab*, some *party per fesse* of the same colours;" whence Gibbon concluded "that heraldry was ingrafted naturally into the sense of the humane race".

[2] Vol. i. p. 356.   [3] Schoolcraft, v. 73,

[4] *Ibid.*, iii. 268.   [5] *Ibid.*, iv. 86.

explained certain features in Greek and other ancient myths and practices as survivals from totemism. The Chimera, a composite creature, lion, goat and serpent, might represent, Lafitau thought, a league of three totem tribes, just as wolf, bear and turtle represented the Iroquois League.

The martyred Père Rasles, again, writing in 1723,[1] says that one stock of the Outaonaks claims descent from a hare (" the great hare was a man of prodigious size "), while another stock derive their lineage from the carp, and a third descends from a bear ; yet they do not scruple, after certain expiatory rites, to eat bear's flesh. Other North American examples are the Kutchin, who have always possessed the system of totems.[2]

It is to be noticed, as a peculiarity of Red Indian totemism which we have not observed (though it may exist) in Africa, that certain stocks claim relations with the sun. Thus Père Le Petit, writing from New Orleans in 1730, mentions the Sun, or great chief of the Natchez Indians.[3] The totem of the privileged class among the Natchez was the sun, and in all myths the sun is regarded as a living being, who can have children, who may be beaten, who bleeds when cut, and is simply on the same footing as men and everything else in the world. Precisely similar evidence comes from South America. In this case our best authority is almost beyond suspicion. He knew the native languages well, being himself a half-caste. He was learned in the European learning of his time ;

---

[1] Kip's *Jesuits in America* i. 33.
[2] Dall's *Alaska*, pp. 196-198.   [3] Kip, ii. 288.

and as a son of the Incas, he had access to all surviving
Peruvian stores of knowledge, and could collect without difficulty the testimonies of his countrymen.   It
will be seen [1] that Don Garcilasso de la Vega could
estimate evidence, and ridiculed the rough methods
and fallacious guesses of Spanish inquirers.   Garcilasso de la Vega was born about 1540, being the son
of an Inca princess and of a Spanish conqueror.   His
book, *Commentarias Reales*,[2] was expressly intended
to rectify the errors of such Spanish writers as
Acosta.   In his account of Peruvian religion, Garcilasso distinguishes between the beliefs of the tribes
previous to the rise of the Inca empire and the sun-
worship of the Incas.   But it is plain, from Garcilasso's own account and from other evidence, that
under the Incas the older faiths and fetichisms
survived, in subordination to sun-worship, just as
Pagan superstitions survived in custom and folk-lore
after the official recognition of Christianity.   Sun-
worship, in Peru, and the belief in a Supreme Creator
there, seem even, like Catholicism in Mexico, China
and elsewhere, to have made a kind of compromise
with the lower beliefs, and to have been content to
allow a certain amount of bowing down in the temples
of the elder faiths.   According, then, to Garcilasso's
account of Peruvian totemism, " An Indian was not
looked upon as honourable unless he was descended
from a fountain, river,[3] or lake, or even from the sea,

---

[1] Appendix B.

[2] See translation in Hakluyt Society's Collection.

[3] Like many Greek heroes. *Odyssey*, iii. 489.   " Orsilochus, the child
begotten of Alpheus."

or from a wild animal, such as a bear, lion, tiger,
eagle, or the bird they call cuntur (condor), or some
other bird of prey ".[1] A certain amount of worship
was connected with this belief in kinship with beasts
and natural objects. Men offered up to their totems
"what they usually saw them eat ".[2] On the sea-
coasts "they worshipped sardines, skates, dog-fish,
and, for want of larger gods, crabs. . . . There was
not an animal, how vile and filthy soever, that they
did not worship as a god," including "lizards, toads
and frogs." Garcilasso (who says they ate the fish
they worshipped) gives his own theory of the origin
of totemism. In the beginning men had only sought
for badges whereby to discriminate one human stock
from another. "The one desired to have a god different from the other. . . . They only thought of
making one different from another." When the Inca
emperors began to civilise the totemistic stocks, they
pointed out that their own father, the sun, possessed
"splendour and beauty" as contrasted with "the
ugliness and filth of the frogs and other vermin they
looked upon as gods".[3] Garcilasso, of course, does
not use the North American word *totem* (or *ote* or
otem) for the family badge which represented the
family ancestors. He calls these things, as a general
rule, *pacarissa*. The sun was the *pacarissa* of the
Incas, as it was of the chief of the Natchez. The
pacarissa of other stocks was the lion, bear, frog, or
what not. Garcilasso accounts for the belief accorded
to the Incas, when they claimed actual descent from
the sun, by observing [4] that "there were tribes among

---

[1] *Comm. Real.,* i. 75.   [2] *Ibid.,* 53.   [3] *Ibid.,* 102.   [4] *Ibid.,* 83.

their subjects who professed similar fabulous descents,
though they did not comprehend how to select ancestors so well as the Incas, but adored animals and
other low and earthly objects ". As to the fact of
the Peruvian worship of beasts, if more evidence is
wanted, it is given, among others, by Cieza de Leon,[1]
who contrasts the adoration of the Roman gods with
that offered in Peru to brutes. " In the important
temple of Pacha-camac (the spiritual deity of Peru)
they worshipped a she-fox or vixen and an emerald."
The devil also " appeared to them and spoke in the
form of a tiger, very fierce ". Other examples of
totemism in South America may be studied in the
tribes on the Amazon.[2] Mr. Wallace found the Pine-
apple stock, the Mosquitoes, Woodpeckers, Herons,
and other totem kindreds. A curious example of
similar ideas is discovered among the Bonis of Guiana.
These people were originally West Coast Africans
imported as slaves, who have won their freedom with
the sword.   While they retain a rough belief in
Gadou (God) and *Didibi* (the devil), they are divided
into totem stocks with animal names. The red ape,
turtle and cayman are among the chief totems.[3]

After this hasty examination of the confused belief
in kinship with animals and other natural objects
which underlies institutions in Australia, West and
South Africa, North and South America, we may
glance at similar notions among the non-Aryan races
of India.   In Dalton's *Ethnology of Bengal*,[4] he tells

---

[1] Cieza de Leon (Hakluyt Society), p. 183.

[2] Acuna, p. 103 ; Wallace, *Travels on Amazon* (1853), pp. 481-506.

[3] Crevaux, *Voyages dans l'Amerique du Sud*, p. 59.   [4] Dalton, p. 63.

us that the Garo clans are divided into *maharis* or *motherhoods*. Children belong to the *mahari* of the mother, just as (in general) they derive their stock name and totem from the mother's side in Australia and among the North American Indians. No man may marry (as among the Red Indians and Australians) a woman belonging to his own stock, motherhood or *mahari*. So far the *maharis* of Bengal exactly correspond to the totem kindred. But do the Maharis also take their names from plants and animals, and so forth? We know that the Killis, similar communities among the Bengal Hos and Mundos, do this.[1] "The Mundaris, like the Oraons, adopt as their tribal distinction the name of some animal, and the flesh of that animal is tabooed to them as food; for example, the eel, the tortoise." This is exactly the state of things in Ashanti. Dalton mentions also[2] a princely family in Nagpur which claims descent from "a great hooded snake". Among the Oraons he found[3] tribes which might not eat young mice (considered a dainty) or tortoises, and a stock which might not eat the oil of the tree which was their totem, nor even sit in its shade. "The family or tribal names" (within which they may not marry) "are usually those of animals or plants, and when this is the case, the flesh of some part of the animal or the fruit of the tree is tabooed to the tribe called after it."

An excellent sketch of totemism in India is given by Mr. H. H. Risley of the Bengal Civil Service:—[4]

---

[1] Dalton, p. 189.   [2] *Ibid.*, p. 166.   [3] *Ibid.*, p. 254.
[4] *The Asiatic Quarterly*, No. 3, Essay on "Primitive Marriage in Bengal"

"At the bottom of the social system, as understood by the average Hindu, stands a large body of non-Aryan castes and tribes, each of which is broken up into a number of what may be called *totemistic* exogamous septs. Each sept bears the name of an animal, a tree, a plant, or of some material object, natural or artificial, which the members of that sept are prohibited from killing, eating, cutting, burning, carrying, *using*, etc." [1]

Mr. Risley finds that both Kolarians, as the Sonthals, and Dravidians, as the Oraons, are in this state of totemism, like the Hos and Mundas. It is most instructive to learn that, as one of these tribes rises in the social scale, it sloughs off its totem, and, abandoning the common name derived from bird, beast, or plant, adopts that of an eponymous ancestor. A tendency in this direction has been observed by Messrs. Fison and Howitt even in Australia. The Mahilis, Koras and Kurmis, who profess to be members of the Hindu community, still retain the totemistic organisation, with names derived from birds, beasts and plants. Even the Jagânnathi Kumhars of Orissa, taking rank immediately below the writer-caste, have the totems tiger, snake, weasel, cow, frog, sparrow and tortoise. The sub-castes of the Khatlya Kumhars explain away their totem-names "as names of certain saints, who, being present at Daksha's Horse-sacrifice, transformed themselves into animals to escape the wrath of Siva,"

---

[1] Here we may note that the origin of exogamy itself is merely part of a strict totemistic prohibition. A man may not "use" an object within the totem kin, nor a woman of the kin. Compare the Greek idiom χρῆσθαι γυναικί.

like the gods of Egypt when they fled in bestial form from the wrath of Set.

Among the non-Aryan tribes the marriage law has the totemistic sanction. No man may marry a woman of his totem kin. When the totem-name is changed for an eponym, the non-Aryan, rising in the social scale, is practically in the same position as the Brahmans, " divided into exogamous sections (*gotras*), the members of which profess to be descended from the mythical *rishi* or inspired saint whose name the *gotra* bears". There is thus nothing to bar the conjecture that the exogamous *gotras* of the whole Brahmans were once a form of totem-kindred, which (like aspiring non-Aryan stocks at the present day) dropped the totem-name and renamed the septs from some eponymous hero, medicine-man, or *Rishi*.

Constant repetition of the same set of facts becomes irksome, and yet is made necessary by the legitimate demand for trustworthy and abundant evidence. As the reader must already have reflected, this living mythical belief in the common confused equality of men, gods, plants, beasts, rivers, and what not, which still regulates savage society,[1] is one of the most prominent features in mythology. Porphyry remarked and exactly described it among the Egyptians—" common and akin to men and gods they believed the beasts to be ".[2] The belief in such equality is alien to modern civilisation. We have shown that it is common and fundamental in savagery. For instance, in the Pacific,

---

[1] See some very curious and disgusting examples of this confusion in Liebrecht's *Zur Volkskunde*, pp. 395, 396 (Heilbronn, 1879).

[2] *De Abst.*, ii. 26.

we might quote Turner,[1] and for Melanesia, Codrington,[2] while for New Zealand we have Taylor.[3] For the Jakuts, along the banks of the Lena in Northern Asia, we have the evidence of Strahlenberg, who writes: "Each tribe of these people look upon some particular creature as sacred, *e.g.*, a swan, goose, raven, etc., and such is not eaten by that tribe" though the others may eat it.[4] As the majority of our witnesses were quite unaware that the facts they described were common among races of whom many of them had never even heard, their evidence may surely be accepted as valid, especially as the beliefs testified to express themselves in marriage laws, in the blood-feud, in abstinence from food, on pillars over graves, in rude heraldry, and in other obvious and palpable shapes. If we have not made out, by the evidence of institutions, that a confused credulity concerning the equality and kinship of man and the objects in nature is actually a ruling belief among savages, and even higher races, from the Lena to the Amazon, from the Gold Coast to Queensland, we may despair of ever convincing an opponent. The survival of the same beliefs and institutions among civilised races, Aryan and others, will later be demonstrated.[5] If we find that the mythology of civilised races here agrees with the actual practical

---

[1] *Nineteen Years in Polynesia*, p. 238, and *Samoa* by the same author. Complete totemism is not asserted here, and is denied for Melanesia.

[2] *Journ. Anthrop. Inst.*, "Religious Practices in Melanesia".

[3] *New Zealand*, "Animal Intermarriage with Men".

[4] *Description of Asia* (1783), p. 383.

[5] Professor Robertson Smith, *Kinship in Arabia*, attempts to show that totemism existed in the Semitic races. The topic must be left to Orientalists.

belief of savages, and if we also find that civilised races retain survivals of the institutions in which the belief is expressed by savages, then we may surely infer that the activity of beasts in the myths of Greece springs from the same sources as the similar activity of beasts in the myths of Iroquois or Kaffirs. That is to say, part of the irrational element in Greek myth will be shown to be derived (whether by inheritance or borrowing) from an ascertained condition of savage fancy.

CHAPTER IV.

THE MENTAL CONDITION OF SAVAGES—MAGIC— METAMORPHOSIS—METAPHYSIC—PSYCHOLOGY.

Claims of sorcerers—Savage scientific speculation—Theory of causation— Credulity, except as to new religious ideas—" Post hoc, ergo propter hoc "—Fundamental ideas of magic—Examples : incantations, ghosts, spirits—Evidence of rank and other institutions in proof of confusions of mind exhibited in magical beliefs.

" I mean eftsoons to have a fling at magicians for their abominable lies and monstrous vanities."—PLINY, *ap. Phil. Holland.*

" Quoy de ceux qui naturellement se changent en loups, en juments, et puis encores en hommes ?" — MONTAIGNE, *Apologie pour Raymond de Sebonde.*

THE second feature in the savage intellectual condition which we promised to investigate was the belief in magic and sorcery. The world and all the things in it being conceived of vaguely as sensible and rational, are supposed to obey the commands of certain members of each tribe, such as chiefs, jugglers, or conjurors. These conjurors, like Zeus or Indra, can affect the weather, work miracles, assume what shapes, animal, vegetable, or inorganic, they please, and can meta-morphose other persons into similar shapes. It has already been shown that savage man has regarded all *things* as *persons* much on a level with himself. It has now to be shown *what kind of person he conceives himself to be.* He does not look on men as civilised races regard them, that is, as beings with strict limitations. On the other hand, he thinks of certain members of his tribe as exempt from most of the limitations, and capable of working every miracle that tradition has ever attributed to prophets or gods. Nor are such miraculous powers, such practical omnipotence, supposed by savages to be at all rare among themselves. Though highly valued, miraculous attainments are not believed to be unusual. This must be kept steadily in mind. When myth-making man regards the sky or sun or wind as a person, he does not mean merely a person with the limitations recognised by modern races. He means a person with the miraculous powers of the medicine-man. The sky, sun, wind or other elemental personage can converse with the dead, and can turn himself and his neighbours into animals, stones and trees.

To understand these functions and their exercise, it is necessary to examine what may be called savage science, savage metaphysics, and the savage theory of the state of the dead. The medicine-man's supernatural claims are rooted in the general savage view of the world, of what is possible, and of what (if anything) is impossible. The savage, even more than the civilised man, may be described as a creature " moving about in worlds not realised ". He feels, no less than civilised man, the need of making the world intelligible, and he is active in his search for causes and effects. There is much " speculation in these eyes that he doth glare withal ". This is a statement which has been denied by some persons who have lived with savages. Thus Mr. Bates, in his *Naturalist*

on the Amazon,[1] writes : "Their want of curiosity
is extreme. . . . Vicente (an Indian companion) did
not know the cause of thunder and lightning. I
asked him who made the sun, the stars, the trees.
He didn't know, and had never heard the subject
mentioned in his tribe." But Mr. Bates admits that
even Vicente had a theory of the configuration of
the world. "The necessity of a theory of the earth
and water had been felt, and a theory had been
suggested." Again, Mr. Bates says about a certain
Brazilian tribe, "Their sluggish minds seem unable
to conceive or feel the want of a theory of the soul";
and he thinks the cause of this indolence is the lack
" of a written language or a leisured class ". Now
savages, as a rule, are all in the "leisured class," all
sportsmen. Mr. Herbert Spencer, too, has expressed
scepticism about the curiosity attributed to savages.
The point is important, because, in our view, the
medicine-man's powers are rooted in the savage theory
of things, and if the savage is too sluggish to invent
or half consciously evolve a theory of things, our
hypothesis is baseless. Again, we expect to find in
savage myths the answer given by savages to their
own questions. But this view is impossible if savages
do not ask themselves, and never have asked themselves, any questions at all about the world. On this
topic Mr. Spencer writes : "Along with absence of
surprise there naturally goes absence of intelligent
curiosity ".[2] Yet Mr. Spencer admits that, according
to some witnesses, "the Dyaks have an insatiable
curiosity," the Samoans "are usually very inquisitive,'

[1] Vol. ii. p. 162.   [2] *Sociology,* p. 98.

and "the Tahitians are remarkably curious and in-quisitive". Nothing is more common than to find travellers complaining that savages, in their ardently inquiring curiosity, will not leave the European for a moment to his own undisturbed devices. Mr. Spencer's savages, who showed no curiosity, displayed this impassiveness when Europeans were trying to make them exhibit signs of surprise. Impassivity is a point of honour with many uncivilised races, and we cannot infer that a savage has no curiosity because he does not excite himself over a mirror, or when his European visitors try to swagger with their mechanical appliances. Mr. Herbert Spencer founds, on the statements of Mr. Bates already quoted, a notion that " the savage, lacking ability to think and the accompanying desire to know, is without tendency to speculate ". He backs Mr. Bates's experience with Mungo Park's failure to " draw " the negroes about the causes of day and night. They had never indulged a conjecture nor formed an hypothesis on the matter. Yet Park avers that "the belief in one God is entire and universal among them ". This he "pronounces without the smallest shadow of doubt". As to "primitive man," according to Mr. Spencer, " the need for explanations about surrounding appearances does not occur to him". We have disclaimed all knowledge about " primitive man," but it is easy to show that Mr. Spencer grounds his belief in the lack of speculation among savages on a frail foundation of evidence.

Mr. Spencer has admitted speculation, or at least curiosity, among New Caledonians, New Guinea people, Dyaks, Samoans and Tahitians. Even where he denies its existence, as among the Amazon tribes mentioned by Mr. Bates, we happen to be able to show that Mr. Bates was misinformed. Another traveller, the American geologist, Professor Hartt of Cornell University, lived long among the tribes of the Amazon. But Professor Hartt did not, like Mr. Bates, find them at all destitute of theories of things—theories expressed in myths, and testifying to the intellectual activity and curiosity which demands an answer to its questions. Professor Hartt, when he first became acquainted with the Indians of the Amazon, knew that they were well supplied with myths, and he set to work to collect them. But he found that neither by coaxing nor by offers of money could he persuade an Indian to relate a myth. Only by accident, " while wearily paddling up the Parana-mirim of the Ituki," did he hear the steersman telling stories to the oarsmen to keep them awake. Professor Hartt furtively noted down the tale, and he found that by " setting the ball rolling," and narrating a story himself, he could make the natives throw off reserve and add to his stock of tales. " After one has obtained his first myth, and has learned to recite it accurately and spiritedly, the rest is easy." The tales published by Professor Hartt are chiefly animal stories, like those current in Africa and among the Red Indians, and Hartt even believed that many of the legends had been imported by Negroes. But as the majority of the Negro myths, like those of the Australians, give a " reason why " for the existence of some phenomenon or other, the argument against early man's curiosity and vivacity of intellect is rather injured, even if the Amazonian myths were imported from Africa. Mr. Spencer based his disbelief in the intellectual curiosity of the Amazonian tribes and of Negroes on the reports of Mr. Bates and of Mungo Park. But it turns out that both Negroes and Amazonians have stories which do satisfy an un-scientific curiosity, and it is even held that the Negroes lent the Amazonians these very stories.[1] The Kamschadals, according to Steller, "give them-selves a reason why for everything, according to their own lively fancy, and do not leave the smallest matter uncriticised ".[2] As far, then, as Mr. Spencer's ob-jections apply to existing savages, we may consider them overweighed by the evidence, and we may believe in a naïve savage curiosity about the world and desire for explanations of the causes of things. Mr. Tylor's opinion corroborates our own: " Man's craving to know the causes at work in each event he witnesses, the reasons why each state of things he surveys is such as it is and no other, is no product of high civilisation, but a characteristic of his race down to its lowest stages. Among rude savages it is already an intellectual appetite, whose satisfaction claims many of the moments not engrossed by war or sport, food or sleep. Even in the Botocudo or the Australian, scien-tific speculation has its germ in actual experience."[3] It will be shown later that the food of the savage intellectual appetite is offered and consumed in the shape of explanatory myths.

[1] See *Amazonian Tortoise-Myths*, pp. 5, 37, 40 ; and compare Mr. Harris's Preface to *Nights with Uncle Remus*.

[2] Steller, p. 267. *Cf.* Farrer's *Primitive Manners*, p. 274.

[3] *Primitive Culture*, i. 369.

But we must now observe that the "actual experience," properly so called, of the savage is so
limited and so coloured by misconception and superstition, that his knowledge of the world varies very
much from the conceptions of civilised races. He
seeks an explanation, a theory of things, based on his
experience. But his knowledge of physical causes
and of natural laws is exceedingly scanty, and he is
driven to fall back upon what we may call metaphysical, or, in many cases "supernatural" explanations. The narrower the range of man's knowledge of
physical causes, the wider is the field which he has
to fill up with hypothetical causes of a metaphysical
or "supernatural" character. These "supernatural"
causes themselves the savage believes to be matters of
experience. It is to his mind a matter of experience
that all nature is personal and animated; that men
may change shapes with beasts; that incantations and
supernatural beings can cause sunshine and storm.

A good example of this is given in Charlevoix's
work on French Canada.[1] Charlevoix was a Jesuit
father and missionary among the Hurons and other
tribes of North America. He thus describes the
philosophy of the Red Men : "The Hurons attribute
the most ordinary effects to supernatural causes".[2] In
the same page the good father himself attributes the
welcome arrival of rainy weather and the cure of
certain savage patients to the prayers of Père Brébeuf
and to the exhibition of the sacraments. Charlevoix
had considerably extended the field in which natural
effects are known to be produced by natural causes.

---

[1] *Histoire de la France-Nouvelle.*   [2] Vol. i. p. 191.

He was much more scientifically minded than his savage flock, and was quite aware that an ordinary clock with a pendulum cannot bring bad luck to a whole tribe, and that a weather-cock is not a magical machine for securing unpleasant weather. The Hurons, however, knowing less of natural causes and nothing of modern machinery, were as convinced that his clock was ruining the luck of the tribe and his weather-cock spoiling the weather, as Father Charlevoix could be of the truth of his own inferences. One or two other anecdotes in the good father's history and letters help to explain the difference between the philosophies of wild and of Christian men. The Père Brébeuf was once summoned at the instigation of a Huron wizard or "medicine-man" before a council of the tribe. His judges told the father that nothing had gone right since he appeared among them. To this Brébeuf replied by "drawing the attention of the savages to the absurdity of their principles". He admitted[1] the premise that nothing had turned out well in the tribe since his arrival. "But the reason," said he, "plainly is that God is angry with your hardness of heart." No sooner had the good father thus demonstrated the absurdity of savage principles of reasoning, than the malignant Huron wizard fell down dead at his feet! This event naturally added to the confusion of the savages.

Coincidences of this sort have a great effect on savage minds. Catlin, the friend of the Mandan tribe, mentions a chief who consolidated his power by aid of a little arsenic, bought from the whites. The chief

[1] Vol. i. p. 192.

used to prophesy the sudden death of his opponents, which always occurred at the time indicated. The natural results of the administration of arsenic were attributed by the barbarous people to supernatural powers in the possession of the chief.[1] Thus the philosophy of savages seeks *causas cognoscere rerum*, like the philosophy of civilised men, but it flies hastily to a hypothesis of "supernatural" causes which are only guessed at, and are incapable of demonstration. This frame of mind prevails still in civilised countries, as the Bishop of Nantes showed when, in 1846, he attributed the floods of the Loire to " the excesses of the press and the general disregard of Sunday ". That "supernatural" causes exist and may operate, it is not at all our intention to deny. But the habit of looking everywhere for such causes, and of assuming their interference at will, is the main characteristic of savage speculation. The peculiarity of the savage is that he thinks human agents can work supernaturally, whereas even the Bishop reserved his supernatural explanations for the Deity. On this belief in man's power to affect events beyond the limits of natural possibility is based the whole theory of *magic*, the whole power of sorcerers. That theory, again, finds incessant expression in myth, and therefore deserves our attention.

The theory requires for its existence an almost boundless credulity. This credulity appears to Europeans to prevail in full force among savages. Bosman is amazed by the African belief that a spider created the world. Moffat is astonished at the South African

[1] Catlin, *Letters*, ii. 117.

notion that the sea was accidentally created by a girl.
Charlevoix says, "Les sauvages sont d'une facilité
à croire ce qu'on leur dit, que les plus facheuse
expériences n'ont jamais pu guérir".[1] But it is a
curious fact that while savages are, as a rule, so
credulous, they often laugh at the religious doctrines
taught them by missionaries. Elsewhere they recognise certain essential doctrines as familiar forms of
old. Dr. Moffat remarks, "To speak of the Creation,
the Fall and the Resurrection, seemed more fabulous,
extravagant and ludicrous to them than their own
vain stories of lions and hyænas" Again, "The
Gospel appeared too preposterous for the most foolish
to believe".[2] While the Zulus declared that they used
to accept their own myths without inquiry,[3] it was a
Zulu who suggested to Bishop Colenso his doubts
about the historical character of the Noachian Deluge.
Hearne[4] knew a Red Man, Matorabhee, who, "though
a perfect bigot with regard to the arts and tricks of
the jugglers, could yet by no means be impressed
with a belief of any part of *our* religion". Lieutenant
Haggard, R.N., tells the writer that during an eclipse
at Lamoo he ridiculed the native notion of driving
away a beast which devours the moon, and explained
the real cause of the phenomenon. But his native
friend protested that "he could not be expected to
believe such a story". Yet other savages aver an old
agreement with the belief in a moral Creator.

We have already seen sufficient examples of credu-

---

[1] Vol. ii. p. 378. [2] *Missionary Labours*, p. 245.
[3] Callaway, *Religion of Amazulus*, i. 35.
[4] *Journey among the Indians*, 1795, p. 350.

lity in savage doctrines about the equal relations of
men and beasts, stars, clouds and plants. The same
readiness of belief, which would be surprising in a
Christian child, has been found to regulate the rudimentary political organisations of grey barbarians.
Add to this credulity a philosophy which takes resemblance, or contiguity in space, or nearness in time as
a sufficient reason for predicating the relations of cause
and effect, and we have the basis of savage physical
science. Yet the metaphysical theories of savages,
as expressed in Maori, Polynesian, and Zuñi hymns,
often amaze us by their wealth of abstract ideas.
Coincidence elsewhere stands for cause.

Post hoc, ergo propter hoc, is the motto of the savage
philosophy of causation. The untutored reasoner
speculates on the principles of the Egyptian clergy,
as described by Herodotus.[1] "The Egyptians have
discovered more omens and prodigies than any other
men; for when aught prodigious occurs, they keep
good watch, and write down what follows; and then,
if anything like the prodigy be repeated, they expect
the same events to follow as before." This way of
looking at things is the very essence of superstition.

Savages, as a rule, are not even so scientific as the
Egyptians. When an untoward event occurs, they
look for its cause among all the less familiar circumstances of the last few days, and select the determining
cause very much at random. Thus the arrival of the
French missionaries among the Hurons was coincident
with certain unfortunate events; therefore it was
argued that the advent of the missionaries was the

[1] II. p. 82.

cause of the misfortune. When the Bechuanas suffered from drought, they attributed the lack of rain to the arrival of Dr. Moffat, and especially to his beard, his church bell, and a bag of salt in his possession. Here there was not even the pretence of analogy between cause and effect. Some savages might have argued (it is quite in their style), that as salt causes thirst, a bag of salt causes drought; but no such case could be made out against Dr. Moffat's bell and beard. To give an example from the beliefs of English peasants. When a cottage was buried by a little avalanche in 1772, the accident was attributed to the carelessness of the cottagers, who had allowed a light to be taken out of their dwelling in Christmas-tide.[1] We see the same confusion between antecedence and consequence in time on one side, and cause and effect on the other, when the Red Indians aver that birds actually bring winds and storms or fair weather. They take literally the sense of the Rhodian swallow-song :—

> The swallow hath come,
> Bringing fair hours,
> Bringing fair seasons,
> On black back and white breast.[2]

Again, in the Pacific the people of one island always attribute hurricanes to the machinations of the people of the nearest island to windward. The wind comes from them; therefore (as their medicine-men can notoriously influence the weather), they must have sent the wind. This unneighbourly act is a *casus belli*, and through the whole of a group of islands the

---

[1] *Shropshire Folk-Lore*, by Miss Burne, iii. 401.
[2] Brinton, *Myths of New World*, p. 107.

banner of war, like the flag of freedom in Byron, flies
against the wind.   The chief principle, then, of savage
science is that antecedence and consequence in time
are the same as effect and cause.[1]   Again, savage
science holds that *like affects like* , that you can injure
a man, for example, by injuring his effigy.   On these
principles the savage explains the world to himself,
and on these principles he tries to subdue to himself
the world.   Now the putting of these principles into
practice is simply the exercise of art magic, an art to
which nothing seems impossible.   The belief that his
Shamans or medicine-men practise this art is universal
among savages.   It seriously affects their conduct, and
is reflected in their myths.

The one general rule which governs all magical
reasoning is, that casual connection in thought is
equivalent to causative connection in fact.   Like suggests like to human thought by association of ideas;
wherefore like influences like, or produces analogous
effects in practice.   Any object once in a man's possession, especially his hair or his nails, is supposed to be
capable of being used against him by a sorcerer   The
part suggests the whole.   A lock of a man's hair was
part of the man ; to destroy the hair is to destroy its
former owner.   Again, whatever event follows another
in time suggests it, and may have been caused by it.
Accompanying these ideas is the belief that nature
is peopled by invisible spiritual powers, over which
magicians and sorcerers possess influence.   The magic
of the lower races chiefly turns on these two beliefs,
First, "man having come to associate in thought those

[1] See account of Zuñi metaphysics in chapter on American Divine Myths.

things which he found by experience to be connected in fact, proceeded erroneously to invert their action, and to conclude that association in thought must involve similar connection in reality. He thus attempted to discover, to foretell, and to cause events, by means of processes which we now see to have only an ideal significance."[1] Secondly, man endeavoured to make disembodied spirits of the dead, or any other spirits, obedient to his will. Savage philosophy presumes that the beliefs are correct, and that their practical application is successful. Examples of the first of the two chief magical ideas are as common in unscientific modern times or among unscientific modern people as in the savage world.

The physicians of the age of Charles II. were wont to give their patients "mummy powder," that is, pulverised mummy. They argued that the mummy had lasted for a very long time, and that the patients ought to do so likewise. Pliny imagined that diamonds must be found in company with gold, because these are the most perfect substances in the world, and like should draw to like. *Aurum potabile*, or drinkable gold, was a favourite medical nostrum of the Middle Ages, because gold, being perfect, should produce perfect health. Among savages the belief that like is caused by like is exemplified in very many practices. The New Caledonians, when they wish their yam plots to be fertile, bury in them with mystic ceremonies certain stones which are naturally shaped like yams. The Melanesians have reduced this kind of magic to a system. Among them certain stones have

[1] *Primitive Culture*, i. 14.

a magical efficacy, which is determined in each case
by the shape of the stone. "A stone in the shape of
a pig, of a bread-fruit, of a yam, was a most valuable
find. No garden was planted without the stones which
were to increase the crop." [1] Stones with a rude
resemblance to beasts bring the Zuñi luck in the chase.

The spiritual theory in some places is mixed up
with the " like to like " theory, and the magical stones
are found where the spirits have been heard twittering
and whistling. "A large stone lying with a number
of small ones under it, like a sow among her sucklings,
was good for a childless woman." [2] It is the savage
belief that stones reproduce their species, a belief con-
sonant with the general theory of universal animation
and personality. The ancient belief that diamonds
gendered diamonds is a survival from these ideas.
"A stone with little disks upon it was good to bring
in money; any fanciful interpretation of a mark was
enough to give a character to the stone and its associated *Vui*" or spirit in Melanesia. In Scotland,
stones shaped like various parts of the human body
are expected to cure the diseases with which these
members may be afflicted. "These stones were called
by the names of the limbs which they represented, as
'eye-stone,' 'head-stone'." The patient washed the
affected part of the body, and rubbed it well with
the stone corresponding. [3]

To return from European peasant-magic to that of
savages, we find that when the Bushmen want wet

---

[1] Rev. R. H. Codrington, *Journ. Anth. Inst.*, February, 1881.
[2] Codrington, *Journ. Anth. Soc.*, x. iii. 276.
[3] Gregor, *Folk-Lore of North-East Counties*, p. 40.

weather they light fires, believing that the black smoke
clouds will attract black rain clouds ; while the Zulus
sacrifice black cattle to attract black clouds of rain.[1]
Though this magic has its origin in savage ignorance,
it survives into civilisation. Thus the sacrifices of
the Vedic age were imitations of the natural phenomena which the priests desired to produce.[2] " C'était
un moyen de faire tombre la pluie en réalisant, par les
réprésentations terrestres des eaux du nuage et de
l'éclair, les conditions dans lesquelles celui-ci détermine
dans le ciel l'épanchement de celles-là." A good example
of magical science is afforded by the medical practice
of the Dacotahs of North America.[3] When any one
is ill, an image of his disease, a boil or what not, is
carved in wood. This little image is then placed in
a bowl of water and shot at with a gun. The image
of the disease being destroyed, the disease itself is
expected to disappear. Compare the magic of the
Philistines, who made golden images of the sores
which plagued them and stowed them away in the
ark.[4] The custom of making a wax statuette of an
enemy, and piercing it with pins or melting it before
the fire, so that the detested person might waste as
his semblance melted, was common in mediæval Europe,
was known to Plato, and is practised by Negroes.
Some Australians take some of the hair of an enemy,
mix it with grease and the feathers of the eagle, and
burn it in the fire. This is " bar " or black magic.
The boarding under the chair of a magistrate in

[1] Callaway, i. 92.
[2] Bergaigne, *Religion Védique*, i. 126-138, i., vii., viii.
[3] Schoolcraft, iv. 491.   [4] 1 Samuel vi. 4, 5.

Barbadoes was lifted not long ago, and the ground beneath was found covered with wax images of litigants stuck full of pins.

The war-magic of the Dacotahs works in a similar manner. Before a party starts on the war-trail, the chief, with various ceremonies, takes his club and stands before his tent. An old witch bowls hoops at him; each hoop represents an enemy, and for each he strikes a foeman is expected to fall. A bowl of sweetened water is also set out to entice the spirits of the enemy.[1] The war-magic of the Aryans in India does not differ much in character from that of the Dacotahs. "If any one wishes his army to be victorious, he should go beyond the battle-line, cut a stalk of grass at the top and end, and throw it against the hostile army with the words, *Prasahe kas trapas-yati?*—O Prâsahâ, who sees thee? If one who has such knowledge cuts a stalk of grass and throws the parts at the hostile army, it becomes split and dissolved, just as a daughter-in-law becomes abashed and faints when seeing her father-in-law,"—an allusion, apparently, to the widespread *tabu* which makes fathers-in-law, daughters-in-law, sons-in-law, and mothers-in-law avoid each other.[2]

The hunt-dances of the Red Indians and Australians are arranged like their war-magic. Effigies of the bears, deer, or kangaroos are made, or some of the hunters imitate the motions of these animals. The rest of the dancers pretend to spear them, and it is hoped that this will ensure success among the real bears and kangaroos.

[1] Schoolcraft, iv. 496.   [2] *Aitareya Brahmana*, iii. 22.

Here is a singular piece of magic in which Europeans
and Australian blacks agree. Boris Godunoff made
his servants swear never to injure him by casting
spells with the dust on which his feet or his carriage
wheels had left traces.[1] Mr. Howitt finds the same
magic among the Kurnai.[2] "Seeing a Tatungolung
very lame, I asked him what was the matter. He
said, 'Some fellow has put *bottle* in my foot'. I found
he was probably suffering from acute rheumatism.
He explained that some enemy must have found his
foot-track and have buried in it a piece of broken bottle.
The magic influence, he believed, caused it to enter his
foot." On another occasion a native told Mr. Howitt
that he had seen black fellows putting poison in his
foot-tracks. Bosman mentions a similar practice among
the people of Guinea. In Scottish folk-lore a screw
nail is fixed into the footprint of the person who is
to be injured.

Just as these magical efforts to influence like by
like work their way into Vedic and other religions, so
they are introduced into the religion of the savage.
His prayers are addresses to some sort of superior being,
but the efficacy of the prayer is often eked out by a
little magic, unless indeed we prefer to suppose that
the words of the supplication are interpreted by
gesture-speech. Sproat writes: "Set words and
gestures are used according to the thing desired. For
instance, in praying for salmon, the native rubs the
backs of his hands, looks upwards, and mutters the
words, 'Many salmon, many salmon'. If he wishes

---

[1] Rambaud's *History of Russia*, English trans., i. 351.
[2] *Kamilaroi and Kurnai*, p. 250.

for deer, he carefully rubs both eyes ; or, if it is geese,
he rubs the back of his shoulder, uttering always in a
sing-song way the accustomed formula. . . . All these
practices in praying no doubt have a meaning. We
may see a steady hand is needed in throwing the
salmon-spear, and clear eyesight in finding deer in the
forest." [1]

In addition to these forms of symbolical magic (which
might be multiplied to any extent), we find among
savages the belief in the power of songs of *incantation*.
This is a feature of magic which specially deserves our
attention. In myths, and still more in *märchen* or
household tales, we shall constantly find that the most
miraculous effects are caused when the hero pronounces
a few lines of rhyme. In Rome, as we have all read
in the Latin Delectus, it was thought that incantations
could draw down the moon. In the *Odyssey* the
kinsfolk of Odysseus sing "a song of healing" over
the wound which was dealt him by the boar's tusk.
Jeanne d'Arc, wounded at Orleans, refused a similar
remedy. Sophocles speaks of the folly of muttering
incantations over wounds that need the surgeon's knife.
The song that salved wounds occurs in the *Kalewala*,
the epic poem of the Finns. In many of Grimm's
märchen, miracles are wrought by the repetition of
snatches of rhyme. This belief is derived from the
savage state of fancy. According to Kohl,[2] "Every
sorrowful or joyful emotion that opens the Indian's
mouth is at once wrapped up in the garb of a *wabano-
nagamowin (chanson magicale)*. If you ask one of
them to sing you a simple innocent hymn in praise of

[1] *Savage Life*, p. 208.   [2] Page 395.

Nature, a spring or jovial hunting stave, he never gives you anything but a form of incantation, with which he says you will be able to call to you all the birds from the sky, and all the foxes and wolves from their caves and burrows." [1] The giant's daughter in the Scotch *märchen, Nicht, Nought, Nothing,* is thus enabled to call to her aid "all the birds of the sky". In the same way, if you ask an Indian for a love-song, he will say that a philtre is really much more efficacious. The savage, in short, is extremely practical. His arts, music and drawing, exist not *pour l'art*, but for a definite purpose, as methods of getting something that the artist wants. The young lover whom Kohl knew, like the lover of Bombyca in Theocritus, believed in having an image of himself and an image of the beloved. Into the heart of the female image he thrust magic powders, and he said that this was common, lovers adding songs, "partly elegiac, partly malicious, and almost criminal forms of incantation". [2]

Among the Indo-Aryans the *masaminik* or incantations of the Red Man are known as *mantras.* [3] These are usually texts from the Veda, and are chanted over the sick and in other circumstances where magic is believed to be efficacious. Among the New Zealanders the incantations are called *karakias*, and are employed in actual life. There is a special *karakia* to raise the wind. In Maori myths the hero is very handy with his *karakia.* Rocks split before him, as before girls

---

[1] *Cf.* Comparetti's *Traditional Poetry of the Finns.*
[2] *Kitchi Gami*, pp. 395, 397.
[3] Muir, *Sanskrit Texts*, v. 441, "Incantations from the Atharva Veda".

who use incantations in Kaffir and Bushman tales. He assumes the shape of any animal at will, or flies in the air, all by virtue of the *karakia* or incantation.[1]

Without multiplying examples in the savage belief that miracles can be wrought by virtue of physical *correspondances*, by like acting on like, by the part affecting the whole, and so forth, we may go on to the magical results produced by the aid of spirits. These may be either spirits of the dead or spiritual essences that never animated mortal men. Savage magic or science rests partly on the belief that the world is peopled by a "choir invisible," or rather by a choir only occasionally visible to certain gifted people, sorcerers and diviners. An enormous amount of evidence to prove the existence of these tenets has been collected by Mr. Tylor, and is accessible to all in the chapters on "Animism" in his *Primitive Culture*. It is not our business here to account for the universality of the belief in spirits. Mr. Tylor, following Lucretius and Homer, derives the belief from the reasonings of early men on the phenomena of dreams, fainting, shadows, visions caused by narcotics, hallucinations, and other facts which suggest the hypothesis of a separable life apart from the bodily organism. It would scarcely be fair not to add that the kind of "facts" investigated by the Psychical Society—such "facts" as the appearance of men at the moment of death in places remote from the scene of their decease, with such real or delusive experiences as the noises

[1] Taylor's *New Zealand ;* Theal's *Kaffir Folk-Lore, South-African Folk-Lore Journal*, passim ; Shortland's *Traditions of the New Zealanders*, pp. 130-135.

and visions in haunted houses—are familiar to savages. Without discussing these obscure matters, it may be said that they influence the thoughts even of some scientifically trained and civilised men. It is natural, therefore, that they should strongly sway the credulous imagination of backward races, in which they originate or confirm the belief that life can exist and manifest itself after the death of the body.[1]

Some examples of savage " ghost-stories," precisely analogous to the " facts" of the Psychical Society's investigations, may be adduced. The first is curious because it offers among the Kanekas an example of a belief current in Breton folk-lore. The story is vouched for by Mr. J. J. Atkinson, late of Noumea, New Caledonia. Mr. Atkinson, we have reason to believe, was unacquainted with the Breton parallel. To him one day a Kaneka of his acquaintance paid a visit, and seemed loth to go away. He took leave, returned, and took leave again, till Mr. Atkinson asked him the reason of his behaviour. He then explained that he was about to die, and would never see his English friend again. As he seemed in perfect health, Mr. Atkinson rallied him on his hypochondria ; but the poor fellow replied that his fate was sealed. He had lately met in the wood one whom he took for the Kaneka girl of his heart ; but he became aware too late that she was no mortal woman, but a wood-spirit in the guise of the beloved. The result would be his death within three days, and, as a matter of fact, he died. This is the groundwork of the old Breton ballad of *Le Sieur Nan*, who dies after his

[1] See the author's *Making of Religion*, 1898.

intrigue with the forest spectre.[1] A tale more like a common modern ghost-story is vouched for by Mr. C. J. Du Ve, in Australia. In the year 1860, a Maneroo black fellow died in the service of Mr. Du Ve. "The day before he died, having been ill some time, he said that in the night his father, his father's friend, and a female spirit he could not recognise, had come to him and said that he would die next day, and that they would wait for him. Mr. Du Ve adds that, though previously the Christian belief had been explained to this man, it had entirely faded, and that he had gone back to the belief of his childhood." Mr. Fison, who prints this tale in his *Kamilaroi and Kurnai*,[2] adds, "I could give many similar instances which have come within my own knowledge among the Fijians, and, strange to say, the dying man in all these cases kept his appointment with the ghosts to the very day".

In the *Cruise of the Beagle* is a parallel anecdote of a Fuegian, Jimmy Button, and his father's ghost.

Without entering into a discussion of ghosts, it is plain that the kind of evidence, whatever its value may be, which convinces many educated Europeans of the existence of "veridical" apparitions has also played its part in the philosophy of uncivilised races. On this belief in apparitions, then, is based the power of the savage sorcerers and necromants, of the men who converse with the dead and are aided by disembodied spirits. These men have greatly influenced

---

[1] It may, of course, be conjectured that the French introduced this belief into New Caledonia.

[2] Page 247.

the beginnings of mythology. Among certain Australian tribes the necromants are called Birraark.[1] "The Kurnai tell me," says Mr. Howitt, "that a Birraark was supposed to be initiated by the 'Mrarts (ghosts) when they met him wandering in the bush. . . . It was from the ghosts that he obtained replies to questions concerning events passing at a distance or yet to happen, which might be of interest or moment to his tribe." Mr. Howitt prints an account of a spiritual *séance* in the bush.[2] "The fires were let go down. The Birraark uttered a cry 'coo-ee' at intervals. At length a distant reply was heard, and shortly afterwards the sound as of persons jumping on the ground in succession. A voice was then heard in the gloom asking in a strange intonation, 'What is wanted?' Questions were put by the Birraark and replies given. At the termination of the *séance*, the spirit-voice said, 'We are going'. Finally, the Birraark was found in the top of an almost inaccessible tree, apparently asleep."[3] There was one Birraark at least to every clan. The Kurnai gave the name of "Brewin" (a powerful evil spirit) to a Birraark who was once carried away for several days by the Mrarts or spirits.[4] It is a belief with the Australians, as,

[1] *Kamilaroi and Kurnai*, p. 253.   [2] Page 254.

[3] In the Jesuit *Relations* (1637), p. 51, we read that the Red Indian sorcerer or Jossakeed was credited with power to vanish suddenly away out of sight of the men standing around him. Of him, as of Homeric gods, it might be said, "Who has power to see him come or go against his will?"

[4] Here, in the first edition, occurred the following passage: "The conception of Brewin is about as near as the Kurnai get to the idea of a God; their conferring of his name on a powerful sorcerer is therefore a point of importance and interest". Mr. Howitt's later knowledge demonstrates an error here.

according to Bosman, it was with the people of the
Gold Coast, that a very powerful wizard lives far
inland, and the Negroes held that to this warlock the
spirits of the dead went to be judged according to the
merit of their actions in life.   Here we have a doctrine
answering to the Greek belief in "the wizard Minos,"
Æacus, and Rhadamanthus, and to the Egyptian idea
of Osiris as judge of the departed.[1]   The pretensions
of the sorcerer to converse with the dead are attested
by Mr. Brough Smyth.[2] "A sorcerer lying on his
stomach spoke to the deceased, and the other sitting
by his side received the precious messages which the
dead man told."   As a natural result of these beliefs,
the Australian necromant has great power in the
tribe.   Mr. Howitt mentions a case in which a group
of kindred, ceasing to use their old totemistic surname,
called themselves the children of a famous dead Birraark, who thus became an eponymous hero, like Ion
among the Ionians.[3]   Among the Scotch Highlanders
the position and practice of the seer were very like
those of the Birraark.   "A person," says Scott,[4] "was
wrapped up in the skin of a newly slain bullock and
deposited beside a waterfall or at the bottom of a
precipice, or in some other strange, wild and unusual
situation, where the scenery around him suggested
nothing but objects of horror.   In this situation he
revolved in his mind the question proposed and what-

[1] Bosman in Pinkerton, xvi. p. 401.

[2] *Aborigines of Australia*, i. 197.

[3] In Victoria, after dark the wizard goes up to the clouds and brings
down a good spirit. Dawkins, p. 57. For eponymous medicine-men see
Kamilaroi and Kurnai, p. 231.

[4] *Lady of the Lake*, note 1 to Canto iv.

ever was impressed on him by his exalted imagination *passed for the inspiration of the disembodied spirits* who haunt these desolate recesses." A number of examples are given in Martin's *Description of the Western Islands.*[1] In the *Century* magazine (July, 1882) is a very full report of Thlinkeet medicine-men and metamorphoses.

The sorcerer among the Zulus is, apparently, of a naturally hysterical and nervous constitution. "He hears the spirits who speak by whistlings speaking to him."[2] Whistling is also the language of the ghosts in New Caledonia, where Mr. Atkinson informs us that he has occasionally put an able-bodied Kaneka to ignominious flight by whistling softly in the dusk. The ghosts in Homer make a similar sound, "and even as bats flit gibbering in the secret place of a wondrous cavern, . . . even so the souls gibbered as they fared together" (*Odyssey*, xxiv. 5). "The familiar spirits make him" (that Zulu sorcerer) "acquainted with what is about to happen, and then he divines for the people." As the Birraarks learn songs and dance-music from the Mrarts, so the Zulu Inyanga or diviners learn magical couplets from the Itongo or spirits.[3]

The evidence of institutions confirms the reports about savage belief in magic. The political power of the diviners is very great, as may be observed from the fact that a hereditary chief needs their consecration to make him a chief *de jure.*[4] In fact, the qualities of the diviner are those which give his sacred authority to

[1] P. 112.　　[2] Callaway, *Religious System of the Amazulus*, p. 265.
[3] On all this, see "Possession" in *The Making of Religion*.
[4] Callaway, p. 340.

the chief.   When he has obtained from the diviners all
their medicines and information as to the mode of using
the *isitundu* (a magical vessel), it is said that he often
orders them to be killed.   Now, the chief is so far a
medicine-man that he is lord of the air.   " The heaven
is the chief's," say the Zulus; and when he calls out
his men, "though the heaven is clear, it becomes
clouded by the great wind that arises ".   Other Zulus
explain this as the mere hyperbole of adulation.
"The word of the chief gives confidence to his troops;
they say, 'We are going; the chief has already seen
all that will happen in his vessel'.   Such then are
chiefs; they use a vessel for divination."[1]   The makers
of rain are known in Zululand as "heaven-herds" or
"sky-herds," who herd the heaven that it may not
break out and do its will on the property of the people.
These men are, in fact, νεφεληγερέται, "cloud-gatherers,"
like the Homeric Zeus, the lord of the heavens.   Their
name of "herds of the heavens" has a Vedic sound.
"The herd that herds the lightning," say the Zulus,
"does the same as the herder of the cattle; he does as
he does by whistling; he says, 'Tshu-i-i-i.   Depart
and go yonder.   Do not come here.'"   Here let it be
observed that the Zulus conceive of the thunder-clouds
and lightning as actual creatures, capable of being
herded like sheep.   There is no metaphor or allegory
about the matter,[2] and no forgetfulness of the original
meaning of words.   The cloud-herd is just like the cow-
herd, except that not every man, but only sorcerers,
and they who have eaten the " lightning-bird" (a bird

[1] Callaway, *Religious System of the Amazules*, p. 343.
[2] *Ibid.*, p. 385.

shot near the place where lightning has struck the earth), can herd the clouds of heaven. The same ideas prevail among the Bushmen, where the rain-maker is asked " to milk a nice gentle female rain " ; the rain-clouds are her hair. Among the Bushmen Rain is a person. Among the Red Indians no metaphor seems to be intended when it is said that " it is always birds who make the wind, except that of the east ". The Dacotahs once killed a thunder-bird[1] behind Little Crow's village on the Missouri. It had a face like a man with a nose like an eagle's bill.[2]

The political and social powers which come into the hands of the sorcerers are manifest, even in the case of the Australians. Tribes and individuals can attempt few enterprises without the aid of the man who listens to the ghosts. Only he can foretell the future, and, in the case of the natural death of a member of the tribe, can direct the vengeance of the survivors against the hostile magician who has committed a murder by "*bar*" or magic. Among the Zulus we have seen that sorcery gives the sanction to the power of the chief "The winds and weather are at the command" of Bosman's "great fetisher". Inland from the Gold Coast,[3] the king of Loango, according to the Abbé Proyart, "has credit to make rain fall on earth". Similar beliefs, with like political results, will be found to follow from the superstition of magic among the Red Indians of North America. The difficulty of writing about sorcerers among the Red Indians is caused by the abundance of the evidence. Charlevoix

[1] Schoolcraft, iii. 486.   [2] Compare Callaway, p. 119.
[3] Pinkerton, xvi. 401.

and the other early Jesuit missionaries found that
the *jongleurs*, as Charlevoix calls the Jossakeeds or
medicine-men, were their chief opponents. As among
the Scotch Highlanders, the Australians and the
Zulus, the Red Indian *jongleur* is visited by the
spirits. He covers a hut with the skin of the animal
which he commonly wears, retires thither, and there
converses with the bodiless beings.[1] The good missionary like Mr. Moffat in Africa, was convinced that the
exercises of the Jossakeeds were verily supernatural.
" Ces seducteurs ont un véritable commerce avec le père
du mensonge."[2]   This was denied by earlier and
wiser Jesuit missionaries. Their political power was
naturally great. In time of war " ils avancent et
retardent les marches comme il leur plait ".   In our
own century it was a medicine-man, Ten Squa Ta
Way, who by his magical processes and superstitious
rites stirred up a formidable war against the United
States.[3] According to Mr. Pond,[4] the native name of
the Dacotah medicine-men, " Wakan," signifies " men
supernaturally gifted ".   Medicine-men are believed to
be " wakanised " by mystic intercourse with supernatural beings. The business of the wakanised man
is to discern future events, to lead and direct parties
on the war-trail, " to raise the storm or calm the
tempest, to converse with the lightning or thunder as
with familiar friends ".[5] The wakanised man, like
the Australian Birraark and the Zulu diviner, " dictates

---

[1] Charlevoix, i. 105. See " Savage Spiritualism " in *Cock Lane and
Common Sense.*

[2] *Ibid.*, iii. 362.   [3] Catlin, ii. 17.

[4] In Schoolcraft, iv. 402.   [5] Pond, in Schoolcraft, iv. 647.

chants and prayers ". In battle " every Dacotah warrior
looks to the Wakan man as almost his only resource ".
Belief in Wakan men is, Mr. Pond says, universal among
the Dacotahs, except where Christianity has under-
mined it. "Their influence is deeply felt by every individual of the tribe, and controls all their affairs." The
Wakan man's functions are absorbed by the general
or war-chief of the tribe, and in Schoolcraft (iv. 495),
Captain Eastman prints copies of native scrolls showing the war-chief at work as a wizard. *" The war-
chief who leads the party to war is always one of these
medicine-men."* In another passage the medicine-men
are described as "having a voice in the sale of land ".
It must be observed that the Jossakeed, or medicine-
man, pure and simple, exercises a power which is not
in itself hereditary. Chieftainship, when associated
with inheritance of property, is hereditary ; and when
the chief, as among the Zulus, absorbs supernatural
power, then the same man becomes diviner and chief,
and is a person of great and sacred influence. The
liveliest account of the performances of the Maori
"tohunga" or sorcerer is to be found in *Old New
Zealand,*[1] by the Pakeha Maori, an English gentleman
who had lived with the natives like one of themselves.
The *tohunga,* says this author,[2] presided over "all
those services and customs which had something
approaching to a religious character. They also pretended to power by means of certain familiar spirits,
to foretell future events, and even in some cases to
control them. . . . The spirit 'entered into' them, and,
on being questioned, gave a response in a sort of half-

[1] Auckland, 1863.　　　　[2] Page 148.

whistling, half-articulate voice, supposed to be the proper
language of spirits." In New South Wales, Mrs. Lang-
lot Parker has witnessed a similar exhibition. The
"spirits" told the truth in this case. The Pakeha Maori
was present in a darkened village-hall when the spirit
of a young man, a great friend of his own, was called
up by a *tohunga*. "Suddenly, without the slightest
warning, a voice came out of the darkness. . . . The
voice all through, it is to be remembered, was not the
voice of the *tohunga*, but a strange melancholy sound,
like the sound of a wind blowing into a hollow vessel.
'It is well with me; my place is a good place.' The
spirit gave an answer to a question which proved
to be correct, and then 'Farewell,' cried the spirit
from deep beneath the ground. 'Farewell,' again,
from high in air. 'Farewell,' once more came moan-
ing through the distant darkness of the night." As
chiefs in New Zealand no less than *tohungas* can
exercise the mystical and magical power of *tabu*, that
is, of imparting to any object or person an inviolable
character, and can prevent or remit the mysterious
punishment for infringement of *tabu*, it appears
probable that in New Zealand, as well as among
the Zulus and Red Indians, chiefs have a tendency
to absorb the sacred character and powers of the
tohungas. This is natural enough, for a *tohunga*, if
he plays his cards well, is sure to acquire property
and hereditary wealth, which, in combination with
magical influence, are the necessary qualifications for
the office of the chieftain.

Here is the place to mention a fact which, though
at first sight it may appear to have only a social

interest, yet bears on the development of mythology. Property and rank seem to have been essential to each other in the making of social rank, and where one is absent among contemporary savages, there we do not find the other. As an example of this, we might take the case of two peoples who, like the Homeric Ethiopians, are the outermost of men, and dwell far apart at the ends of the world. The Eskimos and the Fuegians, at the extreme north and south of the American continent, agree in having little or no private property and no chiefs. Yet magic is providing a kind of basis of rank. The bleak plains of ice and rock are, like Attica, " the mother of men without master or lord ". Among the " house-mates " of the smaller settlements there is no head-man, and in the larger gatherings Dr. Rink says that " still less than among the house-mates was any one belonging to such a place to be considered a chief ". The songs and stories of the Eskimo contain the praises of men who have risen up and killed any usurper who tried to be a ruler over his " place-mates ". No one could possibly establish any authority on the basis of property, because " superfluous property, implements, etc., rarely existed ". If there are three boats in one household, one of the boats is " borrowed " by the community, and reverts to the general fund. If we look at the account of the Fuegians described in Admiral Fitzroy's cruise, we find a similar absence of rank produced by similar causes. " The perfect equality among the individuals composing the tribes must for a long time retard their civilisation. . . . At present even a piece of cloth is torn in shreds and distributed, and no one individual

becomes richer than another. On the other hand, it is
difficult to understand how a chief can arise till there
is property of some sort by which he might manifest
and still increase his authority." In the same book,
however, we get a glimpse of one means by which
authority can be exercised. "The doctor-wizard of
each party has much influence over his companions."
Among the Eskimos this element in the growth of
authority also exists. A class of wizards called
Angakut have power to cause fine weather, and, by
the gift of second-sight and magical practices, can
detect crimes, so that they necessarily become a kind
of civil magistrates. These Angekkok or Angakut have
familiar spirits called Torngak, a word connected with
the name of their chief spiritual being, Torngarsak.
The Torngak is commonly the ghost of a deceased
parent of the sorcerer. "These men," says Egede, "are
held in great honour and esteem among this stupid
and ignorant nation, insomuch that nobody dare ever
refuse the strictest obedience when they command
him in the name of Torngarsak." The importance
and actual existence of belief in magic has thus been
attested by the evidence of institutions, even among
Australians, Fuegians and Eskimos.

It is now necessary to pass from examples of tribes
who have superstitious respect for certain individuals,
but who have no property and no chiefs, to peoples
who exhibit the phenomenon of superstitious reverence
attached to wealthy rulers or to judges. To take the
example of Ireland, as described in the *Senchus Mor*,
we learn that the chiefs, just like the Angakut of the
Eskimos, had "power to make fair or foul weather"

in the literal sense of the words.[1] In Africa, in the
same way, as Bosman, the old traveller, says, " As
to what difference there is between one negro and
another, the richest man is the most honoured," yet
the most honoured man has the same magical power
as the poor Angakuts of the Eskimos.

" In the Solomon Islands," says Dr. Codrington,
" there is nothing to prevent a common man from
becoming a chief, if he can show that he has the
mana (supernatural power) for it." [2]

Though it is anticipating a later stage of this inquiry, we must here observe that the sacredness, and
even the magical virtues of barbarous chiefs seem to
have descended to the early leaders of European races.
The children of Odin and of Zeus were "sacred
kings". The Homeric chiefs, like those of the Zulus
and the Red Men, and of the early Irish and Swedes,
exercised an influence over the physical universe.
Homer [3] speaks of " a blameless king, one that fears
the gods, and reigns among many men and mighty,
and the black earth bears wheat and barley, and the
sheep bring forth and fail not, and the sea gives store
of fish, and all out of his good sovereignty ".

The attributes usually assigned by barbarous peoples
to their medicine-men have not yet been exhausted.
We have found that they can foresee and declare the
future ; that they control the weather and the sensible
world ; that they can converse with, visit and employ
about their own business the souls of the dead. It
would be easy to show at even greater length that the

[1] *Early History of Institutions*, p. 195.
[2] *Journ. Anth. Inst.*, x. iii. 287, 300, 309.   [3] *Od.*, xix. 109.

medicine-man has everywhere the power of metamorphosis. He can assume the shapes of all beasts, birds,
fishes, insects and inorganic matters, and he can
subdue other people to the same enchantment. This
belief obviously rests on the lack of recognised distinction between man and the rest of the world, which
we have so frequently insisted on as a characteristic
of savage and barbarous thought. Examples of accredited metamorphosis are so common everywhere,
and so well known, that it would be waste of space to
give a long account of them. In *Primitive Culture*[1]
a cloud of witnesses to the belief in human tigers,
hyænas, leopards and wolves is collected.[2] Mr.
Lane[3] found metamorphosis by wizards as accredited
a working belief at Cairo as it is among Abipones,
Eskimo, or the people of Ashangoland. In various
parts of Scotland there is a tale of a witch who was shot
at when in the guise of a hare. In this shape she was
wounded, and the same wound was found on her
when she resumed her human appearance. Lafitau,
early in the last century, found precisely the same
tale, except that the wizards took the form of birds,
not of hares, among the Red Indians. The birds were
wounded by the magical arrows of an old medicine-man,
Shonnoh Koui Eretsi, and these bolts were found in
the bodies of the human culprits. In Japan, as we
learn from several stories in Mr. Mitford's *Tales of
Old Japan*, people chiefly metamorphose themselves
into foxes and badgers. The sorcerers of Honduras[4]

[1] Vol. i. pp. 309-315.
[2] See also M'Lennan on Lykanthropy in *Encyclopædia Britannica*.
[3] *Arabian Nights*, i. 51.   [4] Bancroft, *Races of Pacific Coast*, i. 740.

" possess the power of transforming men into wild
beasts, and were much feared accordingly ". Among
the Cakchiquels, a cultivated people of Guatemala,
the very name of the clergy, *haleb*, was derived from
their power of assuming animal shapes, which they
took on as easily as the Homeric gods.[1] Regnard,
the French dramatist, who travelled among the Lapps
at the end of the seventeenth century (1681), says:
" They believe witches can turn men into cats ; "
and again, " Under the figures of swans, crows,
falcons and geese, they call up tempests and destroy
ships ".[2] Among the Bushmen " sorcerers assume the
forms of beasts and jackals".[3] Dobrizhoffer (1717-91), a
missionary in Paraguay, found that "sorcerers arrogate
to themselves the power of transforming themselves into
tigers".[4] He was present when the Abipones believed
that a conversion of this sort was actually taking
place : " Alas," cried the people, " his whole body is
beginning to be covered with tiger-spots ; his nails are
growing ". Near Loanda, Livingstone found that
a " chief may metamorphose himself into a lion, kill
any one he choses, and then resume his proper form ".[5]
Among the Barotse and Balonda, " while persons are
still alive they may enter into lions and alligators ".[6]
Among the Mayas of Central America " sorcerers
could transform themselves into dogs, pigs and other
animals ; their glance was death to a victim ".[7] The
Thlinkeets think that their Shamans can metamor-

[1] Brinton, *Annals of the Cakchiquels*, p. 46.   [2] Pinkerton, i. 471.
[3] Bleek, *Brief Account of Bushman Folk-Lore*, pp. 15, 40.
[4] English translation of Dobrizhoffer's *Abipones*, i. 163.
[5] *Missionary Travels*, p. 615.   [6] Livingstone, p. 642.
[7] Bancroft, ii.

phose themselves into animals at pleasure ; and a
very old raven was pointed out to Mr. C. E. S. Wood
as an incarnation of the soul of a Shaman.[1] Sir A.
C. Lyall finds a similar belief in flourishing existence
in India. The European superstition of the were-wolf
is too well known to need description. Perhaps the
most curious legend is that told by Giraldus Cam-
brensis about a man and his wife metamorphosed into
wolves by an abbot. They retained human speech,
made exemplary professions of Christian faith, and
sent for priests when they found their last hours
approaching. In an old Norman ballad a girl is
transformed into a white doe, and hunted and slain
by her brother's hounds. The "aboriginal" peoples
of India retain similar convictions. Among the Hos,[2]
an old sorcerer called Pusa was known to turn himself
habitually into a tiger, and to eat his neighbour's goats,
and even their wives. Examples of the power of
sorcerers to turn, as with the Gorgon's head, their
enemies into stone, are peculiarly common in America.[3]
Hearne found that the Indians believed they descended from a dog, who could turn himself into a
handsome young man.[4]

Let us recapitulate the powers attributed all over
the world, by the lower people, to medicine-men.
The medicine-man has all miracles at his command.
He rules the sky, he flies into the air, he becomes
visible or invisible at will, he can take or confer any

[1] *Century* Magazine, July, 1882.

[2] Dalton's *Ethnology of Bengal*, p. 200.

[3] Dorman, pp. 130, 134 ; *Report of Ethnological Bureau*, Washington,
1880-81.

[4] *A Journey*, etc., p. 342.

form at pleasure, and resume his human shape. He can control spirits, can converse with the dead, and can descend to their abodes.

When we begin to examine the gods of *mythology*, savage or civilised, as distinct from deities contemplated, in devotion, as moral and creative guardians of ethics, we shall find that, with the general, though not invariable addition of immortality, they possess the very same accomplishments as the medicine-man, peay, tohunga, jossakeed, birraark, or whatever name for sorcerer we may choose. Among the Greeks, Zeus, mythically envisaged, enjoys in heaven all the attributes of the medicine-man ; among the Iroquois, as Père le Jeune, the old Jesuit missionary, observed,[1] the medicine-man enjoys on earth all the attributes of Zeus. Briefly, the miraculous and supernatural endowments of the gods of *myth*, whether these gods be zoomorphic or anthropomorphic, are exactly the magical properties with which the medicine-man is credited by his tribe. It does not at all follow, as Euemerus and Mr. Herbert Spencer might argue, that the god was once a real living medicine-man. But myth-making man confers on the deities of myth the magical powers which he claims for himself.

[1] *Relations* (1636), p. 114.

CHAPTER V.

NATURE MYTHS.

Savage fancy, curiosity and credulity illustrated in nature myths—In these all phenomena are explained by belief in the general animation of everything, combined with belief in metamorphosis—Sun myths, Asian, Australian, African, Melanesian, Indian, Californian, Brazilian, Maori, Samoan—Moon myths, Australian, Muysca, Mexican, Zulu, Macassar, Greenland, Piute, Malay—Thunder myths—Greek and Aryan sun and moon myths—Star myths—Myths, savage and civilised, of animals, accounting for their marks and habits—Examples of custom of claiming blood kinship with lower animals—Myths of various plants and trees—Myths of stones, and of metamorphosis into stones, Greek, Australian and American—The whole natural philosophy of savages expressed in myths, and survives in folk-lore and classical poetry; and legends of metamorphosis.

THE intellectual condition of savages which has been presented and established by the evidence both of observers and of institutions, may now be studied in savage myths. These myths, indeed, would of themselves demonstrate that the ideas which the lower races entertain about the world correspond with our statement. If any one were to ask himself, from what mental conditions do the following savage stories arise? he would naturally answer that the minds which conceived the tales were curious, indolent, credulous of magic and witchcraft, capable of drawing no line between things and persons, capable of crediting all things with human passions and resolutions. But, as myths analogous to those of savages, when found among civilised peoples, have been ascribed to a psychological condition produced by a disease of language acting after civilisation had made considerable advances, we cannot take the savage myths as proof of what savages think, believe and practice in the course of daily life. To do so would be, perhaps, to argue in a circle. We must therefore study the myths of the undeveloped races in themselves.

These myths form a composite whole, so complex and so nebulous that it is hard indeed to array them in classes and categories. For example, if we look at myths concerning the origin of various phenomena, we find that some introduce the action of gods or extra-natural beings, while others rest on a rude theory of capricious evolution ; others, again, invoke the aid of the magic of mortals, and most regard the great natural forces, the heavenly bodies, and the animals, as so many personal characters capable of voluntarily modifying themselves or of being modified by the most trivial accidents. Some sort of arrangement, however, must be attempted, only the student is to understand that the lines are never drawn with definite fixity, that any category may glide into any other category of myth.

We shall begin by considering some nature myths —myths, that is to say, which explain the facts of the visible universe. These range from tales about heaven, day, night, the sun and the stars, to tales accounting for the red breast of the ousel, the habits of the quail, the spots and stripes of wild beasts, the formation of rocks and stones, the foliage of trees, the shapes of plants. In a sense these myths are the science of savages ; in a sense they are their sacred history ; in a sense they are their fiction and romance. Beginning with the sun, we find, as Mr. Tylor says, that " in early philosophy throughout the world the sun and moon are alive, and, as it were, human in their nature ".[1] The mass of these solar myths is so enormous that only a few examples can be given, chosen almost at random out of the heap. The sun is regarded as a personal being, capable not only of being affected by charms and incantations, but of being trapped and beaten, of appearing on earth, of taking a wife of the daughters of men. Garcilasso de la Vega has a story of an Inca prince, a speculative thinker, who was puzzled by the sun-worship of his ancestors. If the sun be thus all-powerful, the Inca inquired, why is he plainly subject to laws ? why does he go his daily round, instead of wandering at large up and down the fields of heaven ? The prince concluded that there was a will superior to the sun's will, and he raised a temple to the Unknown Power. Now the phenomena which put the Inca on the path of monotheistic religion, a path already traditional, according to Garcilasso, have also struck the fancy of savages. Why, they ask, does the sun run his course like a tamed beast ? A reply suited to a mind which holds that all things are personal is given in myths. Some one caught and tamed the sun by physical force or by art magic.

In Australia the myth says that there was a time when the sun did not set. " It was at all times day,

[1] *Primitive Culture*, i. 288.

and the blacks grew weary. Norralie considered and
decided that the sun should disappear at intervals.
He addressed the sun in an incantation (couched like
the Finnish *Kalewala* in the metre of Longfellow's
Hiawatha) ; and the incantation is thus interpreted :
" Sun, sun, burn your wood, burn your internal
substance, and go down ". The sun therefore now
burns out his fuel in a day, and goes below for fresh
firewood.[1]

In New Zealand the taming of the sun is attributed
to the great hero Maui, the Prometheus of the Maoris.
He set snares to catch the sun, but in vain, for the
sun's rays bit them through. According to another
account, while Norralie wished to hasten the sun's
setting, Maui wanted to delay it, for the sun used to
speed through the heavens at a racing pace. Maui
therefore snared the sun, and beat him so unmercifully
that he has been lame ever since, and travels slowly,
giving longer days. "The sun, when beaten, cried
out and revealed his second great name, Taura-mis-
te-ra."[2] It will be remembered that Indra, in his
abject terror when he fled after the slaying of Vrittra,
also revealed his mystic name. In North America the
same story of the trapping and laming of the sun is
told, and attributed to a hero named Tcha-ka-betch.
In Samoa the sun had a child by a Samoan woman.
He trapped the sun with a rope made of a vine and
extorted presents. Another Samoan lassoed the sun
and made him promise to move more slowly.[3] These
Samoan and Australian fancies are nearly as dignified

---

[1] Brough Smyth, *Aborigines of Victoria*, i. 430.
[2] Taylor, *New Zealand*, p. 131.   [3] Turner, *Samoa*, p. 20.

as the tale in the *Aitareya Brahmana*. The gods, afraid "that the sun would fall out of heaven, pulled him up and tied him with five ropes". These ropes are recognised as verses in the ritual, but probably the ritual is later than the ropes. In Mexico we find that the sun himself (like the stars in most myths) was once a human or pre-human devotee, Nanahuatzin, who leapt into a fire to propitiate the gods.[1] Translated to heaven as the sun, Nanahuatzin burned so very fiercely that he threatened to reduce the world to a cinder. Arrows were therefore shot at him, and this punishment had as happy an effect as the beatings administered by Maui and Tcha-ka-betch. Among the Bushmen of South Africa the sun was once a man, from whose armpit a limited amount of light was radiated round his hut. Some children threw him up into the sky, and there he stuck, and there he shines.[2] In the Homeric hymn to Helios, as Mr. Max Müller observes, "the poet looks on Helios as a half god, almost a hero, who had once lived on earth," which is precisely the view of the Bushmen.[3] Among the Aztecs the sun is said to have been attacked by a hunter and grievously wounded by his arrows.[4] The Gallinomeros, in Central California, seem at least to know that the sun is material and impersonal. They say that when all was dark in the beginning, the animals were constantly jostling each other. After a painful encounter, the hawk and the coyote collected two balls of inflammable substance ; the hawk (Indra was

---

[1] Sahagun, French trans., vii. ii.
[2] Bleek, *Hottentot Fables*, p. 67 ; *Bushman Folk-Lore*, pp. 9, 11.
[3] Compare a Californian solar myth : Bancroft, iii. pp. 85, 86.
[4] Bancroft, iii. 73, quoting Burgoa, i. 128, 196.

occasionally a hawk) flew up with them into heaven,
and lighted them with sparks from a flint. There they
gave light as sun and moon. This is an exception to
the general rule that the heavenly bodies are regarded
as persons. The Melanesian tale of the bringing of
night is a curious contrast to the Mexican, Maori,
Australian and American Indian stories which we
have quoted. In Melanesia, as in Australia, the days
were long, indeed endless, and people grew tired; but
instead of sending the sun down below by an incantation when night would follow in course of nature,
the Melanesian hero went to Night (conceived of as
a person) and begged his assistance. Night (Qong)
received Qat (the hero) kindly, darkened his eyes, gave
him sleep, and, in twelve hours or so, crept up from
the horizon and sent the sun crawling to the west.[1]
In the same spirit Paracelsus is said to have attributed
night, not to the absence of the sun, but to the
apparition of certain stars which radiate darkness.
It is extraordinary that a myth like the Melanesian
should occur in Brazil. There was endless day till
some one married a girl whose father "the great
serpent," was the owner of night. The father sent
night bottled up in a gourd. The gourd was not to
be uncorked till the messengers reached the bride,
but they, in their curiosity, opened the gourd, and let
night out prematurely.[2]

The myths which have been reported deal mainly
with the sun as a person who shines, and at fixed

---

[1] Codrington, *Journ. Anthrop. Inst.*, February, 1881.

[2] *Contes Indiens du Bresil*, pp. 1-9, by Couto de Magalhaes. Rio de
Janeiro, 1883. M. Henri Gaidoz kindly presented the author with this
work.

intervals disappears. His relations with the moon are
much more complicated, and are the subject of endless
stories, all explaining in a romantic fashion why the
moon waxes and wanes, whence come her spots, why
she is eclipsed, all starting from the premise that sun
and moon are persons with human parts and passions.
Sometimes the moon is a man, sometimes a woman,
and the sex of the sun varies according to the fancy
of the narrators. Different tribes of the same race, as
among the Australians, have different views of the sex
of moon and sun. Among the aborigines of Victoria,
the moon, like the sun among the Bushmen, was a
black fellow before he went up into the sky. After
an unusually savage career, he was killed with a stone
hatchet by the wives of the eagle, and now he shines
in the heavens.[1] Another myth explanatory of the
moon's phases was found by Mr. Meyer in 1846 among
the natives of Encounter Bay. According to them the
moon is a woman, and a bad woman to boot. She
lives a life of dissipation among men, which makes
her consumptive, and she wastes away till they drive
her from their company. While she is in retreat, she
lives on nourishing roots, becomes quite plump, re-
sumes her gay career, and again wastes away. The
same tribe, strangely enough, think that the sun also
is a woman. Every night she descends among the
dead, who stand in double lines to greet her and let
her pass. She has a lover among the dead, who has
presented her with a red kangaroo skin, and in this she
appears at her rising. Such is the view of rosy-
fingered Dawn entertained by the blacks of Encounter

[1] Brough Smyth, *Aborigines of Victoria*, i. 432.

Bay. In South America, among the Muyscas of
Bogota, the moon, Huythaca, is the malevolent wife of
the child of the sun ; she was a woman before her
husband banished her to the fields of space.[1] The
moon is a man among the Khasias of the Himalaya.
and he was guilty of the unpardonable offence of
admiring his mother-in-law. As a general rule, the
mother-in-law is not even to be spoken to by the
savage son-in-law. The lady threw ashes in his face
to discourage his passion, hence the moon's spots. The
waning of the moon suggested the most beautiful and
best known of savage myths, that in which the moon
sends a beast to tell mortals that, though they die
like her, like her they shall be born again.[2] Because
the spots in the moon were thought to resemble a hare
they were accounted for in Mexico by the hypothesis
that a god smote the moon in the face with a rabbit ;[3]
in Zululand and Thibet by a fancied translation of a
good or bad hare to the moon.

The Eskimos have a peculiar myth to account for the
moon's spots. Sun and moon were human brother
and sister. In the darkness the moon once attempted
the virtue of the sun. She smeared his face over
with ashes, that she might detect him when a light
was brought. She did discover who her assailant
had been, fled to the sky, and became the sun. The
moon still pursues her, and his face is still blackened
with the marks of ashes.[4] Gervaise[5] says that in

---

[1] Tylor, *Primitive Culture*, i. 353.
[2] Bleek, *Reynard in South Africa*, pp. 69-74.
[3] Sahagun, viii. 2. [4] Crantz's *History of Greenland*, i. 212.
[5] *Royaume de Macaçar*, 1688.

Macassar the moon was held to be with child by the sun, and that when he pursued her and wished to beat her, she was delivered of the earth. They are now reconciled. About the alternate appearance of sun and moon a beautifully complete and adequate tale is told by the Piute Indians of California. No more adequate and scientific explanation could possibly be offered, granting the hypothesis that sun and moon are human persons and savage persons. The myth is printed as it was taken down by Mr. De Quille from the lips of Tooroop Eenah (Desert Father), a chief of the Piutes, and published in a San Francisco newspaper.

"The sun is the father and ruler of the heavens. He is the big chief. The moon is his wife and the stars are their children. The sun eats his children whenever he can catch them. They flee before him, and are all the time afraid when he is passing through the heavens. When he (their father) appears in the morning, you see all the stars, his children, fly out of sight—go away back into the blue of the above—and they do not wake to be seen again until he, their father, is about going to his bed.

"Down deep under the ground—deep, deep, under all the ground—is a great hole. At night, when he has passed over the world, looked down on everything and finished his work, he, the sun, goes into his hole, and he crawls and creeps along it till he comes to his bed in the middle part of the earth. So then he, the sun, sleeps there in his bed all night.

"This hole is so little, and he, the sun, is so big, that he cannot turn round in it; and so he must, when

he has had all his sleep, pass on through, and in the
morning we see him come out in the east. When he,
the sun, has so come out, he begins to hunt up through
the sky to catch and eat any that he can of the stars,
his children, for if he does not so catch and eat he
cannot live. He, the sun, is not all seen. *The shape
of him is like a snake or a lizard.* It is not his head
that we can see, but his belly, filled up with the stars
that times and times he has swallowed.

"The moon is the mother of the heavens and is the
wife of the sun. She, the moon, goes into the same
hole as her husband to sleep her naps. But always
she has great fear of the sun, her husband, and when
he comes through the hole to the *nobee* (tent) deep in
the ground to sleep, she gets out and comes away if
he be cross.

"She, the moon, has great love for her children, the
stars, and is happy to travel among them in the
above; and they, her children, feel safe, and sing and
dance as she passes along. But the mother, she cannot
help that some of her children must be swallowed by
the father every month. *It is ordered that way by
the Pah-ah (Great Spirit), who lives above the place
of all.*

"Every month that father, the sun, does swallow
some of the stars, his children, and then that mother,
the moon, feels sorrow. She must mourn; so she
must put the black on her face for to mourn the dead.
You see the Piute women put black on their faces
when a child is gone. But the dark will wear away
from the face of that mother, the moon, a little and a
little every day, and after a time again we see all

bright the face of her. But soon more of her children
are gone, and again she must put on her face the pitch
and the black."

Here all the phenomena are accounted for, and the
explanation is as advanced as the Egyptian doctrine of
the hole under the earth where the sun goes when he
passes from our view. And still the Great Spirit is
over all : Religion comes athwart Myth.

Mr. Tylor quotes[1] a nature myth about sun, moon
and stars which remarkably corresponds to the speculation of the Piutes. The Mintira of the Malayan
Peninsula say that both sun and moon are women. The
stars are the moon's children ; once the sun had as
many. They each agreed (like the women of Jerusalem
in the famine), to eat their own children ; but the sun
swallowed her whole family, while the moon concealed
hers. When the sun saw this she was exceedingly
angry, and pursued the moon to kill her. Occasionally
she gets a bite out of the moon, and that is an eclipse.
The Hos of North-East India tell the same tale, but
say that the sun cleft the moon in twain for her
treachery, and that she continues to be cut in two and
grow again every month. With these sun and moon
legends sometimes coexists the *religious* belief in a
Creator of these and of all things.

In harmony with the general hypothesis that all
objects in nature are personal, and human or bestial,
in real shape, and in passion and habits, are the
myths which account for eclipses. These have so
frequently been published and commented on[2] that a

[1] *Primitive Culture*, i. 356.
[2] Tylor, *Primitive Culture*, vol. i. ; Lefébure, *Les Yeux d' Horus.*

long statement would be tedious and superfluous.
To the savage mind, and even to the Chinese and the
peasants of some European countries, the need of an
explanation is satisfied by the myth that an evil beast
is devouring the sun or the moon. The people even
try by firing off guns, shrieking, and clashing cymbals,
to frighten the beast (wolf, pig, dragon, or what not)
from his prey. What the hungry monster in the sky
is doing when he is not biting the sun or moon we
are not informed. Probably he herds with the big
bird whose wings, among the Dacotahs of America
and the Zulus of Africa, make thunder; or he may
associate with the dragons, serpents, cows and other
aerial cattle which supply the rain, and show themselves in the waterspout. Chinese, Greenland, Hindoo,
Finnish, Lithunian and Moorish examples of the myth
about the moon-devouring beasts are vouched for by
Grimm.[1] A Mongolian legend has it that the gods
wished to punish the maleficent Arakho for his
misdeeds, but Arakho hid so cleverly that their
limited omnipotence could not find him. The sun,
when asked to turn spy, gave an evasive answer.
The moon told the truth. Arakho was punished, and
ever since he chases sun and moon. When he nearly
catches either of them, there is an eclipse, and the
people try to drive him off by making a hideous
uproar with musical and other instruments.[2] Captain
Beeckman in 1704 was in Borneo, when the natives
declared that the devil " was eating the moon ".

Dr. Brinton in his *Myths and Myth-Makers* gives

[1] *Teutonic Mythology*, English trans., ii. 706.
[2] *Moon-Lore*, by Rev. T. Harley, p. 167.

examples from Peruvians, Tupis, Creeks, Iroquois
and Algonkins.   It would be easy, and is perhaps
superfluous, to go on multiplying proofs of the belief
that sun and moon are, or have been, persons.   In the
Hervey Isles these two luminaries are thought to have
been made out of the body of a child cut in twain by
his parents.   The blood escaped from the half which
is the moon, hence her pallor.[1]   This tale is an exception to the general rule, but reminds us of the
many myths which represent the things in the world
as having been made out of a mutilated man, like the
Vedic Purusha.   It is hardly necessary, except by
way of record, to point out that the Greek myths of
sun and moon, like the myths of savages, start from
the conception of the solar and lunar bodies as
persons with parts and passions, human loves and
human sorrows.   As in the Mongolian myth of
Arakho, the sun "sees all and hears all," and, less
honourable than the Mongolian sun, he plays the spy
for Hephæstus on the loves of Ares and Aphrodite.
He has mistresses and human children, such as Circe
and Æetes.[2]

The sun is all-seeing and all-penetrating.   In a
Greek song of to-day a mother sends a message to an
absent daughter by the sun; it is but an unconscious
repetition of the request of the dying Ajax that the
heavenly body will tell his fate to his old father and
his sorrowing spouse.[3]

Selene, the moon, like Helios, the sun, was a person,
and amorous.   Beloved by Zeus, she gave birth to

[1] Gill, *Myths and Songs*, p. 45.   [3] Sophocles, *Ajax*, 846.
[2] See chapter on Greek Divine Myths.

Pandia, and Pan gained her affection by the simple rustic gift of a fleece.[1] The Australian Dawn, with her present of a red kangaroo skin, was not more lightly won than the chaste Selene. Her affection for Endymion is well known, and her cold white glance shines through the crevices of his mountain grave, hewn in a rocky wall, like the tombs of Phrygia.[2] She is the sister of the sun in Hesiod, the daughter (by his sister) of Hyperion in the Homeric hymns to Helios.

In Greece the aspects of sun and moon take the most ideal human forms, and show themselves in the most gracious myths. But, after all, these retain in their anthropomorphism the marks of the earliest fancy, the fancy of Eskimos and Australians. It seems to be commonly thought that the existence of solar myths is denied by anthropologists. This is a vulgar error. There is an enormous mass of solar myths, but they are not caused by "a disease of language," and—all myths are not solar!

There is no occasion to dwell long on myths of the same character in which the stars are accounted for as transformed human adventurers. It has often been shown that this opinion is practically of world-wide distribution.[3] We find it in Australia, Persia, Greece, among the Bushmen, in North and South America, among the Eskimos, in ancient Egypt, in New Zealand, in ancient India—briefly, wherever we look. The Sanskrit forms of these myths have been said to arise from confusion as to the meaning of words. But is it

[1] Virgil, *Georgics*, iii. 391.   [2] Preller, *Griech. Myth.*, i. 163
[3] *Custom and Myth*, "Star-Myths"; *Primitive Culture*, i. 288, 291; J. G. Müller, *Amerikanischen Urreligionen*, pp. 52, 53.

credible that, in all languages, however different, the
same kind of unconscious puns should have led to the
same mistaken beliefs ?   As the savage, barbarous and
Greek star-myths (such as that of Callisto, first changed
into a bear and then into a constellation) are familiar
to most readers, a few examples of Sanskrit star-stories
are offered here from the *Satapatha Brahmana*.[1]
Fires are not, according to the Brahmana ritual, to be
lighted under the stars called Krittikâs, the Pleiades.
The reason is that the stars were the wives of the bears
(Riksha), for the group known in Brahmanic times as
the Rishis (sages) were originally called the Rikshas
(bears).   But the wives of the bears were excluded
from the society of their husbands, for the bears rise
in the north and their wives in the east.   Therefore
the worshipper should not set up his fires under the
Pleiades, lest he should thereby be separated from the
company of his wife.   The Brahmanas [2] also tell us
that Prajapati had an unholy passion for his daughter,
who was in the form of a doe.   The gods made Rudra
fire an arrow at Prajapati to punish him ; he was
wounded, and leaped into the sky, where he became
one constellation and his daughter another, and the
arrow a third group of stars.   In general, according to
the Brahmanas, " the stars are the lights of virtuous
men who go to the heavenly world ".[3]

Passing from savage myths explanatory of the
nature of celestial bodies to myths accounting for the

---

[1] *Sacred Books of the East*, i. 283-286.   [2] *Aitareya Bramana*, iii. 33.
[3] *Satapatha Brahmana*, vi. 5, 4, 8.   For Greek examples, Hesiod, Ovid,
and the *Catasterismoi*, attributed to Eratosthenes, are useful authorities.
Probably many of the tales in Eratosthenes are late fictions consciously
moulded on traditional data.

formation and colour and habits of beasts, birds and fishes, we find ourselves, as an old Jesuit missionary says, in the midst of a barbarous version of Ovid's *Metamorphoses*. It has been shown that the possibility of interchange of form between man and beast is part of the working belief of everyday existence among the lower peoples. They regard all things as on one level, or, to use an old political phrase, they "level up" everything to equality with the human status. Thus Mr. Im Thurn, a very good observer, found that to the Indians of Guiana "all objects, animate or inaminate, seem exactly of the same nature, except that they differ by the accident of bodily form". Clearly to grasp this entirely natural conception of primitive man, the civilised student must make a great effort to forget for a time all that science has taught him of the differences between the objects which fill the world.[1] "To the ear of the savage animals certainly seem to talk." "As far as the Indians of Guiana are concerned, I do not believe that they distinguish such beings as sun and moon, or such other natural phenomena as winds and storms, from men and other animals, from plants and other inanimate objects, or from any other objects whatsoever." Bancroft says about North American myths, "Beasts and birds and fishes fetch and carry, talk and act, in a way that leaves even Æsop's heroes quite in the shade".[2]

[1] *Journ. Anthrop. Inst.*, xi. 366-369. A very large and rich collection of testimonies as to metamorphosis will be found in J. G. Müller's *Amerikanischen Urreligionen*, p. 62 *et seq. ;* while, for European superstitions, Bodin on *La Démonomanie des Sorciers*, Lyon, 1598, may be consulted.

[2] Vol. iii. p. 127.

The savage tendency is to see in inanimate things animals, and in animals disguised men. M. Réville quotes in his *Religions des Peuples Non-Civilisés*, i. 64, the story of some Negroes, who, the first time they were shown a *cornemuse*, took the instrument for a beast, the two holes for its eyes. The Highlander who looted a watch at Prestonpans, and observing, " She's teed," sold it cheap when it ran down, was in the same psychological condition. A queer bit of savage science is displayed on a black stone tobacco-pipe from the Pacific Coast.[1] The savage artist has carved the pipe in the likeness of a steamer, as a steamer is conceived by him. "Unable to account for the motive power, he imagines the paddle to be linked round the tongue of a coiled serpent, fastened to the tail of the vessel," and so he represents it on the black stone pipe. Nay, a savage's belief that beasts are on his own level is so literal, that he actually makes blood-covenants with the lower animals, as he does with men, mingling his gore with theirs, or smearing both together on a stone ;[2] while to bury dead animals with sacred rites is as usual among the Bedouins and Malagasies to-day as in ancient Egypt or Attica. In the same way the Ainos of Japan, who regard the bear as a kinsman, sacrifice a bear once a year. But, to propitiate the animal and his connections, they appoint him a "mother," an Aino girl, who looks after his comforts, and behaves in a way as maternal as possible. The bear is now a *kinsman*, ὁμομήτριος, and cannot avenge himself within the kin. This, at

---

[1] *Magazine of Art*, January, 1883.
[2] " Malagasy Folk-Tales," *Folk-Lore Journal*, October, 1883.

least, seems to be the humour of it. In Lagarde's *Reliquiœ Juris Ecclesiastici Antiquissimœ* a similar Syrian covenant of kinship with insects is described. About 700 A.D., when a Syrian garden was infested by caterpillars, the maidens were assembled, and one caterpillar was caught. Then one of the virgins was "made its mother," and the creature was buried with due lamentations. The "mother" was then brought to the spot where the pests were, her companions bewailed her, and the caterpillars perished like their chosen kinsman, but without extorting revenge.[1] Revenge was out of their reach. They had been brought within the kin of their foes, and there were no Erinnyes, "avengers of kindred blood," to help them. People in this condition of belief naturally tell hundreds of tales, in which men, stones, trees, beasts, shift shapes, and in which the modifications of animal forms are caused by accident, or by human agency, or by magic, or by metamorphosis. Such tales survive in our modern folk-lore. To make our meaning clear, we may give the European nursery-myth of the origin of the donkey's long ears, and, among other illustrations, the Australian myth of the origin of the black and white plumage of the pelican. Mr. Ralston has published the Russian version of the myth of the donkey's ears. The Spanish form, which is identical with the Russian, is given by Fernan Caballero in *La Gaviota*.

"Listen! do you know why your ears are so big?" (the story is told to a stupid little boy with big ears).

---

[1] We are indebted to Professor Robertson Smith for this example, and to Miss Bird's *Journal*, pp. 90, 97, for the Aino parallel.

" When Father Adam found himself in Paradise with
the animals, he gave each its name; those of *thy*
species, my child, he named 'donkeys'. One day,
not long after, he called the beasts together, and
asked each to tell him its name. They all answered
right except the animals of *thy* sort, and they had
forgotten their name ! Then Father Adam was very
angry, and, taking that forgetful donkey by the ears,
he pulled them out, screaming 'You are called *donkey !*'
And the donkey's ears have been long ever since."
This, to a child, is a credible explanation. So, perhaps, is another survival of this form of science—the
Scotch explanation of the black marks on the had-
dock ; they were impressed by St. Peter's finger and
thumb when he took the piece of money for Cæsar's
tax out of the fish's mouth.

Turning from folk-lore to savage beliefs, we learn
that from one end of Africa to another the honey-bird,
schneter, is said to be an old woman whose son was
lost, and who pursued him till she was turned into a
bird, which still shrieks his name, "Schneter, Schneter".[1]
In the same way the manners of most of the birds
known to the Greeks were accounted for by the myth
that they had been men and women. Zeus, for
example, turned Ceyx and Halcyon into sea-fowls
because they were too proud in their married happi-
ness.[2] To these myths of the origin of various animals
we shall return, but we must not forget the black and
white Australian pelican. Why is the pelican parti-
coloured ?[3] For this reason : After the Flood (the

---

[1] Barth, iii. 358.   [2] Apollodorus, i. 7 (13, 12).
[3] Sahagun, viii. 2, accounts for colours of eagle and tiger. A number
of races explain the habits and marks of animals as the result of a curse or

origin of which is variously explained by the Murri),
the pelican (who had been a black fellow) made a
canoe, and went about like a kind of Noah, trying to
save the drowning. In the course of his benevolent
mission he fell in love with a woman, but she and her
friends played him a trick and escaped from him.
The pelican at once prepared to go on the war-path.
The first thing to do was to daub himself white, as is
the custom of the blacks before a battle. They think
the white pipe-clay strikes terror and inspires respect
among the enemy. But when the pelican was only
half pipe-clayed, another pelican came past, and, "not
knowing what such a queer black and white thing
was, struck the first pelican with his beak and killed
him. Before that pelicans were all black; now they
are black and white. That is the reason." [1]

"That is the reason." Therewith native philosopy
is satisfied, and does not examine in Mr. Darwin's
laborious manner the slow evolution of the colour of
the pelican's plumage. The mythological stories about
animals are rather difficult to treat, because they are
so much mixed up with the topic of totemism. Here
we only examine myths which account by means of a
legend for certain peculiarities in the habits, cries, or
colours and shapes of animals. The Ojibbeways told
Kohl they had a story for every creature, accounting
for its ways and appearance. Among the Greeks, as
among Australians and Bushmen, we find that nearly
every notable bird or beast had its tradition. The

blessing of a god or hero. The Hottentots, the Huarochiri of Peru, the
New Zealanders (Shortland, *Traditions*, p. 57), are among the peoples which
use this myth. [1] Brough Symth, *Aborigines of Australia*, i. 477, 478.

nightingale and the swallow have a story of the most
savage description, a story reported by Apollodorus,
though Homer [1] refers to another, and, as usual, to a
gentler and more refined form of the myth.   Here is
the version of Apollodorus.   " Pandion " (an early king
of Athens) "married Zeuxippe, his mother's sister, by
whom he had two daughters, Procne and Philomela,
and two sons, Erechtheus and Butes.   A war broke
out with Labdas about some debatable land, and
Erechtheus invited the alliance of Tereus of Thrace,
the son of Ares.   Having brought the war, with the
aid of Tereus, to a happy end, he gave him his daughter
Procne to wife.   By Procne, Tereus had a son, Itys,
and thereafter fell in love with Philomela, whom he
seduced, pretending that Procne was dead, whereas
he had really concealed her somewhere in his lands.
Thereon he married Philomela, and cut out her tongue.
But she wove into a robe characters that told the
whole story, and by means of these acquainted Procne
with her sufferings.   Thereon Procne found her sister,
and slew Itys, her own son, whose body she cooked,
and served up to Tereus in a banquet.   Thereafter
Procne and her sister fled together, and Tereus seized
an axe and followed after them.   They were overtaken
at Daulia in Phocis, and prayed to the gods that they
might be turned into birds.   So Procne became the
nightingale, and Philomela the swallow, while Tereus
was changed into a hoopoe." [2]   Pausanias has a different
legend ; Procne and Philomela died of excessive grief.

[1] *Odyssey*, xix. 523.

[2] A Red Indian nightingale-myth is alluded to by J. G. Müller, *Amerik.
Urrel.*, p. 175.   Some one was turned into a nightingale by the sun, and still
wails for a lost lover.

These ancient men and women metamorphosed into birds were *honoured as ancestors* by the Athenians.[1] Thus the unceasing musical wail of the nightingale and the shrill cry of the swallow were explained by a Greek story. The birds were lamenting their old human sorrow, as the honey-bird in Africa still repeats the name of her lost son.

Why does the red-robin live near the dwellings of men, a bold and friendly bird? The Chippeway Indians say he was once a young brave whose father set him a task too cruel for his strength, and made him starve too long when he reached man's estate. He turned into a robin, and said to his father, "I shall always be the friend of man, and keep near their dwellings. I could not gratify your pride as a warrior, but I will cheer you by my songs." [2] The converse of this legend is the Greek myth of the hawk. Why is the hawk so hated by birds? Hierax was a benevolent person who succoured a race hated by Poseidon. The god therefore changed him into a hawk, and made him as much detested by birds, and as fatal to them, as he had been beloved by and gentle to men.[3] The Hervey Islanders explain the peculiarities of several fishes by the share they took in the adventures of Ina, who stamped, for example, on the sole, and so flattened him for ever.[4] In Greece the dolphins were, according to the Homeric hymn to Dionysus, metamorphosed pirates who had insulted the god. But because the

[1] Pausanias, i. v. Pausanias thinks such things no longer occur.
[2] Schoolcraft, ii. 229, 230.
[3] Bœo, quoted by Antoninus Liberalis.
[4] Gill, *South Sea Myths*, pp. 88-95,

dolphin found the hidden sea-goddess whom Poseidon
loved, the dolphin, too, was raised by the grateful sea-
god to the stars.[1] The vulture and the heron, according
to Bœo (said to have been a priestess in Delphi and
the author of a Greek treatise on the traditions about
birds), were once a man named Aigupios (vulture) and
his mother, Boulis. They sinned inadvertently, like
Œdipus and Jocasta; wherefore Boulis, becoming
aware of the guilt, was about to put out the eyes of
her son and slay herself. Then they were changed,
Boulis into the heron, "which tears out and feeds on
the eyes of snakes, birds and fishes, and Aigupios
into the vulture which bears his name". This story,
of which the more repulsive details are suppressed, is
much less pleasing and more savage than the Hervey
Islanders' myth of the origin of pigs. Maaru was an
old blind man who lived with his son Kationgia.
There came a year of famine, and Kationgia had great
difficulty in finding food for himself and his father.
He gave the blind old man puddings of banana roots
and fishes, while he lived himself on sea-slugs and shell-
fish, like the people of Terra del Fuego. But blind
old Maaru suspected his son of giving him the worst
share and keeping what was best for himself. At last
he discovered that Kationgia was really being starved ;
he felt his body, and found that he was a mere living
skeleton. The two wept together, and the father
made a feast of some cocoa-nuts and bread-fruit, which
he had reserved against the last extremity. When all
was finished, he said he had eaten his last meal and
was about to die. He ordered his son to cover him

[1] Artemidorus in his *Love Elegies*, quoted by the Pseud-Eratosthenes.

with leaves and grass, and return to the spot in four
days. If worms were crawling about, he was to
throw leaves and grass over them and come back
four days later. Kationgia did as he was instructed,
and, on his second visit to the grave, found the whole
mass of leaves in commotion. A brood of pigs, black,
white and speckled, had sprung up from the soil ;
famine was a thing of the past, and Kationgia became
a great chief in the island.[1]

" The owl was a baker's daughter " is the fragment
of Christian mythology preserved by Ophelia. The
baker's daughter behaved rudely to our Lord, and was
changed into the bird that looks not on the sun. The
Greeks had a similar legend of feminine impiety by
which they mythically explained the origin of the
owl, the bat and the eagle-owl. Minyas of Orchomenos had three daughters, Leucippe, Arsippe and
Alcathoe, most industrious women, who declined to
join the wild mysteries of Dionysus. The god took
the shape of a maiden, and tried to win them to his
worship. They refused, and he assumed the form of
a bull, a lion, and a leopard as easily as the chiefs of
the Abipones become tigers, or as the chiefs among
the African Barotse and Balonda metamorphose themselves into lions and alligators.[2] The daughters of
Minyas, in alarm, drew lots to determine which of
them should sacrifice a victim to the god. Leucippe
drew the lot and offered up her own son. They then
rushed to join the sacred rites of Dionysus, when
Hermes transformed them into the bat, the owl and the

---

[1] Gill, *Myths and Songs from South Pacific*, pp. 135-138.
[2] Livingstone, *Missionary Travels*, pp. 615, 642.

eagle-owl, and these three hide from the light of the sun.[1]

A few examples of Bushman and Australian myths explanatory of the colours and habits of animals will probably suffice to establish the resemblance between savage and Hellenic legends of this character. The Bushman myth about the origin of the eland (a large antelope) is not printed in full by Dr. Bleek, but he observes that it "gives an account of the reasons for the colours of the gemsbok, hartebeest, eland, quagga and springbok ".[2] Speculative Bushmen seem to have been puzzled to account for the wildness of the eland. It would be much more convenient if the eland were tame and could be easily captured. They explain its wildness by saying that the eland was "spoiled" before Cagn, the creator, or rather maker of most things, had quite finished it. Cagn's relations came and hunted the first eland too soon, after which all other elands grew wild. Cagn then said, "Go and hunt them and try to kill one; that is now your work, for it was you who spoilt them ".[3] The Bushmen have another myth explanatory of the white patches on the breasts of crows in their country. Some men tarried long at their hunting, and their wives sent out crows in search of their husbands. Round each crow's neck was hung a piece of fat to serve as food on the journey. Hence the crows have white patches on breast and neck.

In Australia the origins of nearly all animals appear

---

[1] Nicander, quoted by Antoninus Liberalis.
[2] *Brief Account of Bushmen Folk-Lore*, p. 7.
[3] *Cape Monthly Magazine*, July, 1874.

to be explained in myths, of which a fair collection
is printed in Mr. Brough Symth's *Aborigines of
Victoria*.[1] Still better examples occur in Mrs. Langloh
Parker's *Australian Legends*. Why is the crane
so thin? Once he was a man named Kar-ween, the
second man fashioned out of clay by Pund-jel, a
singular creative being, whose chequered career is
traced elsewhere in our chapter on "Savage Myths
of the Origin of the World and of Man". Kar-ween
and Pund-jel had a quarrel about the wives of the
former, whom Pund-jel was inclined to admire. The
crafty Kar-ween gave a dance (*jugargiull, corobboree*),
at which the creator Pund-jel was disporting himself
gaily (like the Great Panjandrum), when Kar-ween
pinned him with a spear. Pund-jel threw another
which took Kar-ween in the knee-joint, so that he
could not walk, but soon pined away and became a
mere skeleton. "Thereupon Pund-jel made Kar-ween
a crane," and that is why the crane has such attenuated
legs. The Kortume, Munkari and Waingilhe, now
birds, were once men. The two latter behaved un-
kindly to their friend Kortume, who shot them out of
his hut in a storm of rain, singing at the same time
an incantation. The three then turned into birds, and
when the Kortume sings it is a token that rain may
be expected.

Let us now compare with these Australian myths
of the origin of certain species of birds the Greek story
of the origin of frogs, as told by Menecrates and
Nicander.[2] The frogs were herdsmen metamorphosed
by Leto, the mother of Apollo. But, by way of

---

[1] Vol. i. p. 426 *et seq.*   [2] Antoninus Liberalis, xxxv.

showing how closely akin are the fancies of Greeks and Australian black fellows, we shall tell the legend without the proper names, which gave it a fictitious dignity.

THE ORIGIN OF FROGS.

" A woman bore two children, and sought for a water-spring wherein to bathe them. She found a well, but herdsmen drove her away from it that their cattle might drink. Then some wolves met her and led her to a river, of which she drank, and in its waters she bathed her children. Then she went back to the well where the herdsmen were now bathing, and she turned them all into frogs. She struck their backs and shoulders with a rough stone and drove them into the waters, and ever since that day frogs live in marshes and beside rivers."

A volume might be filled with such examples of the kindred fancies of Greeks and savages. Enough has probably been said to illustrate our point, which is that Greek myths of this character were inherited from the period of savagery, when ideas of metamorphosis and of the kinship of men and beasts were real practical beliefs. Events conceived to be common in real life were introduced into myths, and these myths were savage science, and were intended to account for the Origin of Species. But when once this train of imagination has been fired, it burns on both in literature and in the legends of the peasantry. Every one who writes a Christmas tale for children now employs the machinery of metamorphosis, and in European folk-lore, as Fontenelle remarked, stories persist which are precisely similar in kind to the minor myths of savages.

Reasoning in this wise, the Mundas of Bengal thus account for peculiarities of certain animals. Sing Bonga, the chief god, cast certain people out of heaven ; they fell to earth, found iron ore, and began smelting it. The black smoke displeased Sing Bonga, who sent two king crows and an owl to bid people cease to pollute the atmosphere. But the iron smelters spoiled these birds' tails, and blackened the previously white crow, scorched its beak red, and flattened its head. Sing Bonga burned man, and turned woman into hills and waterspouts.[1]

Examples of this class of myth in Indo-Aryan literature are not hard to find. Why is dawn red ? Why are donkeys slow ? Why have mules no young ones ? Mules have no foals because they were severely burned when Agni (fire) drove them in a chariot race. Dawn is red, not because (as in Australia) she wears a red kangaroo cloak, but because she competed in this race with red cows for her coursers. Donkeys are slow because they never recovered from their exertions in the same race, when the Asvins called on their asses and landed themselves the winners.[2] And cows are accommodated with horns for a reason no less probable and satisfactory.[3]

Though in the legends of the less developed peoples men and women are more frequently metamorphosed into birds and beasts than into stones and plants, yet such changes of form are by no means unknown. To the north-east of Western Point there lies a range of

---

[1] Dalton, pp. 186, 187. [2] *Aitareya Brahmana*, ii. 272, iv. 9. [3] iv. 17

hills, inhabited, according to the natives of Victoria,
by a creature whose body is made of stone, and
weapons make no wound in so sturdy a constitution.
The blacks refuse to visit the range haunted by the
mythic stone beast. " Some black fellows were once
camped at the lakes near Shaving Point. They were
cooking their fish when a native dog came up. They
did not give him anything to eat. He became cross
and said, ' You black fellows have lots of fish, but you
give me none '. So he changed them all into a big
rock. This is quite true, for the big rock is there to
this day, and I have seen it with my own eyes." [1]
Another native, Toolabar, says that the women of the
fishing party cried out *yacka torn*, " very good ". A
dog replied *yacka torn*, and they were all changed into
rocks. This very man, Toolabar, once heard a dog
begin to talk, whereupon he and his father fled. Had
they waited they would have become stones. " We
should have been like it, *wallung*," that is, stones.

Among the North American Indians any stone
which has a resemblance to the human or animal figure
is explained as an example of metamorphosis. Three
stones among the Aricaras were a girl, her lover and
her dog, who fled from home because the course of
true love did not run smooth, and who were petrified.
Certain stones near Chinook Point were sea-giants
who swallowed a man. His brother, by aid of fire,
dried up the bay and released the man, still alive,
from the body of the giant. Then the giants were
turned into rocks.[2] The rising sun in *Popol Vuh* (if

[1] Native narrator, ap. Brough Smyth, i. 479.
[2] See authorities ap. Dorman, *Primitive Superstitions*, pp. 130-138.

the evidence of *Popol Vuh*, the Quichua sacred book,
is to be accepted) changed into stone the lion, serpent
and tiger gods. The Standing Rock on the Upper
Missouri is adored by the Indians, and decorated with
coloured ribbons and skins of animals. This stone was
a woman, who, like Niobe, became literally petrified
with grief when her husband took a second wife.
Another stone-woman in a cave on the banks of the
Kickapoo was wont to kill people who came near her,
and is even now approached with great respect. The
Oneidas and Dacotahs claim descent from stones to
which they ascribe animation.[1] Montesinos speaks of
a sacred stone which was removed from a mountain by
one of the Incas. A parrot flew out of it and lodged
in another stone, which the natives still worship.[2] The
Breton myth about one of the great stone circles (the
stones were peasants who danced on a Sunday) is a
well-known example of this kind of myth surviving
in folk-lore. There is a kind of stone Actæon[3] near
Little Muniton Creek, "resembling the bust of a man
whose head is decorated with the horns of a stag".[4] A
crowd of myths of metamorphosis into stone will be
found among the Iroquois legends in *Report of Bureau
of Ethnology*, 1880-81. If men may become stones,

[1] Dorman, p. 133.

[2] Many examples are collected by J. G. Müller, *Amerikanischen Urreligionen*, pp. 97, 110, 125, especially when the stones have a likeness to
human form, p. 17a. "Im der That werden auch einige in Steine, oder in
Thiere and Pflanzen verwandelt." *Cf.* p. 220. Instances (from Balboa) of
men turned into stone by wizards, p. 309.

[3] Preller thinks that Actæon, devoured by his hounds after being changed
into a stag, is a symbol of the vernal year. Palæphatus (*De Fab. Narrat.*)
holds that the story is a moral fable.

[4] Dorman, p. 137.

on the other hand, in Samoa (as in the Greek myth of
Deucalion), stones may become men.[1] Gods, too,
especially when these gods happen to be cuttlefish,
might be petrified. They were chased in Samoa by
an Upolu hero, who caught them in a great net and
killed them. "They were changed into stones, and
now stand up in a rocky part of the lagoon on the
north side of Upolu."[2] Mauke, the first man, came
out of a stone. In short,[3] men and stones and beasts
and gods and thunder have interchangeable forms.
In Mangaia[4] the god Ra was tossed up into the sky
by Maui and became pumice-stone. Many samples
of this petrified deity are found in Mangaia. In
Melanesia matters are so mixed that it is not easy
to decide whether a worshipful stone is the dwelling of
a dead man's soul or is of spiritual merit in itself, or
whether "the stone is the spirit's outward part or
organ". The Vui, or spirit, has much the same relations with snakes, owls and sharks.[5] Qasavara, the
mythical opponent of Qat, the Melanesian Prometheus,
"fell dead from heaven" (like Ra in Mangia), and
was turned into a stone, on which sacrifices are made
by those who desire strength in fighting.

Without delaying longer among savage myths of
metamorphosis into stones, it may be briefly shown
that the Greeks retained this with all the other
vagaries of early fancy. Every one remembers the
use which Perseus made of the Gorgon's head, and
the stones on the coast of Seriphus, which, like the

---

[1] Turner's *Samoa*, p. 299.   [2] *Samoa*, p. 31.   [3] *Op. cit.*, p. 34.
[4] Gill, *Myths and Songs*, p. 60.
[5] Codrington, *Journ. Anthrop. Inst.*, February, 1881.

stones near Western Point in Victoria, had once been
men, the enemies of the hero. "Also he slew the
Gorgon," sings Pindar, "and bare home her head,
with serpent tresses decked, to the island folk a stony
death." Observe Pindar's explanatory remark : "I ween
there is no marvel impossible if gods have wrought
thereto ". In the same pious spirit a Turk in an isle
of the Levant once told Mr. Newton a story of how a
man hunted a stag, and the stag spoke to him. "The
stag spoke?" said Mr. Newton. "Yes, by Allah's
will," replied the Turk. Like Pindar, he was repeating
an incident quite natural to the minds of Australians,
or Bushmen, or Samoans, or Red Men, but, like the
religious Pindar, he felt that the affair was rather
marvellous, and accounted for it by the exercise of
omnipotent power.[1] The Greek example of Niobe
and her children may best be quoted in Mr. Bridges'
translation from the *Iliad* :—

> And somewhere now, among lone mountain rocks
> On Sipylus, where couch the nymphs at night
> Who dance all day by Achelous' stream,
> The once proud mother lies, herself a rock,
> And in cold breast broods o'er the goddess' wrong.
> —*Prometheus the Fire-bringer*.[2]

In the *Iliad* it is added that Cronion made the people
into stones. The attitude of the later Greek mind
towards these myths may be observed in a fragment
of Philemon, the comic poet. "Never, by the gods,
have I believed, nor will believe, that Niobe the stone
was once a woman. Nay, by reason of her calamities
she became speechless, and so, from her silence, was
called a stone." [3]

---

[1] Pindar, *Pyth*. x., Myers's translation.   [2] xxiv. **611.**
[3] The Scholiast on *Iliad*, xxiv. 6, 7.

There is another famous petrification in the *Iliad*.
When the prodigy of the snake and the sparrows had
appeared to the assembled Achæans at Aulis, Zeus
displayed a great marvel, and changed into a stone the
serpent which swallowed the young of the sparrow.
Changes into stone, though less common than changes
into fishes, birds and beasts, were thus obviously not
too strange for the credulity of Greek mythology,
which could also believe that a stone became the
mother of Agdestis by Zeus.

As to interchange of shape between men and women
and *plants*, our information, so far as the lower races
are concerned, is less copious. It has already been
shown that the totems of many stocks in all parts of
the world are plants, and this belief in connection with
a plant by itself demonstrates that the confused belief
in all things being on one level has thus introduced
vegetables into the dominion of myth. As far as
possessing souls is concerned, Mr. Tylor has proved
that plants are as well equipped as men or beasts or
minerals.[1] In India the doctrine of transmigration
" widely and clearly recognises the idea of trees or
smaller plants being animated by human souls ". In
the well-known ancient Egyptian story of " The Two
Brothers," [2] the life of the younger is practically
merged in that of the acacia tree where he has hidden
his heart; and when he becomes a bull and is sacrificed, his spiritual part passes into a pair of Persea
trees. The Yarucaris of Bolivia say that a girl

---

[1] *Primitive Culture*, i. 145; examples of Society Islanders, Dyaks,
Karens, Buddhists.

[2] Maspero, *Contes Egyptiens*, p. 25.

once bewailed in the forest her loverless estate. She happened to notice a beautiful tree, which she adorned with ornaments as well as she might. The tree assumed the shape of a handsome young man—

> She did not find him so remiss,
> But, lightly issuing through,
> He did repay her kiss for kiss,
> With usury thereto.[1]

J. G. Müller, who quotes this tale from Andrée, says it has "many analogies with the tales of metamorphosis of human beings into trees among the ancients, as reported by Ovid". The worship of plants and trees is a well-known feature in religion, and probably implies (at least in many cases) a recognition of personality. In Samoa, metamorphosis into vegetables is not uncommon. For example, the king of Fiji was a cannibal, and (very naturally) "the people were melting away under him". The brothers Toa and Pale, wishing to escape the royal oven, adopted various changes of shape. They knew that straight timber was being sought for to make a canoe for the king, so Pale, when he assumed a vegetable form, became a crooked stick overgrown with creepers, but Toa "preferred standing erect as a handsome straight tree". Poor Toa was therefore cut down by the king's shipwrights, though, thanks to his brother's magic wiles, they did not make a canoe out of him after all.[2] In Samoa the trees are so far human that they not only go to war with each other, but actually embark in canoes to seek out distant enemies.[3]

---

[1] J. G. Müller, *Amerik. Urrel.*, p. 264.
[2] Turner's *Samoa*, p. 219.   [3] *Ibid.*, p. 213.

The Ottawa Indians account for the origin of maize
by a myth in which a wizard fought with and conquered a little man who had a little crown of feathers.
From his ashes arose the maize with its crown of
leaves and heavy ears of corn.[1]

In Mangaia the myth of the origin of the cocoa-nut
tree is a series of transformation scenes, in which the
persons shift shapes with the alacrity of medicine-
men.   Ina used to bathe in a pool where an eel
became quite familiar with her.   At last the fish
took courage and made his declaration.   He was Tuna,
the chief of all eels.   "Be mine," he cried, and Ina
was his.   For some mystical reason he was obliged to
leave her, but (like the White Cat in the fairy tale)
he requested her to cut off his eel's head and bury it.
Regretfully but firmly did Ina comply with his request, and from the buried eel's head sprang two
cocoa trees, one from each half of the brain of Tuna.
As a proof of this be it remarked, that when the nut
is husked we always find on it "the two eyes and
mouth of the lover of Ina".[2]   All over the world,
from ancient Egypt to the wigwams of the Algonkins,
plants and other matters are said to have sprung from
a dismembered god or hero, while men are said to
have sprung from plants.[3]   We may therefore perhaps
look on it as a proved point that the general savage
habit of "levelling up" prevails even in their view of
the vegetable world, and has left traces (as we have
seen) in their myths.

Turning now to the mythology of Greece, we see

[1] *Amerik. Urrel.*, p. 60.   [2] Gill, *Myths and Songs*, p. 79.
[3] *Myths of the Beginning of Things.*

that the same rule holds good. Metamorphosis into plants and flowers is extremely common ; the instances of Daphne, Myrrha, Hyacinth, Narcissus and the sisters of Phæthon at once occur to the memory.

Most of those myths in which everything in Nature becomes personal and human, while all persons may become anything in Nature, we explain, then, as survivals or imitations of tales conceived when men were in the savage intellectual condition. In that stage, as we demonstrated, no line is drawn between things animate and inanimate, dumb or " articulate speaking," organic or inorganic, personal or impersonal. Such a mental stage, again, is reflected in the nature-myths, many of which are merely " ætiological,"—assign a cause, that is, for phenomena, and satisfy an indolent and credulous curiosity.

We may be asked again, " But how did this intellectual condition come to exist ? " To answer that is no part of our business ; for us it is enough to trace myth, or a certain element in myth, to a demonstrable and actual stage of thought. But this stage, which is constantly found to survive in the minds of children, is thus explained or described by Hume in his Essay on Natural Religion : " There is an universal tendency in mankind to conceive all beings like themselves, and to transfer to every object those qualities . . . of which they are intimately conscious ".[1] Now they believe themselves to be conscious of magical and supernatural powers, which they do not, of course, possess. These powers of effecting metamorphosis, of " shape-shifting," of flying, of becoming invisible at

[1] See Appendix B.

will, of conversing with the dead, of miraculously
healing the sick, savages pass on to their gods (as will
be shown in a later chapter), and the gods of myth
survive and retain the miraculous gifts after their
worshippers (become more reasonable) have quite
forgotten that they themselves once claimed similar
endowments.   So far, then, it has been shown that
savage fancy, wherever studied, is wild; that savage
curiosity is keen; that savage credulity is practically
boundless.   These considerations explain the existence
of savage myths of sun, stars, beasts, plants and
stones; similar myths fill Greek legend and the
Sanskrit Brahmanes.   We conclude that, in Greek
and Sanskrit, the myths are relics (whether borrowed
or inherited) of the savage mental *status*.

CHAPTER. VI.

NON-ARYAN MYTHS OF THE ORIGIN OF THE WORLD AND OF MAN.

Confusions of myth—Various origins of man and of things—Myths of Australia, Andaman Islands, Bushmen, Ovaherero, Namaquas, Zulus, Hurons, Iroquois, Diggers, Navajoes, Winnebagoes, Chaldæans, Thlinkeets, Pacific Islanders, Maoris, Aztecs, Peruvians—Similarity of ideas pervading all those peoples in various conditions of society and culture.

THE difficulties of classification which beset the study of mythology have already been described. Nowhere are they more perplexing than when we try to classify what may be styled Cosmogonic Myths. The very word *cosmogonic* implies the pre-existence of the idea of a cosmos, an orderly universe, and this was exactly the last idea that could enter the mind of the myth-makers. There is no such thing as orderliness in their mythical conceptions, and no such thing as an universe. The natural question, "Who made the world, or how did the things in the world come to be?" is the question which is answered by cosmogonic myths. But it is answered piecemeal. To a Christian child the reply is given, "God made all things". We have known this reply discussed by some little girls of six (a Scotch minister's daughters, and naturally metaphysical), one of whom solved all difficulties by the impromptu myth, "God first made a little place

to stand on, and then he made the rest ". But savages
and the myth-makers, whose stories survive into the
civilised religions, could adhere firmly to no such
account as this. Here occurs in the first edition of this
book the following passage : " They (savages) have not,
and had not, the conception of God as we understand
what we mean by the word. They have, and had at
most, only the small-change of the idea " God,"—here
the belief in a moral being who watches conduct ; here
again the hypothesis of a pre-human race of magnified,
non-natural medicine-men, or of extra-natural beings
with human and magical attributes, but often wearing
the fur, and fins, and feathers of the lower animals.
Mingled with these faiths (whether earlier, later, or
coeval in origin with these) are the dread and love of
ancestral ghosts, often transmuting themselves into
worship of an imaginary and ideal first parent of the
tribe, who once more is often a beast or a bird. Here
is nothing like the notion of an omnipotent, invisible,
spiritual being, the creator of our religion; here is
only *la monnaie* of the conception."

It ought to have occurred to the author that he was
here traversing the main theory of his own book,
which is that *religion* is one thing, myth quite
another thing. That many low races of savages entertain, in hours of *religious* thought, an elevated
conception of a moral and undying Maker of Things,
and Master of Life, a Father in Heaven, has already
been stated, and knowledge of the facts has been
considerably increased since this work first appeared
(1887). But the *mythical* conceptions described
in the last paragraph coexist with the religious

conception in the faiths of very low savages, such as the Australians and Andamanese, just as the same contradictory coexistence is notorious in ancient Greece, India, Egypt and Anahuac. In a sense, certain low savages *have* the "conception of God, as we understand what we mean by the word". But that sense, when savages come to spinning fables about origins, is apt to be overlaid and perplexed by the frivolity of their mythical fancy.

With such shifting, grotesque and inadequate fables, the cosmogonic myths of the world are necessarily bewildered and perplexed. We have already seen in the chapter on "Nature Myths" that many things, sun, moon, the stars, "that have another birth," and various animals and plants, are accounted for on the hypothesis that they are later than the appearance of man—that they originally *were* men. To the European mind it seems natural to rank myths of the gods before myths of the making or the evolution of the world, because our religion, like that of the more philosophic Greeks, makes the deity the fount of all existences, *causa causans*, "what unmoved moves," the beginning and the end. But the myth-makers, deserting any such ideas they may possess, find it necessary, like the child of whom we spoke, to postulate a *place* for the divine energy to work from, and that place is the earth or the heavens. Then, again, heaven and earth are themselves often regarded in the usual mythical way, as animated, as persons with parts and passions, and finally, among advancing races, as gods. Into this medley of incongruous and inconsistent conceptions we must introduce what order we may, always remembering that the order is not native to the subject, but is brought in for the purpose of study.

The origin of the world and of man is naturally a problem which has excited the curiosity of the least developed minds. Every savage race has its own myths on this subject, most of them bearing the marks of the childish and crude imagination, whose character we have investigated, and all varying in amount of what may be called philosophical thought.

All the cosmogonic myths, as distinct from religious belief in a Creator, waver between the theory of construction, or rather of reconstruction, and the theory of evolution, very rudely conceived. The earth, as a rule, is mythically averred to have grown out of some original matter, perhaps an animal, perhaps an egg which floated on the waters, perhaps a handful of mud from below the waters. But this conception does not exclude the idea that many of the things in the world, minerals, plants and what not, are fragments of the frame of a semi-supernatural and gigantic being, human or bestial, belonging to a race which preceded the advent of man.[1] Such were the Titans, demi-gods, Nurrumbunguttias in Australia. Various members of this race are found active in myths of the creation, or rather the construction, of man and of the world. Among the lowest races it is to be noted that mythical animals of supernatural power often take the place of beings like the Finnish Wainamoinen, the Greek Prometheus, the Zulu Unkulunkulu, the Red Indian Manabozho, himself usually a great hare.

The ages before the development or creation of man

[1] Macrobius, *Saturnal.*, i. xx.

are filled up, in the myths, with the loves and wars of
supernatural people. The appearance of man is explained in three or four contradictory ways, each of
which is represented in the various myths of most
mythologies. Often man is fashioned out of clay,
or stone, or other materials, by a Maker of all things,
sometimes half-human or bestial, but also half-
divine. Sometimes the first man rises out of the
earth, and is himself confused with the Creator, a
theory perhaps illustrated by the Zulu myth of Unkulunkulu, " The Old, Old One ". Sometimes man
arrives ready made, with most of the animals, from
his former home in a hole in the ground, and he
furnishes the world for himself with stars, sun, moon
and everything else he needs. Again, there are many
myths which declare that man was evolved out of one
or other of the lower animals. This myth is usually
employed by tribesmen to explain the origin of their
own peculiar stock of kindred. Once more, man is
taken to be the fruit of some tree or plant, or not to
have emerged ready-made, but to have grown out of
the ground like a plant or a tree. In some countries,
as among the Bechuanas, the Bœotians, and the Peruvians, the spot where men first came out on earth is
known to be some neighbouring marsh or cave. Lastly,
man is occasionally represented as having been framed
out of a piece of the body of the Creator, or made by
some demiurgic potter out of clay. All these legends
are told by savages, with no sense of their inconsistency.
There is no single orthodoxy on the matter, and we
shall see that all these theories coexist pell-mell
among the mythological traditions of civilised races.

In almost every mythology, too, the whole theory of
the origin of man is crossed by the tradition of a
Deluge, or some other great destruction, followed by
revival or reconstruction of the species, a tale by no
means necessarily of Biblical origin.

In examining savage myths of the origin of man
and of the world, we shall begin by considering those
current among the most backward peoples, where no
hereditary or endowed priesthood has elaborated and
improved the popular beliefs. The natives of Australia furnish us with myths of a purely popular type,
the property, not of professional priests and poets, but
of all the old men and full-grown warriors of the
country. Here, as everywhere else, the student must
be on his guard against accepting myths which are
disguised forms of missionary teaching.[1]

In Southern Australia we learn that the Boon-
oorong, an Australian coast tribe, ascribe the creation
of things to a being named Bun-jel or Pund-jel. He
figures as the chief of an earlier supernatural class of
existence, with human relationships ; thus he "has a
wife, *whose face he has never seen,*" brothers, a son,
and so on. Now this name Bun-jel means "eagle-
hawk," and the eagle-hawk is a totem among certain
stocks. Thus, when we hear that Eagle-hawk is the
maker of men and things we are reminded of the
Bushman creator, Cagn, who now receives prayers of
considerable beauty and pathos, but who is (in some

[1] Taplin, *The Narrinyeri.* "He must also beware of supposing that
the Australians believe in a creator in our sense, because the Narrinyeri,
for example, say that Nurundere 'made everything'. Nurundere is but
an idealised wizard and hunter, with a rival of his species." This occurs in
the first edition, but " making all things " is one idea, wizardry is another.

theories) identified with *kaggen*, the mantis insect, a
creative grasshopper, and the chief figure in Bushman
mythology.[1] Bun-jel or Pund-jel also figures in Australian belief, neither as the creator nor as the eagle-
hawk, but "as an old man who lives at the sources of
the Yarra river, where he possesses great multitudes
of cattle".[2] The term Bun-jel is also used, much like
our "Mr.," to denote the older men of the Kurnai and
Briakolung, some of whom have magical powers. One
of them, Krawra, or "West Wind," can cause the wind to
blow so violently as to prevent the natives from climb-
ing trees; this man has semi-divine attributes. From
these facts it appears that this Australian creator, in
myth, partakes of the character of the totem or worshipful beast, and of that of the wizard or medicine-man.
He carried a large knife, and, when he made the earth,
he went up and down slicing it into creeks and valleys.
The aborigines of the northern parts of Victoria seem
to believe in Pund-jel in what may perhaps be his
most primitive mythical shape, that of an eagle.[3] This
eagle and a crow created everything, and separated
the Murray blacks into their two main divisions, which
derive their names from the crow and the eagle. The
Melbourne blacks seem to make Pund-jel more anthropomorphic. Men are his πλάσματα πηλοῦ, figures
kneaded of clay, as Aristophanes says in the *Birds*.
Pund-jel made two clay images of men, and danced
round them. "He made their hair—one had straight,

---

[1] Bleek, *Brief Account of Bushman Mythology*, p. 6; *Cape Monthly
Magazine*, July, 1874, pp. 1-13; *Kamilaroi and Kurnai*, pp. 210, 324.

[2] *Kamilaroi and Kurnai*, p. 210.

[3] Brough Smyth, *Natives of Victoria*, vol. i. p. 423.

one curly hair—of bark. He danced round them.
He lay on them, and breathed his breath into their
mouths, noses and navels, and danced round them.
Then they arose full-grown young men." Some blacks
seeing a brickmaker at work on a bridge over the
Yarra exclaimed, "Like 'em that Pund-jel make 'em
Koolin". But other blacks prefer to believe that, as
Pindar puts the Phrygian legend, the sun saw men
growing like trees.

The first man was formed out of the gum of a wattle-
tree, and came out of the knot of a wattle-tree. He
then entered into a young woman (though he was the
first man) and was born.[1] The Encounter Bay people
have another myth, which might have been attributed
by Dean Swift to the Yahoos, so foul an origin does
it allot to mankind.

Australian myths of creation are by no means exclusive of a hypothesis of evolution. Thus the Dieyrie,
whose notions Mr. Gason has recorded, hold a very
mixed view. They aver that "the good spirit" Moora-
Moora made a number of small black lizards, liked
them, and promised them dominion. He divided their
feet into toes and fingers, gave them noses and lips,
and set them upright. Down they fell, and Moora-
Moora cut off their tails. Then they walked erect and
were men.[2] The conclusion of the adventures of one
Australian creator is melancholy. He has ceased to
dwell among mortals whom he watches and inspires.
The Jay possessed many bags full of wind; he
opened them, and Pund-jel was carried up by the blast

---

[1] Meyer, *Aborigines of Encounter Bay*. See, later, "Gods of the
Lowest Races".

[2] Gason's *Dieyries*, ap. *Native Tribes of South Australia*, p. 20.

into the heavens. But this event did not occur before Pund-jel had taught men and women the essential arts of life. He had shown the former how to spear kangaroos, he still exists and inspires poets. From the cosmogonic myths of Australia (the character of some of which is in contradiction with the higher religious belief of the people to be later described) we may turn, without reaching a race of much higher civilisation, to the dwellers in the Andaman Islands and their opinions about the origin of things.

The Andaman Islands, in the Bay of Bengal, are remote from any shores, and are protected from foreign influences by dangerous coral reefs, and by the reputed ferocity and cannibalism of the natives. These are Negritos, and are commonly spoken of as most abject savages. They are not, however, without distinctions of rank ; they are clean, modest, moral after marriage, and most strict in the observance of prohibited degrees. Unlike the Australians, they use bows and arrows, but are said to be incapable of striking a light, and, at all events, find the process so difficult that, like the Australians and the farmer in the *Odyssey*,[1] they are compelled " to hoard the seeds of fire ". Their mythology contains explanations of the origin of men and animals, and of their own customs and language.

The Andamanese, long spoken of as " godless," owe much to Mr. Man, an English official, who has made a most careful study of their beliefs.[2] So extraordinary is the contradiction between the relative purity and morality of the *religion* and the savagery of the

[1] *Odyssey*, v. 490.   [2] *Journ. Anthrop. Soc.*, vol. xii. p. 157 *et seq.*

'myths of the Andamanese, that, in the first edition
of this work, I insisted that the " spiritual god " of
the faith must have been " borrowed from the same
quarter as the stone house " in which he is mythically
said to live. But later and wider study, and fresh
information from various quarters, have convinced
me that the relative purity of Andamanese religion,
with its ethical sanction of conduct, may well be, and
probably is, a natural unborrowed development. It
is easy for *myth* to borrow the notion of a stone
house from our recent settlement at Port Blair. But
it would not be easy for *religion* to borrow many
new ideas from an alien creed, in a very few years,
while the noted ferocity of the islanders towards
strangers, and the inaccessibility of their abode,
makes earlier borrowing, on a large scale at least,
highly improbable. The Andamanese god, Puluga,
is " like fire " but invisible, unborn and immortal,
knowing and punishing or rewarding, men's deeds,
even " the thoughts of their hearts ". But when
once mythical fancy plays round him, and stories are
told about him, he is credited with a wife who is an
eel or a shrimp, just as Zeus made love as an ant or a
cuckoo. Puluga was the maker of men ; no particular
myth as to how he made them is given. They tried
to kill him, after the deluge (of which a grotesque
myth is told), but he replied that he was " as hard as
wood ". His legend is in the usual mythical contradiction with the higher elements in his religion.

Leaving the Andaman islanders, but still studying
races in the lowest degree of civilisation, we come to
the Bushmen of South Africa. This very curious and

interesting people, far inferior in material equipment
to the Hottentots, is sometimes regarded as a branch
of that race.[1]   The Hottentots call themselves " Khoi-
khoi," the Bushmen they style "Sa".   The poor Sa
lead the life of pariahs, and are hated and chased by
all other natives of South Africa.   They are hunters
and diggers for roots, while the Hottentots, perhaps
their kinsmen, are cattle-breeders.[2]   Being so ill-
nourished, the Bushmen are very small, but sturdy.
They dwell in, or rather wander through, countries
which have been touched by some ancient civilisation,
as is proved by the mysterious mines and roads of
Mashonaland.   It is singular that the Bushmen possess
a tradition according to which they could once "make
stone things that flew over rivers ".   They have
remarkable artistic powers, and their drawings of men
and animals on the walls of caves are often not inferior
to the designs on early Greek vases.[3]

Thus we must regard the Bushmen as possibly
degenerated from a higher status, though there is
nothing (except perhaps the tradition about bridge-
making) to show that it was more exalted than that
of their more prosperous neighbours, the Hottentots.
The myths of the Bushmen, however, are almost on
the lowest known level.   A very good and authentic
example of Bushman cosmogonic myth was given to
Mr. Orpen, chief magistrate of St. John's territory, by
Qing, King Nqusha's huntsman.   Qing "had never

[1] See " Divine Myths of the Lower Races ".

[2] Hahu, *Tsuni Goam*, p. 4.   See other accounts in Waitz, *Anthropologie*,
ii. 328.

[3] *Custom and Myth*, where illustrations of Bushman art are given, pp
290-295.

seen a white man, but in fighting," till he became
acquainted with Mr. Orpen.[1] The chief force in Bushmen myth is by Dr. Bleek identified with the mantis,
a sort of large grasshopper. Though he seems at least
as "chimerical a beast" as the Aryan creative boar, the
"mighty big hare" of the Algonkins, the large spider
who made the world in the opinion of the Gold Coast
people, or the eagle of the Australians, yet the insect (if insect he be), like the others, has achieved moral qualities
and is addressed in prayer. In his religious aspect he is
nothing less than a grasshopper. He is called Cagn.
"Cagn made all things and we pray to him," said Qing.
"Coti is the wife of Cagn." Qing did not know where
they came from ; "perhaps with the men who brought
the sun". The fact is, Qing "did not dance that dance,"
that is, was not one of the Bushmen initiated into the
more esoteric mysteries of Cagn. Till we, too, are
initiated, we can know very little of Cagn in his religious
aspect. Among the Bushmen, as among the Greeks,
there is "no religious mystery without dancing". Qing
was not very consistent. He said Cagn gave orders and
caused all things to appear and to be made, sun, moon,
stars, wind, mountains, animals, and this, of course, is a
lofty theory of creation. Elsewhere myth avers that
Cagn did not so much create as manufacture the objects
in nature. In his early day "the snakes were also
men". Cagn struck snakes with his staff and turned
them into men, as Zeus, in the Æginetan myth, did
with ants. He also turned offending men into baboons.
In Bushman myth, little as we really know of it,
we see the usual opposition of fable and faith, a

[1] *Cape Monthly Magazine*, July, 1874.

kind creator in religion is apparently a magician in myth.

Neighbours of the Bushmen, but more fortunate in their wealth of sheep and cattle, are the Ovaherero. The myths of the Ovaherero, a tribe dwelling in a part of Hereraland "which had not yet been under the influence of civilisation and Christianity," have been studied by the Rev. H. Reiderbecke, missionary at Otyozondyupa. The Ovaherero, he says, have a kind of tree *Ygdrasil*, a tree out of which men are born, and this plays a great part in their myth of creation. The tree, which still exists, though at a great age, is called the Omumborombonga tree. Out of it came, in the beginning, the first man and woman. Oxen stepped forth from it too, but baboons, as Caliban says of the stars, " came otherwise," and sheep and goats sprang from a flat rock. Black people are so coloured, according to the Ovaherero, because when the first parents emerged from the tree and slew an ox, the ancestress of the blacks appropriated the black liver of the victim. The *Ovakuru Meyuru* or " *old ones* in heaven," once let the skies down with a run, but drew them up again (as the gods of the *Satapatha Brahmana* drew the sun) when most of mankind had been drowned.[1] The remnant pacified the *old ones* (as Odysseus did the spirits of the dead) by the sacrifice of a *black* ewe, a practice still used to appease ghosts by the Ovaherero. The neighbouring Omnambo ascribe the creation of man to Kalunga, who came out of the earth, and made the first three sheep.[2]

[1] An example of a Deluge myth in Africa, where M. Lenormant found none.

[2] *South African Folk-Lore Journal*, ii. pt. v. p. 95.

Among the Namaquas, an African people on the
same level of nomadic culture as the Ovaherero, a
divine or heroic early being called Heitsi Eibib had
a good deal to do with the origin of things. If he
did not exactly make the animals, he impressed on
them their characters, and their habits (like those of
the serpent in Genesis) are said to have been conferred
by a curse, the curse of Heitsi Eibib. A precisely
similar notion was found by Avila among the Indians
of Huarochiri, whose divine culture-hero imposed, by a
curse or a blessing, their character and habits on the
beasts.[1] The lion used to live in a nest up a tree till
Heitsi Eibib cursed him and bade him walk on the
ground. He also cursed the hare, " and the hare ran
away, and is still running ".[2] The name of the first
man is given as Eichaknanabiseb (with a multitude
of " clicks "), and he is said to have met all the animals
on a flat rock, and played a game with them for
copper beads. The rainbow was made by Gaunab,
who is generally a malevolent being, of whom more
hereafter.

Leaving these African races, which, whatever their
relative degrees of culture, are physically somewhat
contemptible, we reach their northern neighbours, the
Zulus. They are among the finest, and certainly
among the least religious, of the undeveloped peoples.
Their faith is mainly in magic and ghosts, but there
are traces of a fading and loftier belief.

The social and political condition of the Zulu is
well understood. They are a pastoral, but not a

[1] *Fables of Yncas* (Hakluyt Society), p. 127.
[2] *Tsuni Goam*, pp. 66, 67.

nomadic people, possessing large kraals or towns. They practise agriculture, and they had, till quite recently, a centralised government and a large army, somewhat on the German system. They appear to have no regular class of priests, and supernatural power is owned by the chiefs and the king, and by diviners and sorcerers, who conduct the sacrifices. Their myths are the more interesting because, whether from their natural scepticism, which confuted Bishop Colenso in his orthodox days, or from acquaintance with European ideas, they have begun to doubt the truth of their own traditions.[1] The Zulu theory of the origin of man and of the world commences with the feats of Unkulunkulu, "the old, old one," who, in some legends, was the first man, "and broke off in the beginning". Like Manabozho among the Indians of North America, and like Wainamoinen among the Finns, Unkulunkulu imparted to men a knowledge of the arts, of marriage, and so forth. His exploits in this direction, however, must be considered in another part of this work. Men in general "came out of a bed of reeds".[2] But there is much confusion about this bed of reeds, named "Uthlanga". The younger people ask where the bed of reeds was; the old men do not know, and neither did their fathers know. But they stick to it that "that bed of reeds still exists". Educated Zulus appear somewhat inclined to take the expression in an allegorical sense, and to understand the reeds either as a kind of protoplasm or as a creator who was mortal.

[1] These legends have been carefully collected and published by Bishop Callaway (Trübner & Co., 1868).

[2] Callaway, p. 9.

" He exists no longer. As my grandfather no longer
exists, he too no longer exists ; he died." Chiefs who
wish to claim high descent trace their pedigree to
Uthlanga, as the Homeric kings traced theirs to Zeus.
The myths given by Dr. Callaway are very contradictory.

In addition to the legend that men came out of a
bed of reeds, other and perhaps even more puerile
stories are current. " Some men say that they were
belched up by a cow ; " others " that Unkulunkulu
split them out of a stone,"[1] which recalls the legend
of Pyrrha and Deucalion. The myth about the cow is
still applied to great chiefs. " He was not born ; he
was belched up by a cow." The myth of the stone
origin corresponds to the Homeric saying about men
" born from the stone or the oak of the old tale ".[2]

In addition to the theory of the natal bed of reeds,
the Zulus, like the Navajoes of New Mexico, and the
Bushmen, believe in the subterranean origin of man.
There was a succession of emigrations from below of
different tribes of men, each having its own Unkulunkulu. All accounts agree that Unkulunkulu is
not worshipped, and he does not seem to be identified
with " the lord who plays in heaven "—a kind of
fading Zeus—when there is thunder. Unkulunkulu
is not worshipped, though ancestral spirits are worshipped, because he lived so long ago that no one can
now trace his pedigree to the being who is at once the

---

[1] Without anticipating a later chapter, the resemblances of these to
Greek myths, as arrayed by M. Bouché Leclercq (*De Origine Generis
Humani*), is very striking.

[2] *Odyssey*, xix. 103.

first man and the creator. His "honour-giving name" is lost in the lapse of years, and the family rites have become obsolete.[1]

The native races of the North American continent (concerning whose civilisation more will be said in the account of their divine myths) occupy every stage of culture, from the truly bestial condition in which some of the Digger Indians at present exist, living on insects and unacquainted even with the use of the bow, to the civilisation which the Spaniards destroyed among the Aztecs.

The original facts about religion in America are much disputed, and will be more appropriately treated later. It is now very usual for anthropologists to say, like Mr. Dorman, "no approach to monotheism had been made before the discovery of America by Europeans, and the Great Spirit mentioned in these (their) books is an introduction by Christianity".[2] "This view will not bear examination," says Mr. Tylor, and we shall later demonstrate the accuracy of his remark.[3] But at present we are concerned, not with what Indian religion had to say about her Gods, but with what Indian myth had to tell about the beginnings of things.

The Hurons, for example (to choose a people in a state of middle barbarism), start in myth from the usual conception of a powerful non-natural race of men dwelling in the heavens, whence they descended,

---

[1] See Zulu religion in *The Making of Religion*, pp. 225-229, where it is argued that ghost worship has superseded a higher faith, of which traces are discernible.

[2] *Origin of Primitive Superstitions*, p. 15.

[3] *Primitive Culture*, 1873, ii. p. 340.

and colonised, not to say constructed, the earth. In
the *Relation de la Nouvelle France*, written by
Père Paul le Jeune, of the Company of Jesus, in
1636, there is a very full account of Huron opinion,
which, with some changes of names, exists among the
other branches of the Algonkin family of Indians.

They recognise as the founder of their kindred a
woman named Ataentsic, who, like Hephæstus in the
Iliad, was banished from the sky. In the upper
world there are woods and plains, as on earth.
Ataentsic fell down a hole when she was hunting
a bear, or she cut down a heaven-tree, and fell with
the fall of this Huron *Ygdrasil*, or she was seduced
by an adventurer from the under world, and was
tossed out of heaven for her fault. However it
chanced, she dropped on the back of the turtle in the
midst of the waters. He consulted the other aquatic
animals, and one of them, generally said to have been
the musk-rat, fished [1] up some soil and fashioned the
earth.[2] Here Ataentsic gave birth to twins, Ioskeha

---

[1] *Relations*, 1633. In this myth one Messou, the Great Hare, is the
beginner of our race. He married a daughter of the Musk-rat.

[2] Here we first meet in this investigation a very widely distributed myth.
The myths already examined have taken the origin of earth for granted.
The Hurons account for its origin; a speck of earth was fished out of the
waters and grew. In M. H. de Charencey's tract *Une Legende Cosmogo-
nique* (Havre, 1884) this legend is traced. M. de Charencey distinguishes (1)
a continental version; (2) an insular version; (3) a mixed and *Hindoo* version
Among continental variants he gives a Vogul version (*Revue de Philologie
et d'Ethnographie*, Paris, 1874, i. 10). Numi Tarom (a god who cooks fish
in heaven) hangs a male and female above the abyss of waters in a silver
cradle. He gives them, later, just earth enough to build a house on. Their
son, in the guise of a squirrel, climbs to Numi Tarom, and receives from
him a duck-skin and a goose-skin. Clad in these, like Yehl in his raven-
skin or Odin in his hawk-skin, he enjoys the powers of the animals, dives
and brings up three handfuls of mud, which grow into our earth. Elempi

and Tawiscara. These represent the usual dualism of myth ; they answer to Osiris and Set, to Ormuzd and Ahriman, and were bitter enemies. According to one form of the myth, the woman of the sky had twins, and what occurred may be quoted from Dr. Brinton. " Even before birth one of them betrayed his restless and evil nature by refusing to be born in the usual manner, but insisting on breaking through his parent's side or arm-pit. He did so, but it cost his mother her life. Her body was buried, and from it sprang the various vegetable productions," pumpkins, maize, beans, and so forth.[1]

nakes men out of clay and snow. The American version M. de Charencey gives from Nicholas Perrot (*Mem. sur les Mœurs*, etc., Paris, 1864, i. 3). Perrot was a traveller of the seventeenth century. The Great Hare takes a hand in the making of earth out of fished-up soil. After giving other North American variants, and comparing the animals that, after three attempts, fish up earth to the dove and raven of Noah, M. de Charencey reaches the Bulgarians. God made Satan, in the skin of a diver, fish up earth out of Lake Tiberias. Three doves fish up earth, in the beginning, in the Galician popular legend (Chodzko, *Contes des Paysans Slaves*, p. 374). In the *insular* version, as in New Zealand, the island is usually fished up with a hook by a heroic angler (Japan, Tonga, Tahiti, New Zealand). The Hindoo version, in which the boar plays the part of musk-rat, or duck, or diver, will be given in "Indian Cosmogonic Myths".

[1] Brinton, *American Hero-Myths*, p. 54. Nicholas Perrot and various Jesuit *Relations* are the original authorities. See "Divine Myths of America". Mr. Leland, in his *Algonkin Tales*, prints the same story, with the names altered to Glooskap and Malsumis, from oral tradition. Compare Schoolcraft, v. 155, and i. 317, and the versions of PP. Charlevoix and Lafitau. In Charlevoix the good and bad brothers are Manabozho and Chokanipok or Chakekanapok, and out of the bones and entrails of the latter many plants and animals were fashioned, just as, according to a Greek myth preserved by Clemens Alexandrinus, parsley and pomegranates arose from the blood and scattered members of Dionysus Zagreus. The tale of Tawiscara's violent birth is told of Set in Egypt, and of Indra in the Veda, as will be shown later. This is a very common fable, and, as Mr. Whitley Stokes tells me, it recurs in old Irish legends of the birth of our Lord. Myth, as usual, invading religion, even Christian religion.

According to another version of the origin of things, the maker of them was one Michabous, or Michabo, the Great Hare. His birthplace was shown at an island called Michilimakinak, like the birthplace of Apollo at Delos. The Great Hare made the earth, and, as will afterwards appear, was the inventor of the arts of life. On the whole, the Iroquois and Algonkin myths agree in finding the origin of life in an upper world beyond the sky. The earth was either fished up (as by Brahma when he dived in the shape of a boar) by some beast which descended to the bottom of the waters, or grew out of the tortoise on whose back Ataentsic fell. The first dwellers in the world were either beasts like Manabozho or Michabo, the Great Hare, or the primeval wolves of the Uinkarets,[1] or the creative musk-rat, or were more anthropomorphic heroes, such as Ioskeha and Tawiscara. As for the things in the world, some were made, some evolved, some are transformed parts of an early non-natural man or animal. There is a tendency to identify Ataentsic, the sky-woman, with the moon, and in the Two Great Brethren, hostile as they are, to recognise moon and sun.[2]

[1] Powell, *Bureau of Ethnology*, i. 44.

[2] Dr. Brinton has endeavoured to demonstrate by arguments drawn from etymology that Michabos, Messou, Missibizi or Manabozho, the Great Hare, is originally a personification of Dawn (*Myths of the New World*, p. 178). I have examined his arguments in the *Nineteenth Century*, January, 1886, which may be consulted, and in *Mélusine*, January, 1887. The hare appears to be one out of the countless primeval beast-culture heroes. A curious piece of magic in a tradition of the Dènè Hareskins may seem to aid Dr. Brinton's theory : " Pendant la nuit il entra, jeta au feu une tête de lièvre blanc et aussitôt le jour se fit ".—Petitot, *Traditions Indiennes*, p. 173. But I take it that the sacrifice of a white hare's head makes light magically, as sacrifice of black beasts and columns of black smoke make rainclouds.

Some of the degraded Digger Indians of California have the following myth of the origin of species. In this legend, it will be noticed, a species of evolution takes the place of a theory of creation. The story was told to Mr. Adam Johnston, who "drew" the narrator by communicating to a chief the Biblical narrative of the creation.[1] The chief said it was a strange story, and one that he had never heard when he lived at the Mission of St. John under the care of a Padre. According to this chief (he ruled over the Po-to-yan-te tribe or Coyotes), the first Indians were coyotes. When one of their number died, his body became full of little animals or spirits. They took various shapes, as of deer, antelopes, and so forth; but as some exhibited a tendency to fly off to the moon, the Po-to-yan-tes now usually bury the bodies of their dead, to prevent the extinction of species. Then the Indians began to assume the shape of man, but it was a slow transformation. At first they walked on all fours, then they would begin to develop an isolated human feature, one finger, one toe, one eye, like the ascidian, our first parent in the view of modern science. Then they doubled their organs, got into the habit of sitting up, and wore away their tails, which they unaffectedly regret, "as they consider the tail quite an ornament". Ideas of the immortality of the soul are said to be confined to the old women of the tribe, and, in short, according to this version, the Digger Indians occupy the modern scientific position.

The Winnebagoes, who communicated their myths to Mr. Fletcher,[2] are suspected of having been in-

[1] Schoolcraft, vol. v. [2] *Ibid.*, iv. 228.

fluenced by the Biblical narrative. They say that the
Great Spirit woke up as from a dream, and found
himself sitting in a chair. As he was all alone, he
took a piece of his body and a piece of earth, and made
a man. He next made a woman, steadied the earth by
placing beasts beneath it at the corners, and created
plants and animals. Other men he made out of bears.
" He created the white man to make tools for the poor
Indians "—a very pleasing example of a teleological
hypothesis and of the doctrine of final causes as
understood by the Winnebagoes. The Chaldean
myth of the making of man is recalled by the legend
that the Great Spirit cut out a piece of himself for the
purpose; the Chaldean wisdom coincides, too, with
the philosophical acumen of the Po-to-yan-te or Coyote
tribe of Digger Indians. Though the Chaldean theory
is only connected with that of the Red Men by its
savagery, we may briefly state it in this place.

According to Berosus, as reported by Alexander
Polyhistor, the universe was originally (as before
Manabozho's time) water and mud. Herein all manner
of mixed monsters, with human heads, goat's horns,
four legs, and tails, bred confusedly. In place of the
Iroquois Ataentsic, a woman called Omoroca presided
over the mud and the menagerie. She, too, like
Ataentsic, is sometimes recognised as the moon.
Affairs being in this state, Bel-Maruduk arrived and
cut Omoroca in two (Chokanipok destroyed Ataentsic),
and out of Omoroca Bel made the world and the things
in it. We have already seen that in savage myth many
things are fashioned out of a dead member of the
extra-natural race. Lastly, Bel cut his own head off,

and with the blood the gods mixed clay and made
men. The Chaldeans inherited very savage fancies.[1]

One ought, perhaps, to apologise to the Chaldeans
for inserting their myths among the fables of the least
cultivated peoples ; but it will scarcely be maintained
that the Oriental myths differ in character from the
Digger Indian and Iroquois explanations of the origin
of things. The Ahts of Vancouver Island, whom Mr.
Sproat knew intimately, and of whose ideas he gives a
cautious account (for he was well aware of the limits
of his knowledge), tell a story of the usual character.[2]
They believe in a member of the extra-natural race,
named Quawteaht, of whom we shall hear more in
his heroic character. As a demiurge "he is undoubtedly represented as the general framer, I do not
say creator, of all things, though some special things
are excepted. He made the earth and water, the
trees and rocks, and all the animals. Some say that
Quawteaht made the sun and moon, but the majority
of the Indians believe that he had nothing to do with
their formation, and that they are deities superior to
himself, though now distant and less active. He
gave names to everything; among the rest, to all the
Indian houses which then existed, although inhabited
only by birds and animals. Quawteaht went away
before the apparent change of the birds and beasts into
Indians, which took place in the following manner :—

" The birds and beasts of old had the spirits of the
Indians dwelling in them, and occupied the various

---

[1] *Cf.* Syncellus, p. 29 ; Euseb., *Chronic. Armen.*, ed. Mai, p. 10 ; Lenormant, *Origines de l'Histoire*, i. 506.

[2] Sproat, *Scenes and Studies of Savage Life*, pp. 210, 211.

coast villages, as the Ahts do at present.   One day a
canoe manned by two Indians from an unknown
country approached the shore.   As they coasted along,
at each house at which they landed, the deer, bear,
elk, and other brute inhabitants fled to the mountains,
and the geese and other birds flew to the woods and
rivers.   But in this flight, the Indians, who had
hitherto been contained in the bodies of the various
creatures, were left behind, and from that time they
took possession of the deserted dwellings and assumed
the condition in which we now see them."

Crossing the northern continent of America to the
west, we are in the domains of various animal culture-
heroes, ancestors and teachers of the human race, and
the makers, to some extent, of the things in the world.
As the eastern tribes have their Great Hare, so the
western tribes have their wolf hero and progenitor, or
their coyote, or their raven, or their dog.   It is possible, and even certain in some cases, that the animal
which was the dominant totem of a race became heir
to any cosmogonic legends that were floating about.

The country of the Papagos, on the eastern side of
the Gulf of California, is the southern boundary of the
province of the coyote or prairie wolf.   The realm of
his influence as a kind of Prometheus, or even as a
demiurge, extends very far northwards.   In the myth
related by Con Quien, the chief of the central Papagos,[1]
the coyote acts the part of the fish in the Sanskrit
legend of the flood, while Montezuma undertakes the
rôle of Manu.   This Montezuma was formed, like the
Adams of so many races, out of potter's clay in the

[1] Davidson, *Indian Affairs Report*, 1865, p. 131 ; Bancroft, iii. 75.

hands of the Great Spirit. In all this legend it seems plain enough that the name of Montezuma is imported from Mexico, and has been arbitrarily given to the hero of the Papagos. According to Mr. Powers, whose manuscript notes Mr. Bancroft quotes (iii. 87), all the natives of California believe that their first ancestors were created directly from the earth of their present dwelling-places, and in very many cases these ancestors were coyotes.

The Pimas, a race who live near the Papagos on the eastern coast of the Gulf of California, say that the earth was made by a being named Earth-prophet. At first it appeared like a spider's web, reminding one of the West African legend that a great spider created the world. Man was made by the Earth-prophet out of clay kneaded with sweat. A mysterious eagle and a deluge play a great part in the later mythical adventures of war and the world, as known to the Pimas.[1]

In Oregon the coyote appears as a somewhat tentative demiurge, and the men of his creation, like the beings first formed by Prajapati in the Sanskrit myth, needed to be reviewed, corrected and considerably augmented. The Chinooks of Oregon believe in the usual race of magnified non-natural men, who preceded humanity.

These semi-divine people were called Ulhaipa by the Chinooks, and Sehuiab by the Lummies. But the coyote was the maker of men. As the first of Nature's journeymen, he made men rather badly, with closed eyes and motionless feet. A kind being, named Ikanam, touched up the coyote's crude essays with

---

[1] Communicated to Mr. Bancroft by Mr. Stout of the Pima Agency.

a sharp stone, opening the eyes of men, and giving
their hands and feet the powers of movement. He
also acted as a "culture-hero," introducing the first
arts.[1]

Moving up the West Pacific coast we reach British
Columbia, where the coyote is not supposed to have
been so active as our old friend the musk-rat in the
great work of the creation. According to the Tacullies,
nothing existed in the beginning but water and a
musk-rat. As the animal sought his food at the
bottom of the water, his mouth was frequently filled
with mud. This he spat out, and so gradually formed
by alluvial deposit an island. This island was small at
first, like earth in the Sanskrit myth in the *Satapatha
Brahmana*, but gradually increased in bulk. The
Tacullies have no new light to throw on the origin of
man.[2]

The Thlinkeets, who are neighbours of the Tacullies
on the north, incline to give crow or raven the chief
rôle in the task of creation, just as some Australians
allot the same part to the eagle-hawk, and the Yakuts
to a hawk, a crow and a teal-duck. We shall hear
much of Yehl later, as one of the mythical heroes of
the introduction of civilisation. North of the Thlinkeets, a bird and a dog take the creative duties, the
Aleuts and Koniagas being descended from a dog.
Among the more northern Tinnehs, the dog who was
the progenitor of the race had the power of assuming
the shape of a handsome young man. He supplied

[1] [Franchere's *Narrative*, 258 ; Gibb's *Chinook Vocabulary ;* Parker's
Exploring Tour, i. 139 ;] Bancroft, iii. 96.
[2] Bancroft, iii. 98 ; Harmon's *Journey*, pp. 302, 303,

the protoplasm of the Tinnehs, as Purusha did that
of the Aryan world, out of his own body. A giant
tore him to pieces, as the gods tore Purusha, and out
of the fragments thrown into the rivers came fish, the
fragments tossed into the air took life as birds, and
so forth.[1] This recalls the Australian myth of the
origin of fish and the Ananzi stories of the origin of
whips.[2]

Between the cosmogonic myths of the barbarous
or savage American tribes and those of the great
cultivated American peoples, Aztecs, Peruvians and
Quiches, place should be found for the legends of
certain races in the South Pacific. Of these, the most
important are the Maoris or natives of New Zealand,
the Mangaians and the Samoans. Beyond the
usual and world-wide correspondences of myth,
the divine tales of the various South Sea isles display
resemblances so many and essential that they must
be supposed to spring from a common and probably
not very distant centre. As it is practically impossible
to separate Maori myths of the making of things
from Maori myths of the gods and their origin, we
must pass over here the metaphysical hymns and
stories of the original divine beings, Rangi and Papa,
Heaven and Earth, and of their cruel but necessary
divorce by their children, who then became the usual
Titanic race which constructs and " airs " the world
for the reception of man.[3] Among these beings, more

---

[1] Hearne, pp. 342, 343 ; Bancroft, iii. 106.
[2] See " Divine Myths of Lower Races ". M. Cosquin, in *Contes de
Lorraine*, vol. i. p. 58, gives the Ananzi story.
[3] See " Divine Myths of Lower Races ".

fully described in our chapter on the gods of the lower
races, is Tiki, with his wife Marikoriko, twilight.
Tane (male) is another of the primordial race, children
of earth and heaven, and between him and Tiki lies
the credit of having made or begotten humanity.
Tane adorned the body of his father, heaven (*Rangi*),
by sticking stars all over it, as disks of pearl-shells
are stuck all over images. He was the parent of trees
and birds, but some trees are original and divine
beings. The first woman was not born, but formed
out of the sun and the echo, a pretty myth. Man
was made by Tiki, who took red clay, and kneaded
it with his own blood, or with the red water of
swamps. The habits of animals, some of which are
gods, while others are descended from gods, follow
from their conduct at the moment when heaven and
earth were violently divorced. New Zealand itself,
or at least one of the isles, was a huge fish caught by
Maui (of whom more hereafter). Just as Pund-jel, in
Australia, cut out the gullies and vales with his knife,
so the mountains and dells of New Zealand were
produced by the knives of Maui's brothers when they
crimped his big fish.[1] Quite apart from those childish
ideas are the astonishing metaphysical hymns about
the first stirrings of light in darkness, of " becoming "
and " being," which remind us of Hegel and Heraclitus,
or of the most purely speculative ideas in the Rig-
Veda.[2] Scarcely less metaphysical are the myths

---

[1] Taylor, *New Zealand*, pp. 115-121; Bastian, *Heilige Sage der Polynesier*,
pp. 36-50; Shortland, *Traditions of New Zealanders*.

[2] See chapter on " Divine Myths of the Lower Races," and on " Indian
Cosmogonic Myths ".

of Mangaia, of which Mr. Gill[1] gives an elaborate account.

The Mangaian ideas of the world are complex, and of an early scientific sort. The universe is like the hollow of a vast cocoa-nut shell, divided into many imaginary circles like those of mediæval speculation. There is a demon at the stem, as it were, of the cocoa-nut, and, where the edges of the imaginary shell nearly meet, dwells a woman demon, whose name means "the very beginning". In this system we observe efforts at metaphysics and physical speculation. But it is very characteristic of rude thought that such extremely abstract conceptions as "the very beginning" are represented as possessing life and human form. The woman at the bottom of the shell was anxious for progeny, and therefore plucked a bit out of her own right side, as Eve was made out of the rib of Adam. This piece of flesh became Vatea, the father of gods and men. Vatea (like Oannes in the Chaldean legend) was half man, half fish. "The Very Beginning" begat other children in the same manner, and some of these became departmental gods of ocean, noon-day, and so forth. Curiously enough, the Mangaians seem to be sticklers for primogeniture. Vatea, as the first-born son, originally had his domain next above that of his mother. But she was pained by the thought that his younger brothers each took a higher place than his; so she pushed his land up, and it is now next below the solid crust on which mortals live in Mangaia. Vatea married a woman from one of the under worlds named Papa, and their children had the regular human

[1] *Myths and Songs from the South Pacific*, pp. 1-22.

form. One child was born either from Papa's head,
like Athene from the head of Zeus, or from her arm-
pit, like Dionysus from the thigh of Zeus. Another
child may be said, in the language of dog-breeders, to
have "thrown back," for he wears the form of a white
or black lizard. In the Mangaian system the sky is a
solid vault of blue stone. In the beginning of things
the sky (like Ouranos in Greece and Rangi in New
Zealand) pressed hard on earth, and the god Ru was
obliged to thrust the two asunder, or rather he was
engaged in this task when Maui tossed both Ru and
the sky so high up that they never came down again.
Ru is now the Atlas of Mangaia, "the sky-supporting
Ru".[1] His lower limbs fell to earth, and became
pumice-stone. In these Mangaian myths we discern
resemblances to New Zealand fictions, as is natural,
and the tearing of the body of "the Very Beginning"
has numerous counterparts in European, American
and Indian fable. But on the whole, the Mangaian
myths are more remarkable for their semi-scientific
philosophy than for their coincidences with the fancies
of other early peoples.

The Samoans, like the Maoris and Greeks, hold that
heaven at first fell down and lay upon earth.[2] The
arrowroot and another plant pushed up heaven, and
"the heaven-pushing place" is still known and pointed
out. Others say the god Ti-iti-i pushed up heaven,
and his feet made holes six feet deep in the rocks
during this exertion. The other Samoan myths chiefly
explain the origin of fire, and the causes of the characteristic forms and habits of animals and plants. The

[1] Gill, p. 59.   [2] Turner's *Samoa*, p. 198,

Samoans, too, possess a semi-mythical, metaphysical cosmogony, starting from *nothing*, but rapidly becoming the history of rocks, clouds, hills, dew and various animals, who intermarried, and to whom the royal family of Samoa trace their origin through twenty-three generations. So personal are Samoan abstract conceptions, that " *Space* had a long-legged stool," on to which a head fell, and grew into a companion for Space. Yet another myth says that the god Tangaloa existed in space, and made heaven and earth, and sent down his daughter, a snipe. Man he made out of the mussel-fish. So confused are the doctrines of the Samoans.[1]

Perhaps the cosmogonic myths of the less cultivated races have now been stated in sufficient number. As an example of the ideas which prevailed in an American race of higher culture, we may take the Quiche legend as given in the *Popol Vuh*, a post-Christian collection of the sacred myths of the nation, written down after the Spanish conquest, and published in French by the Abbé Brasseur de Bourbourg.[2]

The Quiches, like their neighbours the Cakchiquels, were a highly civilised race, possessing well-built towns, roads and the arts of life, and were great agriculturists. Maize, the staple of food among these advanced Americans, was almost as great a god as

---

[1] Turner's *Samoa*, pp. 1-9.

[2] See *Popol Vuh* in Mr. Max Müller's *Chips from a German Workshop*, with a discussion of its authenticity. In his *Annals of the Cakchiquels*, a nation bordering on the Quiches, Dr. Brinton expresses his belief in the genuine character of the text. Compare Bancroft, iii. p. 45. The ancient and original *Popol Vuh*, the native book in native characters, disappeared during the Spanish conquest

Soma among the Indo-Aryans. The Quiches were acquainted with a kind of picture-writing, and possessed records in which myth glided into history. The *Popol Vuh*, or book of the people, gives itself out as a post-Columbian copy of these traditions, and may doubtless contain European ideas. As we see in the *Commentarias Reales* of the half-blood Inca Garcilasso de la Vega, the conquered people were anxious to prove that their beliefs were by no means so irrational and so "devilish" as to Spanish critics they appeared. According to the *Popol Vuh*, there was in the beginning nothing but water and the feathered serpent, one of their chief divine beings; but there also existed somehow, "they that gave life". Their names mean "shooter of blow-pipe at coyote," "at opossum," and so forth. They said "Earth," and there *was* earth, and plants growing thereon. Animals followed, and the Givers of life said "Speak our names," but the animals could only cluck and croak. Then said the Givers, "Inasmuch as ye cannot praise us, ye shall be killed and eaten". They then made men out of clay; these men were weak and watery, and by water they were destroyed. Next they made men of wood and women of the pith of trees. These puppets married and gave in marriage, and peopled earth with wooden mannikins. This unsatisfactory race was destroyed by a rain of resin and by the wild beasts. The survivors developed into apes. Next came a period occupied by the wildest feats of the magnified non-natural race and of animals. The record is like the description of a supernatural pantomime—the nightmare of a god. The Titans upset hills, are turned into stone, and behave like Heitsi Eibib in the Namaqua myths.

Last of all, men were made of yellow and white maize, and these gave more satisfaction, but their sight was contracted. These, however, survived, and became the parents of the present stock of humanity.

Here we have the conceptions of creation and of evolution combined. Men are *made*, but only the fittest survive ; the rest are either destroyed or permitted to develop into lower species. A similar mixture of the same ideas will be found in one of the Brahmanas among the Aryans of India. It is to be observed that the Quiche myths, as recorded in *Popol Vuh*, contain not only traces of belief in a creative word and power, but many hymns of a lofty and beautifully devotional character.

" Hail ! O Creator, O Former ! Thou that hearest and understandest us, abandon us not, forsake us not ! O God, thou that art in heaven and on the earth, O Heart of Heaven, O Heart of Earth, give us descendants and posterity as long as the light endures.''

This is an example of the prayers of the men made out of maize, made especially that they might " call on the name " of the god or gods. Whether we are to attribute this and similar passages to Christian influence (for *Popol Vuh*, as we have it, is but an attempt to collect the fragments of the lost book that remained in men's minds after the conquest), or whether the purer portions of the myth be due to untaught native reflection and piety, it is not possible to determine. It is improbable that the ideas of a hostile race would be introduced into religious hymns by their victims.

Here, as elsewhere in the sacred legends of civilised peoples, various strata of mythical and religious thought coexist.

No American people reached such a pitch of civilisation as the Aztecs of Anahuac, whose capital was the city of Mexico. It is needless here to repeat the story of their grandeur and their fall. Obscure as their history, previous to the Spanish invasion, may be, it is certain that they possessed a highly organised society, fortified towns, established colleges or priesthoods, magnificent temples, an elaborate calendar, great wealth in the precious metals, the art of picture-writing in considerable perfection, and a despotic central government. The higher classes in a society like this could not but develop speculative systems, and it is alleged that shortly before the reign of Montezuma attempts had been made to introduce a pure monotheistic religion. But the ritual of the Aztecs remained an example of the utmost barbarity. Never was a more cruel faith, not even in Carthage. Nowhere did temples reek with such pools of human blood; nowhere else, not in Dahomey and Ashanti, were human sacrifice, cannibalism and torture so essential to the cult that secured the favour of the gods. In these dark fanes—reeking with gore, peopled by monstrous shapes of idols bird-headed or beast-headed, and adorned with the hideous carvings in which we still see the priest, under the mask of some less ravenous forest beast, tormenting the victim—in these abominable temples the Castilian conquerors might well believe that they saw the dwellings of devils.

Yet Mexican religion had its moral and beautiful

aspect, and the gods, or certain of the gods, required from their worshippers not only bloody hands, but clean hearts.

To the gods we return later. The myths of the origin of things may be studied without a knowledge of the whole Aztec Pantheon. Our authorities, though numerous, lack complete originality and are occasionally confused. We have first the Aztec monuments and hieroglyphic scrolls, for the most part undeciphered. These merely attest the hideous and cruel character of the deities. Next we have the reports of early missionaries, like Sahagun and Mendieta, of conquerors, like Bernal Diaz, and of noble half-breeds, such as Ixtlilxochitl.[1]

There are two elements in Mexican, as in Quiche, and Indo-Aryan, and Maori, and even Andaman cosmogonic myth. We find the purer religion and the really philosophic speculation concurrent with such crude and childish stories as usually satisfy the intellectual demands of Ahts, Cahrocs and Bushmen; but of the purer and more speculative opinions we know little. Many of the noble, learned and priestly classes of Aztecs perished at the conquest. The survivors were more or less converted to Catholicism, and in their writings probably put the best face possible on the native religion. Like the Spanish clergy, their instructors, they were inclined to explain away their national gods by a system of euhemerism, by taking

[1] Bancroft's *Native Races of Pacific Coast of North America*, vol. iii., contains an account of the sources, and, with Sahagun and Acosta, is mainly followed here. See also J. G. Müller, *Ur. Amerik. Rel.*, p. 507. See chapter on the "Divine Myths of Mexico".

it for granted that the gods and culturé-heroes had
originally been ordinary men, worshipped after their
decease. This is almost invariably the view adopted
by Sahagun. Side by side with the confessions, as it
were, of the clergy and cultivated classes coexisted
the popular beliefs, the myths of the people, partaking
of the nature of folk-lore, but not rejected by the
priesthood.

Both strata of belief are represented in the surviving
cosmogonic myths of the Aztecs. Probably we may
reckon in the first or learned and speculative class
of tales the account of a series of constructions and
reconstructions of the world. This idea is not peculiar
to the higher mythologies, the notion of a deluge and
recreation or renewal of things is almost universal,
and even among the untutored Australians there are
memories of a flood and of an age of ruinous winds.
But the theory of definite epochs, calculated in accordance with the Mexican calendar, of epochs in which
things were made and re-made, answers closely to the
Indo-Aryan conception of successive *kalpas*, and can
only have been developed after the method of reckoning
time had been carried to some perfection. " When
heaven and earth were fashioned, they had already
been four times created and destroyed," say the fragments of what is called the Chimalpopoca manuscript.
Probably this theory of a series of *kalpas* is only one
of the devices by which the human mind has tried to
cheat itself into the belief that it can conceive a
beginning of things. The earth stands on an elephant,
the elephant on a tortoise, and it is going too far to
ask what the tortoise stands on. In the same way the

world's beginning seems to become more intelligible
or less puzzling when it is thrown back into a series
of beginnings and endings. This method also was in
harmony with those vague ideas of evolution and of
the survival of the fittest which we have detected in
myth. The various tentative human races of the *Popol
Vuh* degenerated or were destroyed because they did
not fulfil the purposes for which they were made. In
Brahmanic myth we shall see that type after type was
condemned and perished because it was inadequate, or
inadequately equipped—because it did not harmonise
with its environment.[1] For these series of experi-
mental creations and inefficient evolutions vast spaces
of time were required, according to the Aztec and
Indo-Aryan philosophies. It is not impossible that
actual floods and great convulsions of nature may have
been remembered in tradition, and may have lent
colour and form to these somewhat philosophic myths
of origins. From such sources probably comes the
Mexican hypothesis of a water-age (ending in a deluge),
an earth-age (ending in an earthquake), a wind-age
(ending in hurricanes), and the present dispensation,
to be destroyed by fire.

The less philosophic and more popular Aztec legend
of the commencement of the world is mainly remarkable for the importance given in it to objects of stone.
For some reason, stones play a much greater part in
American than in other mythologies. An emerald was

[1] As an example of a dim evolutionary idea, note the myths of the
various ages as reported by Mendieta, according to which there were five
earlier ages "or suns" of bad quality, so that the contemporary human
beings were unable to live on the fruits of the earth.

worshipped in the temple of Pachacamac, who was, according to Garcilasso, the supreme and spiritual deity of the Incas. The creation legend of the Cakchiquels of Guatemala [1] makes much of a mysterious, primeval and animated obsidian stone. In the Iroquois myths [2] stones are the leading characters. Nor did Aztec myth escape this influence.

There was a god in heaven named Citlalatonac, and a goddess, Citlalicue. When we speak of "heaven" we must probably think of some such world of ordinary terrestrial nature above the sky as that from which Ataentsic fell in the Huron story. The goddess gave birth to a flint-knife, and flung the flint down to earth. This abnormal birth partly answers to that of the youngest of the Adityas, the rejected abortion in the Veda, and to the similar birth and rejection of Maui in New Zealand. From the fallen flint-knife sprang our old friends the magnified non-natural beings with human characteristics, "the gods," to the number of 1600. The gods sent up the hawk (who in India and Australia generally comes to the front on these occasions), and asked their mother, or rather grandmother, to help them to make men, to be their servants. Citlalicue rather jeered at her unconsidered offspring. She advised them to go to the lord of the homes of the departed, Mictlanteuctli, and borrow a bone or some ashes of the dead who are with him. We must never ask for consistency from myths. This statement implies that men had already been in existence, though they were not yet created. Perhaps they had perished

[1] Brinton, *Annals of the Cakchiquels.*
[2] Erminie Smith, *Bureau of Ethnol. Report,* ii.

in one of the four great destructions. With difficulty
and danger the gods stole a bone from Hades, placed
it in a bowl, and smeared it with their own blood, as
in Chaldea and elsewhere. Finally, a boy and a girl
were born out of the bowl. From this pair sprang
men, and certain of the gods, jumping into a furnace,
became sun and moon. To the sun they then, in Aztec
fashion, sacrificed themselves, and there, one might
think, was an end of them. But they afterwards
appeared in wondrous fashions to their worshippers,
and ordained the ritual of religion. According to
another legend, man and woman (as in African myths)
struggled out of a hole in the ground.[1]

The myths of the peoples under the empire of the
Incas in Peru are extremely interesting, because
almost all mythical formations are found existing
together, while we have historical evidence as to the
order and manner of their development. The Peru of
the Incas covered the modern state of the same name,
and included Ecuador, with parts of Chili and Bolivia.
M. Réville calculates that the empire was about 2500
miles in length, four times as long as France, and that
its breadth was from 250 to 500 miles. The country,
contained three different climatic regions, and was
peopled by races of many different degrees of culture,
all more or less subject to the dominion of the Children
of the Sun. The three regions were the dry strip
along the coast, the fertile and cultivated land about
the spurs of the Cordilleras, and the inland mountain

---

[1] Authorities : Ixtlil. ; Kingsborough, ix. pp. 205, 206 ; Sahagun, *Hist.
Gen.*, i. 3, vii. 2 ; J. G. Müller, p. 510, where Müller compares the Delphic
conception of ages of the world ; Bancroft, iii. pp. 60, 65.

regions, inhabited by the wildest races.   Near Cuzco,
the Inca capital, was the Lake of Titicaca, the Medi-
terranean, as it were, of Peru, for on the shores of this
inland sea was developed the chief civilisation of the
new world.

As to the institutions, myths and religion of the
empire, we have copious if contradictory information.
There are the narratives of the Spanish conquerors,
especially of Pizarro's chaplain, Valverde, an ignorant bigoted fanatic.   Then we have somewhat later
travellers and missionaries, of whom Cieza de Leon
(his book was published thirty years after the conquest,
in 1553) is one of the most trustworthy.   The "Royal
Commentaries" of Garcilasso de la Vega, son of an
Inca lady and a Spanish conqueror, have often already
been quoted.   The critical spirit and sound sense of
Garcilasso are in remarkable contrast to the stupid
orthodoxy of the Spaniards, but some allowance must
be made for his fervent Peruvian patriotism.   He had
heard the Inca traditions repeated in boyhood, and
very early in life collected all the information which
his mother and maternal uncle had to give him, or
which could be extracted from the *quipus* (the records
of knotted cord), and from the commemorative pictures
of his ancestors.   Garcilasso had access, moreover, to
the "torn papers" of Blas Valera, an early Spanish
missionary of unusual sense and acuteness.   Christoval
de Moluna is also an excellent authority, and much
may be learned from the volume of *Rites and Laws
of the Yncas.*[1]

---

[1] A more complete list of authorities, including the garrulous Acosta, is
published by M. Réville in his *Hibbert Lectures*, pp. 136, 137.   Garcilasso,

The political and religious condition of the Peruvian empire is very clearly conceived and stated by Garcilasso. Without making due allowance for that mysterious earlier civilisation, older than the Incas, whose cyclopean buildings are the wonder of travellers, Garcilasso attributes the introduction of civilisation to his own ancestors. Allowing for what is confessedly mythical in his narrative, it must be admitted that he has a firm grasp of what the actual history must have been. He recognises a period of savagery before the Incas, a condition of the rudest barbarism, which still existed on the fringes and mountain recesses of the empire. The religion of that period was mere magic and totemism. From all manner of natural objects, but chiefly from beasts and birds, the various savage stocks of Peru claimed descent, and they revered and offered sacrifice to their totemic ancestors.[1] Garcilasso adds, what is almost incredible, that the Indians tamely permitted themselves to be eaten by their totems, when these were carnivorous animals. They did this with the less reluctance as they were cannibals, and accustomed to breed children for the purposes of the *cuisine* from captive women taken in war.[2] Among the *huacas* or idols, totems, fetishes and other adorable objects of the Indians, worshipped before and retained

Cieza de Leon, Christoval de Moluna, Acosta and the *Rites and Laws* have all been translated by Mr. Clements Markham, and are published, with the editor's learned and ingenious notes, in the collection of the Hakluyt Society. Care must be taken to discriminate between what is reported about the Indians of the various provinces, who were in very different grades of culture, and what is told about the Incas themselves.

[1] *Com. Real.*, vol. i., chap. ix., x., xi. pp. 47-53.

[2] Cieza de Leon, xii., xv., xix., xxi., xxiii., xxvi., xxviii., xxxii. Cieza is speaking of people in the valley of Cauca, in New Granada.

after the introduction of the Inca sun-totem and solar cult, Garcilasso names trees, hills, rocks, caves, fountains, emeralds, pieces of jasper, tigers, lions, bears, foxes, monkeys, condors, owls, lizards, toads, frogs, sheep, maize, the sea, " for want of larger gods, crabs " and bats. The bat was also the totem of the Zotzil, the chief family of the Cakchiquels of Guatemala, and the most high god of the Cakchiquels was worshipped in the shape of a bat. We are reminded of religion as it exists in Samoa. The explanation of Blas Valera was that in each totem (*pacarissa*) the Indians adored the devil.

Athwart this early religion of totems and fetishes came, in Garcilasso's narrative, the purer religion of the Incas, with what he regards as a philosophic development of a belief in a Supreme Being. According to him, the Inca sun-worship was really a totemism of a loftier character. The Incas "knew how to choose gods better than the Indians ". Garcilasso's theory is that the earlier totems were selected chiefly as distinguishing marks by the various stocks, though, of course, this does not explain why the animals or other objects of each family were worshipped or were regarded as ancestors, and the blood-connections of the men who adored them. The Incas, disdaining crabs, lizards, bats and even serpents and lions, " chose " the sun. Then, just like the other totemic tribes, they feigned to be of the blood and lineage of the sun.

This fable is, in brief, the Inca myth of the origin of civilisation and of man, or at least of their breed of men. As M. Réville well remarks, it is obvious that the Inca claim is an adaptation of the local myth of

Lake Titicaca, the inland sea of Peru. According to that myth, the Children of the Sun, the ancestors of the Incas, came out of the earth (as in Greek and African legends) at Lake Titicaca, or reached its shores after wandering from the hole or cave whence they first emerged. The myth, as adapted by the Incas, takes for granted the previous existence of mankind, and, in some of its forms, the Inca period is preceded by the deluge.

Of the Peruvian myth concerning the origin of things, the following account is given by a Spanish priest, Christoval de Moluna, in a report to the Bishop of Cuzco in 1570.[1] The story was collected from the lips of ancient Peruvians and old native priests, who again drew their information in part from the painted records reserved in the temple of the sun near Cuzco. The legend begins with a deluge myth ; a cataclysm ended a period of human existence. All mankind perished except a man and woman, who floated in a box to a distance of several hundred miles from Cuzco. There the creator commanded them to settle, and there, like Pund-jel in Australia, he made clay images of men of all races, attired in their national dress, and then animated them. They were all fashioned and painted as correct models, and were provided with their national songs and with seed-corn. They then were put into the earth, and emerged all over the world at the proper places, some (as in Africa and Greece) coming out of fountains, some out of trees, some out of caves. For this reason they made *huacas* (worshipful objects or fetishes) of the trees, caves and fountains. Some

---

[1] *Rites and Laws of the Yncas*, p. 4, Hakluyt Society, 1873.

of the earliest men were changed into stones, others
into falcons, condors and other creatures which we
know were totems in Peru. Probably this myth of
metamorphosis was invented to account for the reverence paid to totems or *pacarissas* as the Peruvians called
them. In Tiahuanaco, where the creation, or rather
manufacture of men took place, the creator turned many
sinners into stones. The sun was made in the shape
of a man, and, as he soared into heaven, he called out
in a friendly fashion to Manco Ccapac, the Ideal first
Inca, " Look upon me as thy father, and worship me
as thy father ". In these fables the creator is called
Pachyachachi, " Teacher of the world ". According to
Christoval, the creator and his sons were " eternal and
unchangeable ". Among the Canaris men descend
from the survivor of the deluge, and a beautiful bird
with the face of a woman, a siren in fact, but known
better to ornithologists as a macaw. " The chief cause,"
says the good Christoval, " of these fables was ignorance
of God."

The story, as told by Cieza de Leon, runs thus : [1]
A white man of great stature (in fact, " a magnified
non-natural man ") came into the world, and gave
life to beasts and human beings. His name was
Ticiviracocha, and he was called the Father of the
Sun.[2] There are likenesses of him in the temple, and
he was regarded as a moral teacher. It was owing
apparently to this benevolent being that four mysterious brothers and sisters emerged from a cave—

---

[1] *Second Part of the Chronicles of Peru*, p 5.
[2] See *Making of Religion*, pp. 265-270.   Name and God are much disputed.

Children of the Sun, fathers of the Incas, teachers of savage men. Their own conduct, however, was not exemplary, and they shut up in a hole in the earth the brother of whom they were jealous. This incident is even more common in the *märchen* or household tales than in the regular tribal or national myths of the world.[1] The buried brother emerged again with wings, and " without doubt he must have been some devil," says honest Cieza de Leon. This brother was Manco Ccapac, the heroic ancestor of the Incas, and he turned his jealous brethren into stones. The whole tale is in the spirit illustrated by the wilder romances of the *Popol Vuh*.

Garcilasso gives three forms of this myth. According to " the old Inca," his maternal uncle, it was the sun which sent down two of his children, giving them a golden staff, which would sink into the ground at the place where they were to rest from wandering. It sank at Lake Titicaca. About the current myths Garcilasso says generally that they were " more like dreams" than straightforward stories ; but, as he adds, the Greeks and Romans also " invented fables worthy to be laughed at, and in greater number than the Indians. The stories of one age of heathenism may be compared with those of the other, and in many points they will be found to agree." This critical position of Garcilasso's will be proved correct when we reach the myths of Greeks and Indo-Aryans. The myth as narrated north-east of Cuzco speaks of the four brothers and four sisters who came out of caves,

---

[1] The story of Joseph and the *märchen* of *Jean de l'Ours* are well-known examples.

and the caves in Inca times were panelled with gold and silver.

Athwart all these lower myths, survivals from the savage stage, comes what Garcilasso regards as the philosophical Inca belief in Pachacamac. This deity, to Garcilasso's mind, was purely spiritual: he had no image and dwelt in no temple; in fact, he is that very God whom the Spanish missionaries proclaimed. This view, though the fact has been doubted, was very probably held by the *Amautas*, or philosophical class in Peru.[1] Cieza de Leon says "the name of this devil, Pachacamac, means creator of the world ". Garcilasso urges that Pachacamac was the *animus mundi;* that he did not "make the world," as Pund-jel and other savage demiurges made it, but that he was to the universe what the soul is to the body.

Here we find ourselves, if among myths at all, among the myths of metaphysics—rational myths; that is, myths corresponding to our present stage of thought, and therefore intelligible to us. Pachacamac "made the sun, and lightning, and thunder, and of these the sun was worshipped by the Incas ". Garcilasso denies that the moon was worshipped. The reflections of the sceptical or monotheistic Inca, who declared that the sun, far from being a free agent, "seems like a thing held to its task," are reported by Garcilasso, and appear to prove that solar worship was giving way, in the minds of educated Peruvians, a hundred years before the arrival of Pizarro and Valverde with his missal.[2]

---

[1] *Com. Real.*, vol. i. p. 106.
[2] Garcilasso, viii. 8, quoting Blas Valera.

From this summary it appears that the higher Peruvian religion had wrested to its service, and to the dynastic purposes of the Incas, a native myth of the familiar class, in which men come ready made out of holes in the ground. But in Peru we do not find nearly such abundance of other savage origin myths as will be proved to exist in the legends of Greeks and Indo-Aryans. The reason probably is that Peru left no native literature ; the missionaries disdained stories of " devils," and Garcilasso's common sense and patriotism were alike revolted by the incidents of stories " more like dreams " than truthful records. He therefore was silent about them. In Greece and India, on the other hand, the native religious literature pre-served myths of the making of man out of clay, of his birth from trees and stones, of the fashioning of things out of the fragments of mutilated gods and Titans, of the cosmic egg, of the rending and wounding of a personal heaven and a personal earth, of the fishing up from the waters of a tiny earth which grew greater, of the development of men out of beasts, with a dozen other such notions as are familiar to contemporary Bushmen, Australians, Digger Indians, and Cahrocs. But in Greece and India these ideas coexist with myths and religious beliefs as purely spiritual and metaphysical as the belief in the Pachacamac of Garci-lasso and the *Amautas* of Peru.

CHAPTER VII.

INDO-ARYAN MYTHS—SOURCES OF EVIDENCE.

Authorities—Vedas—Brahmanas—Social condition of Vedic India—Arts—
Ranks—War—Vedic fetishism—Ancestor worship—Date of Rig-Veda
Hymns doubtful—Obscurity of the Hymns—Difficulty of interpreting
the real character of Veda—Not primitive but sacerdotal—The moral
purity not innocence but refinement.

BEFORE examining the myths of the Aryans of India,
it is necessary to have a clear notion of the nature of
the evidence from which we derive our knowledge of
the subject. That evidence is found in a large and
incongruous mass of literary documents, the heritage
of the Indian people. In this mass are extremely
ancient texts (the *Rig-Veda*, and the *Atharva-Veda*),
expository comments of a date so much later that the
original meaning of the older documents was sometimes
lost (the Brahmanas), and poems and legendary collections of a period later still, a period when the whole
character of religious thought had sensibly altered. In
this literature there is indeed a certain continuity; the
names of several gods of the earliest time are preserved
in the legends of the latest. But the influences of
many centuries of change, of contending philosophies,
of periods of national growth and advance, and of
national decadence and decay, have been at work on
the mythology of India. Here we have myths that

were perhaps originally popular tales, and are probably
old ; here again, we have later legends that certainly
were conceived in the narrow minds of a pedantic and.
ceremonious priesthood. It is not possible, of course,
to analyse in this place all the myths of all the
periods; we must be content to point out some which
seem to be typical examples of the working of the
human intellect in its earlier or its later childhood, in
its distant hours of barbaric beginnings, or in the
senility of its sacerdotage.

The documents which contain Indian mythology
may be divided, broadly speaking, into four classes.
First, and most ancient in date of composition, are the
collections of hymns known as the *Vedas*. Next, and
(as far as date of collection goes) far less ancient, are
the expository texts called the *Brahmanas*. Later
still, come other manuals of devotion and of sacred
learning, called *Sutras* and *Upanishads ;* and last are
the epic poems (*Itihasas*), and the books of legends
called *Puranas*. We are chiefly concerned here with
the Vedas and Brahmanas. A gulf of time, a period of
social and literary change, separates the Brahmanas
from the Vedas. But the epics and Puranas differ perhaps even still more from the Brahmanas, on account of
vast religious changes which brought new gods into
the Indian Olympus, or elevated to the highest place
old gods formerly of low degree. From the composition of the first Vedic hymn to the compilation of the
latest Purana, religious and mythopœic fancy was
never at rest.

Various motives induced various poets to assign, on
various occasions, the highest powers to this or the

other god. The most antique legends were probably
omitted or softened by some early Vedic bard (Rishi) of
noble genius, or again impure myths were brought
from the obscurity of oral circulation and foisted into
literature by some poet less divinely inspired. Old
deities were half-forgotten, and forgotten deities were
resuscitated. Sages shook off superstitious bonds,
priests forged new fetters on ancient patterns for
themselves and their flocks. Philosophy explained
away the more degrading myths; myths as degrading
were suggested to dark and servile hearts by unscientific etymologies. Over the whole mass of ancient
mythology the new mythology of a debased Brahmanic
ritualism grew like some luxurious and baneful parasite.
It is enough for our purpose if we can show that even
in the purest and most antique mythology of India
the element of traditional savagery survived and played
its part, and that the irrational legends of the Vedas and
Brahmanas can often be explained as relics of savage
philosophy or faith, or as novelties planned on the
ancient savage model, whether borrowed or native
to the race.

The oldest documents of Indian mythology are the
Vedas, usually reckoned as four in number. The
oldest, again, of the four, is the *Sanhita* (" collection ")
of the *Rig-Veda*. It is a purely lyrical assortment of
the songs " which the Hindus brought with them from
their ancient homes on the banks of the Indus ". In
the manuscripts, the hymns are classified according
to the families of poets to whom they are ascribed.
Though composed on the banks of the Indus by sacred
bards, the hymns were compiled and arranged in India

proper. At what date the oldest hymns of which this collection is made up were first chanted it is impossible to say with even approximate certainty. Opinions differ, or have differed, between 2400 B.C. and 1400 B.C. as the period when the earliest sacred lyrics of the Veda may first have been listened by gods and men. In addition to the *Rig-Veda* we have the *Sanhita* of the *Sama-Veda*, " an anthology taken from the *Rik-Samhita*, comprising those of its verses which were intended to be chanted at the ceremonies of the soma sacrifice ".[1] It is conjectured that the hymns of the *Sama-Veda* were borrowed from the *Rig-Veda* before the latter had been edited and stereotyped into its present form. Next comes the *Yajur-Veda*, " which contains the formulas for the entire sacrificial ceremonial, and indeed forms its proper foundations," the other Vedas being devoted to the soma sacrifice.[2] The *Yajur-Veda* has two divisions, known as the *Black* and the *White Yajur*, which have common matter, but differ in arrangement. The *Black Yajur-Veda* is also called the *Taittirya*, and it is described as " a motley undigested jumble of different pieces ".[3] Last comes *Atharva-Veda*, not always regarded as a Veda properly speaking. It derives its name from an old semi-mythical priestly family, the Atharvans, and is full of magical formulæ, imprecations, folk-lore and spells. There are good reasons for thinking this late as a

---

[1] Weber, *History of Indian Literature*, Eng. transl., p. 63.

[2] *Ibid.*, p. 86.

[3] *Ibid.*, p. 87. The name *Taittirya* is derived from a partridge, or from a Rishi named Partridge in Sanskrit. There is a story that the pupils of a sage were turned into partridges, to pick up sacred texts.

collection, however early may be the magical ideas expressed in its contents.[1]

Between the Vedas, or, at all events, between the oldest of the Vedas, and the compilation of the Brahmanas, these "canonised explanations of a canonised text,"[2] it is probable that some centuries and many social changes intervened.[3]

If we would criticise the documents for Indian mythology in a scientific manner, it is now necessary that we should try to discover, as far as possible, the social and religious condition of the people among whom the Vedas took shape. Were they in any sense "primitive," or were they civilised? Was their religion in its obscure beginnings or was it already a special and peculiar development, the fruit of many ages of thought? Now it is an unfortunate thing that scholars have constantly, and as it were involuntarily, drifted into the error of regarding the Vedas as if they were "primitive," as if they exhibited to us the "germs" and "genesis" of religion and mythology, as if they contained the simple though strange utterances of *primitive* thought.[4] Thus Mr. Whitney declares, in his *Oriental and Linguistic Studies,* "that the Vedas exhibit to us the very earliest germs of the

---

[1] Barth (*Les Religions de l'Inde,* p. 6) thinks that the existence of such a collection as the *Atharva-Veda* is implied, perhaps, in a text of the *Rig-Veda,* x. 90, 9.

[2] Whitney, *Oriental and Linguistic Studies,* First Series, p. 4.

[3] Max Müller, *Biographical Essays,* p. 20. "The prose portions presuppose the hymns, and, to judge from the utter inability of the authors of the Brahmanas to understand the antiquated language of the hymns, these Brahmanas must be ascribed to a much later period than that which gave birth to the hymns."

[4] *Ibid., Rig-Veda Sanhita,* p. vii.

Hindu culture". Mr. Max Müller avers that "no country can be compared to India as offering opportunities for a real study of the genesis and growth of religion ".[1] Yet the same scholar observes that " even the earliest specimens of Vedic poetry belong to the modern history of the race, and that the early period of the historical growth of religion had passed away before the Rishis (bards) could have worshipped their Devas or bright beings with sacred hymns and invocations ". Though this is manifestly true, the sacred hymns and invocations of the Rishis are constantly used as testimony bearing on the beginning of the historical growth of religion. Nay, more; these remains of " the modern history of the race" are supposed to exhibit mythology in the process of making, as if the race had possessed no mythology before it reached a comparatively modern period, the Vedic age. In the same spirit, Dr. Muir, the learned editor of *Sanskrit Texts*, speaks in one place as if the Vedic hymns " illustrated the natural workings of the human mind in the period of its infancy ".[2] A brief examination of the social and political and religious condition of man, as described by the poets of the Vedas, will prove that his infancy had long been left behind him when the first Vedic hymns were chanted

As Barth observes, the very ideas which permeate

---

[1] *Hibbert Lectures,* p. 131.

[2] Nothing can prove more absolutely and more briefly the late character of Vedic faith than the fact that the faith had already to be defended against the attacks of sceptics. The impious denied the existence of Indra because he was invisible. *Rig-Veda,* ii. 12, 5; viii. 89, 3; v. 30, 1-2; vi. 27, 3 Bergaigne, ii. 167. " Es gibt keinen Indra, so hat der eine und der ander gesagt " (Ludwig's version).

the Veda, the idea of the mystic efficacy of sacrifice,
of *brahma*, prove that the poems are profoundly
sacerdotal; and this should have given pause to the
writers who have persisted in representing the hymns
as the work of primitive shepherds praising their gods
as they feed their flocks.[1] In the Vedic age the ranks
of society are already at least as clearly defined as in
Homeric Greece. "We men," says a poet of the *Rig-
Veda*,[2] "have all our different imaginations and designs.
The carpenter seeks something that is broken, the
doctor a patient, the priest some one who will offer
libations. . . . The artisan continually seeks after
a man with plenty of gold. . . . I am a poet, my
father is a doctor, and my mother is a grinder of corn."
Chariots and the art of the chariot-builder are as
frequently spoken of as in the *Iliad*. Spears, swords,
axes and coats of mail were in common use. The art
of boat-building or of ship-building was well known.
Kine and horses, sheep and dogs, had long been
domesticated. The bow was a favourite weapon, and
warriors fought in chariots, like the Homeric Greeks
and the Egyptians. Weaving was commonly practised.
The people probably lived, as a rule, in village settlements, but cities or fortified places were by no means
unknown.[3] As for political society, "kings are
frequently mentioned in the hymns," and "it was

---

[1] *Les Religions de l'Inde*, p. 27.   [2] ix. 112.

[3] Ludwig, *Rig-Veda*, iii. 203. The burgs were fortified with wooden
palisades, capable of being destroyed by fire. "Cities" may be too
magnificent a word for what perhaps were more like *pahs*. But compare
Kaegi, *The Rig-Veda*, note 42, Engl. transl. Kaegi's book (translated by
Dr. Arrowsmith, Boston, U.S., 1886) is probably the best short manual of
the subject.

regarded as eminently beneficial for a king to entertain a family priest," on whom he was expected to confer thousands of kine, lovely slaves and lumps of gold. In the family polygamy existed, probably as the exception. There is reason to suppose that the brother-in-law was permitted, if not expected, to "raise up seed" to his dead brother, as among the Hebrews.[1] As to literature, the very structure of the hymns proves that it was elaborate and consciously artistic. M. Barth writes : "It would be a great mistake to speak of the primitive *naïveté* of the Vedic poetry and religion ".[2] Both the poetry and the religion, on the other hand, display in the highest degree the mark of the sacerdotal spirit. The myths, though originally derived from nature-worship, in an infinite majority of cases only reflect natural phenomena through a veil of ritualistic corruptions.[3] The rigid division of castes is seldom recognised in the *Rig-Veda*. We seem to see caste in the making.[4] The Rishis and priests of the princely families were on their way to becoming the all-

---

[1] Deut. xxv. 5 ; Matt. xxii. 24.

[2] *Revue de l'Histoire des Religions*, i. 245.   [3] Ludwig, iii. 262.

[4] On this subject see Muir, i. 192, with the remarks of Haug. "From all we know, the real origin of caste seems to go back to a time anterior to the composition of the Vedic hymns, though its development into a regular system with insurmountable barriers can be referred only to the later period of the Vedic times." Roth approaches the subject from the word *brahm*, that is, prayer with a mystical efficacy, as his starting-point. From *brahm*, prayer, came *brahma*, he who pronounces the prayers and performs the rite. This celebrant developed into a priest, whom to entertain brought blessings on kings. This domestic chaplaincy (conferring peculiar and even supernatural benefits) became hereditary in families, and these, united by common interests, exalted themselves into the Brahman caste. But in the Vedic age gifts of prayer and poetry alone marked out the *purohitas*, or men put forward to mediate between gods and mortals. Compare Ludwig, iii. 221.

powerful Brahmans. The kings and princes were on their way to becoming the caste of Kshatriyas or warriors. The mass of the people was soon to sink into the caste of Vaisyas and broken men. Non-Aryan aborigines and others were possibly developing into the caste of Sudras. Thus the spirit of division and of ceremonialism had still some of its conquests to achieve. But the extraordinary attention given and the immense importance assigned to the details of sacrifice, and the supernatural efficacy constantly attributed to a sort of magical asceticism (*tapas*, austere fervour), prove that the worst and most foolish elements of later Indian society and thought were in the Vedic age already in powerful existence.

Thus it is self-evident that the society in which the Vedic poets lived was so far from being *primitive* that it was even superior to the higher barbarisms (such as that of the Scythians of Herodotus and Germans of Tacitus), and might be regarded as safely arrived at the threshold of civilisation. Society possessed kings, though they may have been kings of small communities, like those who warred with Joshua or fought under the walls of Thebes or Troy. Poets were better paid than they seem to have been at the courts of Homer or are at the present time. For the tribal festivals special priests were appointed, " who distinguished themselves by their comprehensive knowledge of the requisite rites and by their learning, and amongst whom a sort of rivalry is gradually developed, according as one tribe or another is supposed to have more or less prospered by its sacrifices ".[1] In the

[1] Weber, p. 37.

family marriage is sacred, and traces of polyandry
and of the levirate, surviving as late as the epic
poems, were regarded as things that need to be
explained away. Perhaps the most barbaric feature
in Vedic society, the most singular relic of a distant
past, is the survival, even in a modified and symbolic
form, of human sacrifice.[1]

As to the religious condition of the Vedic Aryans,
we must steadily remember that in the Vedas we have
the views of the Rishis only, that is, of sacred poets
on their way to becoming a sacred caste. Necessarily
they no more represent the *popular* creeds than the
psalmists and prophets, with their lofty monotheistic
morality, represent the popular creeds of Israel. The
faith of the Rishis, as will be shown later, like that
of the psalmists, has a noble moral aspect. Yet certain
elements of this higher creed are already found in the
faiths of the lowest savages. The Rishis probably
did not actually *invent* them. Consciousness of sin,
of imperfection in the sight of divine beings, has been
developed (as it has even in Australia) and is often
confessed. But on the whole the religion of the
Rishis is practical—it might almost be said, is magical.
They desire temporal blessings, rain, sunshine, long
life, power, wealth in flocks and herds. The whole
purpose of the sacrifices which occupy so much of
their time and thought is to obtain these good things.
The sacrifice and the sacrificer come between gods and
men. On the man's side is faith, munificence, a

---

[1] Wilson, *Rig-Veda*, i. p. 59-63; Muir, i. ii.; Wilson, *Rig-Veda* i. p.
xxiv., ii. 8 (ii. 90); *Aitareya Brahmana*, Haug's version, vol. ii. pp. 462,
469.

compelling force of prayer and of intentness of will.
The sacrifice invigorates the gods to do the will of
the sacrificer; it is supposed to be mystically celebrated in heaven as well as on earth—the gods are
always sacrificing. Often (as when rain is wanted)
the sacrifice imitates the end which it is desirable to
gain.[1] In all these matters a minute ritual is already
observed. The mystic word *brahma*, in the sense of
hymn or prayer of a compelling and magical efficacy,
has already come into use. The *brahma* answers
almost to the Maori *karakia* or incantation and charm.
"This *brahma* of Visvamitra protects the tribe of
Bharata." "Atri with the fourth prayer discovered
the sun concealed by unholy darkness."[2] The complicated ritual, in which prayer and sacrifice were
supposed to exert a constraining influence on the
supernatural powers, already existed, Haug thinks,
in the time of the chief Rishis or hymnists of the
Rig-Veda.[3]

In many respects the nature of the idea of the divine,
as entertained by the Rishis of the *Rig-Veda*, is still
matter for discussion. In the chapter on Vedic gods
such particulars as can be ascertained will be given.
Roughly speaking, the religion is mainly, though not
wholly, a cult of departmental gods, originally, in
certain cases, forces of Nature, but endowed with
moral earnestness. As to fetishism in the Vedas the

---

[1] Compare "The Prayers of Savages" in J. A. Farrer's *Primitive
Manners*, and Ludwig, iii. 262-296, and see Bergaigne, *La Religion
Védique*, vol. i. p. 121.

[2] See texts in Muir, i. 242.

[3] Preface to translation of *Aitareya Brahmana*, p. 36.

opinions of the learned are divided. M. Bergaigne [1]
looks on the whole ritual as, practically, an organised
fetishism, employed to influence gods of a far higher
and purer character. Mr Max Müller remarks, "that
stones, bones, shells, herbs and all the other so-called
fetishes, are simply absent in the old hymns, though
they appear in more modern hymns, particularly those
of the *Atharva-Veda*. When artificial objects are
mentioned and celebrated in the *Rig-Veda*, they are
only such as might be praised even by Wordsworth or
Tennyson—chariots, bows, quivers, axes, drums, sacrificial vessels and similar objects. They never assume
any individual character; they are simply mentioned
as useful or precious, it may be as sacred." [2]

When the existence of fetish "herbs" is denied by
Mr. Max Müller, he does not, of course, forget Soma,
that divine juice. It is also to be noted that in modern
India, as Mr. Max Müller himself observes, Sir Alfred
Lyall finds that "the husbandman prays to his plough
and the fisher to his net," these objects being, at
present, fetishes. In opposition to Mr. Max Müller,
Barth avers that the same kind of fetishism which
flourishes to-day flourishes in the *Rig-Veda*. "Mountains, rivers, springs, trees, herbs are invoked as so
many powers. The beasts which live with man—the
horse, the cow, the dog, the bird and the animals
which imperil his existence—receive a cult of praise
and prayer. Among the instruments of ritual, some
objects are more than things consecrated—they are

---

[1] *La Religion Védique*, vol. i. p. 123. "Le culte est assimilable dans
une certaine mesure aux incantations, aux pratiques magiques."

[2] *Hibbert Lectures*, p. 198.

divinities; and the war-chariot, the weapons of defence
and offence, the plough, are the objects not only
of benedictions but of prayers."[1]   These absolute
contradictions on matters of fact add, of course, to
the difficulty of understanding the early Indo-Aryan
religion.   One authority says that the Vedic people
were fetish-worshippers; another authority denies it.

Were the Rishis ancestor-worshippers?   Barth has
no doubt whatever that they were.   In the *pitris* or
fathers he recognises ancestral spirits, now "companions of the gods, and gods themselves.   At their
head appear the earliest celebrants of the sacrifice,
Atharvan, the Angiras, the Kavis (the *pitris*, *par
excellence*) equals of the greatest gods, spirits who, *by
dint of sacrifice*, drew forth the world from chaos, gave
birth to the sun and lighted the stars,"—cosmical
feats which, as we have seen, are sometimes attributed
by the lower races to their idealised mythic ancestors,
the "old, old ones" of Australians and Ovahereroes.

A few examples of invocations of the ancestral
spirits may not be out of place.[2]   "May the Fathers
protect me in my invocation of the gods."   Here is a
curious case, especially when we remember how the
wolf, in the North American myth, scattered the stars
like spangles over the sky: "The fathers have adorned
the sky with stars".[3]

---

[1] Barth, *Les Religions de l'Inde*, p. 7, with the Vedic texts.

[2] *Rig-Veda*, vi. 52, 4.

[3] *Ibid.*, x. 68, xi.

Mr. Whitney (*Oriental and Linguistic Studies*, First Series, p. 59) gives
examples of the ceremony of feeding the Aryan ghosts.   "The fathers are
supposed to assemble, upon due invocation, about the altar of him who
would pay them homage, to seat themselves upon the straw or matting

Important as is the element of ancestor-worship in the evolution of religion, Mr. Max Müller, in his *Hibbert Lectures*, merely remarks that thoughts and feelings about the dead " supplied some of the earliest and most important elements of religion"; but how these earliest elements affect his system does not appear. On a general view, then, the religion of the Vedic poets contained a vast number of elements in solution—elements such as meet us in every quarter of the globe. The belief in ancestral ghosts, the adoration of fetishes, the devotion to a moral ideal, contemplated in the persons of various deities, some of whom at least have been, and partly remain, personal natural forces, are all mingled, and all are drifting towards a kind of pantheism, in which, while everything is divine, and gods are reckoned by millions, the worshipper has glimpses of one single divine essence. The ritual, as we have seen, is more or less magical in character. The general elements of the beliefs are found, in various proportions, everywhere; the pantheistic mysticism is almost peculiar to India. It is, perhaps, needless to repeat that a faith so very composite, and already so strongly differentiated, cannot possibly be "primitive," and that the beliefs and practices of a race so highly organised in society and so well equipped in material civilisation as the Vedic Aryans cannot possibly be "near the beginning". Far from expecting to find in the Veda the primitive myths of the Aryans, we must remember that myth had already, when these hymns were sung, become

spread for each of the guests invited, and to partake of the offerings set before them." The food seems chiefly to consist of rice, sesame and honey.

obnoxious to the religious sentiment. "Thus," writes
Barth, "the authors of the hymns have expurgated,
or at least left in the shade, a vast number of legends
older than their time; such, for example, as the
identity of soma with the moon, as the account of the
divine families, of the parricide of Indra, and a long
list might be made of the *reticences* of the Veda. . . .
It would be difficult to extract from the hymns a
chapter on the loves of the gods. The goddesses are
veiled, the adventures of the gods are scarcely touched
on in passing. . . . We must allow for the moral
delicacy of the singers, and for their dislike of speaking too precisely about the gods. Sometimes it seems
as if their chief object was to avoid plain speaking.
. . . But often there is nothing save jargon and indolence of mind in this voluntary obscurity, for
already in the Veda the Indian intellect is deeply
smitten with its inveterate malady of affecting mystery the more, the more it has nothing to conceal;
the mania for scattering symbols which symbolise no
reality, and for sporting with riddles which it is not
worth while to divine." [1] Barth, however, also recognises amidst these confusions, " the inquietude of a
heart deeply stirred, which seeks truth and redemp-
tion in prayer". Such is the natural judgment of
the clear French intellect on the wilfully obscure,
tormented and evasive intellect of India.

It would be interesting were it possible to illuminate
the criticism of Vedic religion by ascertaining which
hymns in the *Rig-Veda* are the most ancient, and
which are later. Could we do this, we might draw

---

[1] *Les Religions de l'Inde*, p. 21.

inferences as to the comparative antiquity of the religious ideas in the poems. But no such discrimination of relative antiquity seems to be within the reach of critics. M. Bergaigne thinks it impossible at present to determine the relative age of the hymns by any philological test. The ideas expressed are not more easily arrayed in order of date. We might think that the poems which contain most ceremonial allusions were the latest. But Mr. Max Müller says that "even the earliest hymns have sentiments worthy of the most advanced ceremonialists ".[1]

The first and oldest source of our knowledge of Indo-Aryan myths is the *Rig-Veda*, whose nature and character have been described. The second source is the *Atharva-Veda* with the Brahmanas. The peculiarity of the *Atharva* is its collection of magical incantations spells and fragments of folk-lore. These are often, doubtless, of the highest antiquity. Sorcery and the arts of medicine-men are earlier in the course of evolution than priesthood. We meet them everywhere among races who have not developed the institution of an order of priests serving national gods. As a collection, the *Atharva-Veda* is later than the *Rig-Veda*, but we need not therefore conclude that the *ideas* of the *Atharva* are " a later development of the more primitive ideas of the *Rig-Veda*". Magic is *quod semper, quod ubique, quod ab omnibus ;* the ideas of the *Atharva-Veda* are everywhere ; the peculiar notions of the *Rig-Veda* are the special property of an advanced and highly differentiated people. Even in the present collected shape,

[1] *History of Sanskrit Literature,* p. 556.

M. Barth thinks that many hymns of the *Atharva* are not much later than those of the *Rig-Veda.* Mr. Whitney, admitting the lateness of the *Atharva as a collection,* says, " This would not necessarily imply that the main body of the *Atharva* hymns were not already in existence when the compilation of the *Rig-Veda* took place ".[1] The *Atharva* refers to some poets of the *Rig* (as certain hymnists in the *Rig* also do) as earlier men. If in the *Rig* (as Weber says) " there breathes a lively natural feeling, a warm love of nature, while in the *Atharva,* on the contrary, there predominates an anxious apprehension of evil spirits and their magical powers," it by no means follows that this apprehension is of later origin than the lively feeling for Nature. Rather the reverse. There appears to be no doubt [2] that the style and language of the *Atharva* are later than those of the *Rig.* Roth, who recognises the change. in language and style, yet considers the *Atharva* " part of the old literature ".[3] He concludes that the *Atharva* contains many pieces which, " both by their style and ideas, are shown to be contemporary with the older hymns of the *Rig-Veda*". In religion, according to Muir,[4] the *Atharva* shows progress in the direction of monotheism in its celebration of Brahman, but it also introduces serpent-worship.

As to the *Atharva,* then, we are free to suppose, if we like, that the dark magic, the evil spirits, the incantations, are old parts of Indian, as of all other popular beliefs, though they come later into literature than the poetry about Ushas and the morality of Varuna.

[1] *Journal of the American Oriental Society,* iv. 253.
[2] Muir, ii. 446.   [3] *Ibid.,* ii. 448.   [4] *Ibid.,* ii. 451.

The same remarks apply to our third source of information, the Brahmanas. These are indubitably comments on the sacred texts very much more modern in form than the texts themselves. But it does not follow, and this is most important for our purpose, that the myths in the Brahmanas are all later than the Vedic myths or corruptions of the *Veda*. Muir remarks,[1] " The *Rig-Veda*, though the oldest collection, does not necessarily contain everything that is of the greatest age in Indian thought or tradition. We know, for example, that certain legends, bearing the impress of the highest antiquity, such as that of the deluge, appear first in the Brahmanas." We are especially interested in this criticism, because most of the myths which we profess to explain as survivals of savagery are narrated in the Brahmanas. If these are necessarily late corruptions of Vedic ideas, because the collection of the Brahmanas is far more modern than that of the *Veda*, our argument is instantly disproved. But if ideas of an earlier stratum of thought than the Vedic stratum may appear in a later collection, as ideas of an earlier stratum of thought than the Homeric appear in poetry and prose far later than Homer, then our contention is legitimate. It will be shown in effect that a number of myths of the Brahmanas correspond in character and incident with the myths of savages, such as Cahrocs and Ahts. Our explanation is, that these tales partly survived, in the minds perhaps of conservative local priesthoods, from the savage stage of thought, or were borrowed from aborigines in that stage, or were moulded in more

[1] Muir, iv. 450.

recent times on surviving examples of that wild early
fancy.

In the age of the Brahmanas the people have spread
southwards from the basin of the Indus to that of the
Ganges. The old sacred texts have begun to be scarcely
comprehensible. The priesthood has become much
more strictly defined and more rigorously constituted.
Absurd as it may seem, the Vedic metres, like the
Gayatri, have been personified, and appear as active
heroines of stories presumably older than this personification. The Asuras have descended from the rank
of gods to that of the heavenly opposition to Indra's
government; they are now a kind of fiends, and the
Brahmanas are occupied with long stories about the
war in heaven, itself a very ancient conception. Varuna
becomes cruel on occasion, and hostile. Prajapati
becomes the great mythical hero, and inherits the
wildest myths of the savage heroic beasts and birds.

The priests are now Brahmans, a hereditary divine
caste, who possess all the vast and puerile knowledge
of ritual and sacrificial minutiæ. As life in the opera
is a series of songs, so life in the Brahmanas is a
sequence of sacrifices. Sacrifice makes the sun rise
and set, and the rivers run this way or that.

The study of Indian myth is obstructed, as has been
shown, by the difficulty of determining the relative
dates of the various legends, but there are a myriad of
other obstacles to the study of Indian mythology. A
poet of the Vedas says, "The chanters of hymns go
about enveloped in mist, and unsatisfied with idle talk"

---

[1] *Rig-Veda*, x. 82, 7, but compare Bergaigne, *op. cit.*, iii. 72, "envel-
oppés de nuées et de murmures".

The ancient hymns are still "enveloped in mist," owing to the difficulty of their language and the variety of modern renderings and interpretations. The heretics of Vedic religion, the opponents of the orthodox commentators in ages comparatively recent, used to complain that the Vedas were simply nonsense, and their authors "knaves and buffoons". There are moments when the modern student of Vedic myths is inclined to echo this petulant complaint. For example, it is difficult enough to find in the *Rig-Veda* anything like a categoric account of the gods, and a description of their personal appearance. But in *Rig-Veda*, viii. 29, 1, we read of one god, "a youth, brown, now hostile, now friendly; a golden lustre invests him". Who is this youth? "Soma as the moon," according to the commentators. M. Langlois thinks the sun is meant. Dr. Aufrecht thinks the troop of Maruts (spirits of the storm), to whom, he remarks, the epithet "dark-brown, tawny" is as applicable as it is to their master, Rudra. This is rather confusing, and a mythological inquirer would like to know for certain whether he is reading about the sun or soma, the moon, or the winds.

To take another example; we open Mr. Max Müller's translation of the *Rig-Veda* at random, say at page 49. In the second verse of the hymn to the Maruts, Mr. Müller translates, "They who were born together, self-luminous, with the spotted deer (the clouds), the spears, the daggers, the glittering ornaments. I hear their whips almost close by, as they crack them in their hands; they gain splendour on their way." Now Wilson translates this passage, "Who, borne by spotted deer, were born self-luminous, with weapons,

war-cries and decorations.   I hear the cracking of
their whips in their hands, wonderfully inspiring
courage in the fight."   Benfey has, " Who with stags
and spears, and with thunder and lightning, self-
luminous, were born.   Hard by rings the crack of
their whip as it sounds in their hands; bright fare
they down in storm."   Langlois translates, " Just born
are they, self-luminous.   Mark ye their arms, their
decorations, their car drawn by deer ?   Hear ye their
clamour ? Listen ! 'tis the noise of the whip they hold
in their hands, the sound that stirs up courage in the
battle."   This is an ordinary example of the diversities
of Vedic translation.   It is sufficiently puzzling, nor is
the matter made more transparent by the variety of
opinion as to the meaning of the "deer" along with
which the Maruts are said (by some of the translators)
to have been born.   This is just the sort of passage on
which a controversy affecting the whole nature of Vedic
mythological ideas might be raised.   According to a
text in the *Yajur Veda*, gods, and men, and beasts,
and other matters were created from various portions
of the frame of a divine being named Prajapati.[1]   The
god Agni, Brahmans and the goat were born from the
mouth of Prajapati.   From his breast and arms came
the god Indra (sometimes spoken of as a ram), the
sheep, and of men the Rajanya.   Cows and gods called
Visvadevas were born together from his middle.   Are
we to understand the words "they who were born
together with the spotted deer" to refer to a myth of
this kind—a myth representing the Maruts and deer
as having been born at the same birth, as Agni came

[1] Muir, *Sanskrit Texts*, 2nd edit., i. 16.

with the goat, and Indra with the sheep? This is just
the point on which the Indian commentators were
divided.[1] Sayana, the old commentator, says, "The
legendary school takes them for deer with white spots;
the etymological school, for the many-coloured lines of
clouds". The modern legendary (or anthropological)
and etymological (or philological) students of mythology are often as much at variance in their attempts to
interpret the traditions of India.

Another famous, and almost comic, example of the
difficulty of Vedic interpretation is well known. In
Rig-Veda, x. 16, 4, there is a funeral hymn. Agni,
the fire-god, is supplicated either to *roast a goat* or to
warm the soul of the dead and convey it to paradise.
Whether the soul is to be thus comforted or the goat
is to be grilled, is a question that has mightily puzzled
Vedic doctors.[2] Professor Müller and M. Langlois are
all for "the immortal soul", the goat has advocates,
or had advocates, in Aufrecht, Ludwig and Roth. More
important difficulties of interpretation are illustrated by
the attitude of M. Bergaigne in *La Religion Védique*,
and his controversy with the great German lexico-
graphers. The study of mythology at one time made
the Vedas its starting-point. But perhaps it would be
wise to begin from something more intelligible, something less perplexed by difficulties of language and
diversities of interpretation.

In attempting to criticise the various Aryan myths,
we shall be guided, on the whole, by the character of
the myths themselves. Pure and elevated conceptions

[1] Max Müller, *Rig-Veda Sanhita*, trans., vol. i. p. 59.
[2] Muir, v. 217.

we shall be inclined to assign to a pure and elevated
condition of thought (though such conceptions do, recog-
nisably, occur in the lowest known religious strata), and
we shall make no difficulty about believing that Rishis
and singers capable of noble conceptions existed in an
age very remote in time, in a society which had many
of the features of a lofty and simple civilisation.   But
we shall not, therefore, assume that the hymns of
these Rishis are in any sense "primitive," or throw
much light on the infancy of the human mind, or on
the "origin" of religious and heroic myths.   Impure,
childish and barbaric conceptions, on the other
hand, we shall be inclined to attribute to an impure,
childish, and barbaric condition of thought; and we
shall again make no difficulty about believing that
ideas originally conceived when that stage of thought
was general have been retained and handed down to a
far later period.   This view of the possible, or rather
probable, antiquity of many of the myths preserved
in the Brahmanas is strengthened, if it needed
strengthening, by the opinion of Dr. Weber.[1]   "We
must indeed assume generally with regard to many of
those legends (in the Brahmanas of the *Rig-Veda*) that
they had already gained a rounded independent shape
in tradition before they were incorporated into the
Brahmanas; and of this we have frequent evidence in
the *distinctly archaic character of their language,*
compared with that of the rest of the text."

We have now briefly stated the nature and probable
relative antiquity of the evidence which is at the
disposal of Vedic mythologists.   The chief lesson we

[1] *History of Indian Literature*, English trans., p. 47.

would enforce is the necessity of suspending the judgment when the Vedas are represented as examples of primitive and comparatively pure and simple natural religion. They are not primitive; they are highly differentiated, highly complex, extremely enigmatic expressions of fairly advanced and very peculiar religious thought. They are not morally so very pure as has been maintained, and their purity, such as it is, seems the result of conscious reticence and wary selection rather than of primeval innocence. Yet the bards or editors have by no means wholly excluded very ancient myths of a thoroughly savage character. These will be chiefly exposed in the chapter on "Indo-Aryan Myths of the Beginnings of Things," which follows.

CHAPTER VIII.

INDIAN MYTHS OF THE ORIGIN OF THE WORLD AND OF MAN.

Comparison of Vedic and savage myths—The metaphysical Vedic account
   of the beginning of things—Opposite and savage fable of world made
   out of fragments of a man—Discussion of this hymn—Absurdities of
   Brahmanas—Prajapati, a Vedic Unkulunkulu or Qat—Evolutionary
   myths—Marriage of heaven and earth—Myths of *Puranas*, their
   savage parallels—Most savage myths are repeated in *Brahmanas*.

IN discussing the savage myths of the origin of the
world and of man, we observed that they were as
inconsistent as they were fanciful.   Among the fancies
embodied in the myths was noted the theory that the
world, or various parts of it, had been formed out of
the body of some huge non-natural being, a god, or
giant, or a member of some ancient mysterious race.
We also noted the myths of the original union of
heaven and earth, and their violent separation as
displayed in the tales of Greeks and Maoris, to which
may be added the Acagchemem nation in California.[1]
Another feature of savage cosmogonies, illustrated
especially in some early Slavonic myths, in Australian
legends, and in the faith of the American races, was
the creation of the world, or the recovery of a drowned
world by animals, as the raven, the dove and the

[1] Bancroft, v. 162.

coyote. The hatching of all things out of an egg
was another rude conception, chiefly noted among the
Finns. The Indian form occurs in the *Satapatha Brahmana*.[1] The preservation of the human race in the
Deluge, or the creation of the race after the Deluge,
was yet another detail of savage mythology; and for
many of these fancies we seemed to find a satisfactory origin in the exceedingly credulous and confused
state of savage philosophy and savage imagination.

The question now to be asked is, do the traditions
of the Aryans of India supply us with myths so
closely resembling the myths of Nootkas, Maoris
and Australians that we may provisionally explain
them as stories originally due to the invention of
savages? This question may be answered in the
affirmative. The Vedas, the Epics and the Puranas
contain a large store of various cosmogonic traditions
as inconsistent as the parallel myths of savages We
have an Aryan Ilmarinen, Tvashtri, who, like the
Finnish smith, forged "the iron vault of hollow
heaven" and the ball of earth.[2] Again, the earth is
said to have sprung, as in some Mangaian fables,
"from a being called Uttanapad".[3] Again, Brah-
manaspati, "blew the gods forth like a blacksmith,"
and the gods had a hand in the making of things.
In contrast with these childish pieces of anthropomorphism, we have the famous and sublime speculations of an often-quoted hymn.[4] It is thus that the
poet dreams of the days before being and non-being
began :—

[1] *Sacred Books of the East*, i. 216.   [2] Muir, v. 354.
[3] *Rig-Veda*, x. 72, 4.   [4] *Ibid.*, x. 126.

" There was then neither non-entity nor entity;
there was no atmosphere nor sky above. What
enveloped [all]? . . . Was it water, the profound
abyss ? Death was not then, nor immortality : there
was no distinction of day or night. That One breathed
calmly, self-supported ; then was nothing different
from it, or above it. In the beginning darkness
existed, enveloped in darkness. All this was un-
distinguishable water. That One which lay void and
wrapped in nothingness was developed by the power
of fervour. Desire first arose in It, which was the
primal germ of mind [and which] sages, searching
with their intellect, have discovered to be the bond
which connects entity with non-entity. The ray [or
cord] which stretched across these [worlds], was it
below or was it above ? There were there impreg-
nating powers and mighty forces, a self-supporting
principle beneath and energy aloft. Who knows ?
who here can declare whence has sprung, whence
this creation ? The gods are subsequent to the
development of this [universe] ; who then knows
whence it arose ? From what this creation arose, and
whether [any one] made it or not, he who in the
highest heaven is its ruler, he verily knows, or [even]
he does not know." [1]

Here there is a Vedic hymn of the origin of things,
from a book, it is true, supposed to be late, which is
almost, if not absolutely, free from mythological ideas.
The " self-supporting principle beneath and energy
aloft " may refer, as Dr. Muir suggests, to the father,
heaven above, and the mother, earth beneath. The

[1] Muir, *Sanskrit Texts*, 2nd edit., v. 357.

"bond between entity and non-entity" is sought in a favourite idea of the Indian philosophers, that of *tapas* or "fervour". The other speculations remind us, though they are much more restrained and temperate in character, of the metaphysical chants of the New Zealand priests, of the Zuñis, of *Popol Vuh*, and so on. These belong to very early culture.

What is the relative age of this hymn? If it could be proved to be the oldest in the Veda, it would demonstrate no more than this, that in time exceedingly remote the Aryans of India possessed a philosopher, perhaps a school of philosophers, who applied the minds to abstract speculations on the origin of things. It could not prove that mythological speculations had not preceded the attempts of a purer philosophy. But the date cannot be ascertained. Mr. Max Müller cannot go farther than the suggestion that the hymn is an expression of the *perennis quœdam philosophia* of Leibnitz. We are also warned that a hymn is not necessarily modern because it is philosophical.[1] Certainly that is true; the Zuñis, Maoris, and Mangaians exhibit amazing powers of abstract thought. We are not concerned to show that this hymn is late; but it seems almost superfluous to remark that ideas like those which it contains can scarcely be accepted as expressing man's earliest theory of the origin of all things. We turn from such ideas to those which the Aryans of India have in common with black men and red men, with far-off Finns and Scandinavians, Chaldæans, Haidahs, Cherokees, Murri and Maori, Mangaians and Egyptians.

[1] *History of Sanskrit Literature*, p. 568.

The next Vedic account of creation which we propose to consider is as remote as possible in character
from the sublime philosophic poem. In the *Purusha
Sukta*, the ninetieth hymn of the tenth book of the
Rig-Veda Sanhita, we have a description of the
creation of all things out of the severed limbs of a
magnified non-natural man, Purusha.   This conception
is of course that which occurs in the Norse myths of
the rent body of Ymir. Borr's sons took the body
of the Giant Ymir and of his flesh formed the
earth, of his blood seas and waters, of his bones
mountains, of his teeth rocks and stones, of his hair
all manner of plants, of his skull the firmament, of
his brains the clouds, and so forth.   In Chaldean
story, Bel cuts in twain the magnified non-natural
woman Omorca, and converts the halves of her body
into heaven and earth.   Among the Iroquois in North
America, Chokanipok was the giant whose limbs,
bones and blood furnished the raw material of many
natural objects; while in Mangaia portions of Ru,
in Egypt of Set and Osiris, in Greece of Dionysus
Zagreus were used in creating various things, such as
stones, plants and metals. The same ideas precisely
are found in the ninetieth hymn of the tenth book
of the *Rig-Veda*. Yet it is a singular thing that, in
all the discussions as to the antiquity and significance
of this hymn which have come under our notice, there
has not been one single reference made to parallel
legends among Aryan or non-Aryan peoples.   In
accordance with the general principles which guide
us in this work, we are inclined to regard any
ideas which are at once rude in character and widely

distributed, both among civilised and uncivilised
races, as extremely old, whatever may be the age of
the literary form in which they are presented. But
the current of learned opinions as to the date of the
Purusha Sukta, the Vedic hymn about the sacrifice of
Purusha and the creation of the world out of fragments of his body, runs in the opposite direction.
The hymn is not regarded as very ancient by most
Sanskrit scholars. We shall now quote the hymn,
which contains the data on which any theory as to its
age must be founded :—[1]

" Purusha has a thousand heads, a thousand eyes, a
thousand feet. On every side enveloping the earth,
he overpassed (it) by a space of ten fingers. Purusha
himself is this whole (universe), whatever is and whatever shall be. . . . When the gods performed a sacrifice
with Purusha as the oblation, the spring was its butter,
the summer its fuel, and the autumn its (accompanying)
offering. This victim, Purusha, born in the beginning,
they immolated on the sacrificial grass. With him the
gods, the Sadhyas, and the Rishis sacrificed. From that
universal sacrifice were provided curds and butter. It
formed those aerial (creatures) and animals both wild
and tame. From that universal sacrifice sprang the
the Ric and Saman verses, the metres and Yajush.
From it sprang horses, and all animals with two rows
of teeth ; kine sprang from it ; from it goats and sheep.
When (the gods) divided Purusha, into how many parts
did they cut him up ? What was his mouth ? What
arms (had he) ? What (two objects) are said (to have
been) his thighs and feet ? The Brahman was his

---

[1] *Rig-Veda,* x. 90 ; Muir, *Sanskrit Texts,* 2nd edit., i. 9.

mouth; the Rajanya was made his arms; the being
(called) the Vaisya, he was his thighs; the Sudra sprang
from his feet. The moon sprang from his soul (Mahas),
the sun from his eye, Indra and Agni from his mouth,
and Vaiyu from his breath   From his navel arose the
air, from his head the sky, from his feet the earth,
from his ear the (four) quarters; in this manner (the
gods) formed the world. When the gods, performing
sacrifice, bound Purusha as a victim, there were seven
sticks (stuck up) for it (around the fire), and thrice
seven pieces of fuel were made. With sacrifice the
gods performed the sacrifice. These were the earliest
rites. These great powers have sought the sky, where
are the former Sadhyas, gods."

The myth here stated is plain enough in its essential
facts. The gods performed a sacrifice with a gigantic
anthropomorphic being (Purusha = Man) as the victim.
Sacrifice is not found, as a rule, in the religions of the
most backward races of all; it is, relatively, an innova-
tion, as shall be shown later. His head, like the head
of Ymir, formed the sky, his eye the sun, animals
sprang from his body. The four castes are connected
with, and it appears to be implied that they sprang
from, his mouth, arms, thighs and feet. It is obvious
that this last part of the myth is subsequent to the
formation of castes. This is one of the chief arguments
for the late date of the hymn, as castes are not distinctly recognised elsewhere in the *Rig-Veda*. Mr.
Max Müller [1] believes the hymn to be " modern both
in its character and in its diction," and this opinion he
supports by philological arguments. Dr. Muir [2] says

[1] *Ancient Sanskrit Literature*, 570.   [2] *Sanskrit Texts*, 2nd edit., i. 12.

that the hymn "has every character of modernness both in its diction and ideas ". Dr Haug, on the other hand,[1] in a paper read in 1871, admits that the present form of the hymn is not older than the greater part of the hymns of the tenth book, and than those of the *Atharva Veda ;* but he adds, " The ideas which the hymn contains are certainly of a primeval antiquity. . . . In fact, the hymn is found in the *Yajur-Veda* among the formulas connected with human sacrifices, which were formerly practised in India." We have expressly declined to speak about " primeval antiquity," as we have scarcely any evidence as to the myths and mental condition for example, even of palæolithic man ; but we may so far agree with Dr. Haug as to affirm that the fundamental idea of the *Purusha Sukta,* namely, the creation of the world or portions of the world out of the fragments of a fabulous anthropomorphic being is common to Chaldeans, Iroquois, Egyptians, Greeks, Tinnehs, Mangaians and Aryan Indians. This is presumptive proof of the antiquity of the ideas which Dr. Muir and Mr. Max Müller think relatively modern. The savage and brutal character of the invention needs no demonstration. Among very low savages, for example, the Tinnehs of British North America, not a man, not a god, but a *dog,* is torn up, and the fragments are made into animals.[2] On the Paloure River a beaver suffers in the manner of Purusha. We may, for these reasons, regard the chief idea of the myth as extremely ancient—infinitely more ancient than the diction of the hymn.

As to the mention of the castes, supposed to be a

[1] *Sanskrit Texts*, 2nd edit., ii. 463. [2] Hearne's *Journey*, pp. 342-343.

comparatively modern institution, that is not an essential part of the legend. When the idea of creation out of a living being was once received it was easy to extend the conception to any institution, of which the origin was forgotten. The Teutonic race had a myth which explained the origin of the classes eorl, ceorl and thrall (earl, churl and slave). A South American people, to explain the different ranks in society, hit on the very myth of Plato, the legend of golden, silver and copper races, from which the ranks of society have descended. The Vedic poet, in our opinion, merely extended to the institution of caste a myth which had already explained the origin of the sun, the firmament, animals, and so forth, on the usual lines of savage thought. The *Purusha Sukta* is the type of many other Indian myths of creation, of which the following[1] one is extremely noteworthy. " Prajapati desired to propagate. He formed the Trivrit (*stoma*) from his mouth. After it were produced the deity Agni, the metre Gayatri, . . . of men the Brahman, of beasts the goat ; . . . from his breast, and from his arms he formed the Panchadasa (*stoma*). After it were created the God Indra, the Trishtubh metre, . . of men the Rajanya, of beasts the sheep. Hence they are vigorous, because they were created from vigour. From his middle he formed the Saptadasa (*stoma*). After it were created the gods called the Visvadevas, the Jagati metre, . . . of men the Vaisya, of beasts kine. Hence they are to be eaten, because they were created from the receptacle of food." The form in which we receive this myth is

---

[1] *Taittirya Sanhita,* or *Yajur-Veda,* vii. i. 1-4 ; Muir, 2nd edit., i. 15.

obviously later than the institution of caste and the technical names for metres. Yet surely any statement that kine " are to be eaten " must be older than the universal prohibition to eat that sacred animal the cow. Possibly we might argue that when this theory of creation was first promulgated, goats and sheep were forbidden food.[1]

Turning from the Vedas to the Brahmanas, we find a curiously savage myth of the origin of species.[2] According to this passage of the Brahmana, "this universe was formerly soul only, in the form of Purusha". He caused himself to fall asunder into two parts. Thence arose a husband and a wife. "He cohabited with her; from them men were born. She reflected, 'How does he, after having produced me from himself, cohabit with me? Ah, let me disappear.' She became a cow, and the other a bull, and he cohabited with her. From them kine were produced." After a series of similar metamorphoses of the female into all animal shapes, and a similar series of pursuits by the male in appropriate form, "in this manner pairs of all sorts of creatures down to ants were created". This myth is a parallel to the various Greek legends about the amours in bestial form of Zeus, Nemesis, Cronus, Demeter and other gods and goddesses. In the Brahmanas this myth is an explanation of the origin of species, and such an explanation as could scarcely have occurred to a civilised mind. In other

---

[1] Mr. M'Lennan has drawn some singular inferences from this passage, connecting, as it does, certain gods and certain classes of men with certain animals, in a manner somewhat suggestive of totemism (*Fornightly Review*), February, 1870.

[2] *Satapatha Brahmana*, xiv. 4, 2; Muir, 2nd edit., i. 25.

myths in the Brahmanas, Prajapati creates men from
his body, or rather the fluid of his body becomes a
tortoise, the tortoise becomes a man (*purusha*), with
similar examples of speculation.[1]

Among all these Brahmana myths of the part taken
by Prajapati in the creation or evoking of things, the
question arises who *was* Prajapati ? His *rôle* is that
of the great Hare in American myth; he is a kind of
demiurge, and his name means " The Master of Things
Created," like the Australian Biamban, " Master,"
and the American title of the chief Manitou,
" Master of Life ".[2] Dr. Muir remarks that, as the
Vedic mind advances from mere divine beings who
" reside and operate in fire " (Agni), " dwell and shine
in the sun" (Surya), or " in the atmosphere " (Indra),
towards a conception of deity, " the farther step would
be taken of speaking of the deity under such new
names as Visvakarman and Prajapati ". These are
" appellatives which do not designate any limited
functions connected with any single department of
Nature, but the more general and abstract notions of
divine power operating in the production and government of the universe ". Now the interesting point
is that round this new and abstract *name* gravitate
the most savage and crudest myths, exactly the myths
we meet among Hottentots and Nootkas. For example,
among the Hottentots it is Heitsi Eibib, among the
Huarochiri Indians it is Uiracocha, who confers,
by curse or blessing, on the animals their proper
attributes and characteristics.[3] In the *Satapatha*

[1] Similar tales are found among the *Khonds*.
[2] Bergaigne, iii. 40.   [3] Avila, *Fables of the Yncas*, p. 127.

Brahmana it is Prajapati who takes this part, that falls to rude culture-heroes of Hottentots and Huarochiris.[1] How Prajapati made experiments in a kind of state-aided evolution, so to speak, or evolution superintended and assisted from above, will presently be set forth.

In the Puranas creation is a process renewed after each kalpa, or vast mundane period Brahma awakes from his slumber, and finds the world a waste of water. Then, just as in the American myths of the coyote, and the Slavonic myths of the devil and the doves, a boar or a fish or a tortoise fishes up the world out of the waters. That boar fish, tortoise, or what not, is Brahma or Vishnu. This savage conception of the beginnings of creation in the act of a tortoise, fish, or boar is not first found in the Puranas, as Dr. Muir points out, but is indicated in the *Black Yajur Veda* and in the *Satapatha Brahmana*.[2] In the *Satapatha Brahmana*, xiv 1, 2, 11, we discover the idea, so common in savage myths—for example, in that of the Navajoes—that the earth was at first very small, a mere patch, and grew bigger after the animal fished it up. "Formerly this earth was only so large, of the size of a span. A boar called Emusha raised her up." Here the boar makes no pretence of being the incarnation of a god, but is a mere boar *sans phrase*, like the creative coyote of the Papogas and Chinooks, or the musk-rat of the Tacullies. This is a good example of the development of myths. Savages begin, as we saw, by mythically regarding various animals, spiders grasshoppers, ravens, eagles, cockatoos, as the creators

[1] English translation, ii. 361.   [2] Muir, 2nd edit., vol. i. p. 52.

or recoverers of the world.   As civilisation advances,
those animals still perform their beneficent functions,
but are looked on as gods in disguise   In time the
animals are often dropped altogether, though they
hold their place with great tenacity in the cosmogonic
traditions of the Aryans in India.   When we find the
Satapatha Brahmana alleging[1] " that all creatures are
descended from a tortoise," we seem to be among the
rude Indians of the Pacific Coast.   But when the
tortoise is identified with Aditya, and when Adityas
prove to be solar deities, sons of Aditi, and when
Aditi is recognised by Mr. Müller as the Dawn, we
see that the Aryan mind has not been idle, but has
added a good deal to the savage idea of the descent of
men and beasts from a tortoise.[2]

Another feature of savage myths of creation we
found to be the introduction of a crude theory of
evolution.   We saw that among the Potoyante tribe
of the Digger Indians, and among certain Australian
tribes, men and beasts were supposed to have been
slowly evolved and improved out of the forms first of
reptiles and then of quadrupeds.   In the mythologies of
the more civilised South American races, the idea of
the survival of the fittest was otherwise expressed.
The gods made several attempts at creation, and each
set of created beings proving in one way or other
unsuited to its environment, was permitted to die out
or degenerated into apes, and was succeeded by a set

[1] Muir, 2nd edit., vol. i. p. 54.

[2] See Ternaux Compans' *Nouvelles Annales des Voyages*, lxxxvi. p. 5.
For Mexican traditions, " Mexican and Australian Hurricane World's End,'
Bancroft, v. 64.

better adapted for survival.[1] In much the same way
the *Satapatha Brahmana*[2] represents mammals as
the last result of a series of creative experiments.
"Prajapati created living beings, which perished for
want of food   Birds and serpents perished thus.
Prajapati reflected, 'How is it that my creatures perish
after having been formed?' He perceived this: 'They
perish from want of food'. In his own presence he
caused milk to be supplied to breasts. He created
living beings, which, resorting to the breasts, were
thus preserved. These are the creatures which did not
perish."

The common myth which derives the world from
a great egg—the myth perhaps most familiar in its
Finnish shape—is found in the *Satapatha Brahmana*.[3]
"In the beginning this universe was waters, nothing
but waters. The waters desired: 'How can we be
reproduced?' So saying, they toiled, they performed
austerity. While they were performing austerity, a
golden egg came into existence. It then became a
year. . . . From it in a year a man came into existence, who was Prajapati. . . . He conceived progeny
in himself; with his mouth he created the gods."
According to another text,[4] "Prajapati took the form
of a tortoise". The tortoise is the same as Aditya.[5]

It is now time to examine the Aryan shape of the

---

[1] This myth is found in *Popol Vuh*. A Chinook myth of the same sort,
Bancroft, v. 95.

[2] ii. 5, 11 ; Muir, 2nd edit., i. 70.

[3] xi. 1, 6, 1 ; Muir, *Journal of Royal Asiatic Society*, 1863.

[4] *Satapatha Brahmana*, vii. 4, 3, 5.

[5] *Aitareya Brahmana*, iii. 34 (11, 219), a very discreditable origin of
species.

widely spread myth about the marriage of heaven and
earth, and the fortunes of their children We have
already seen that in New Zealand heaven and earth
were regarded as real persons, of bodily parts and
passions, united in a secular embrace. We shall apply
the same explanation to the Greek myth of Gaea and
of the mutilation of Cronus. In India, Dyaus (heaven)
answers to the Greek Uranus and the Maori Rangi,
while Prithivi (earth) is the Greek Gaea, the Maori
Papa. In the Veda, heaven and earth are constantly
styled "parents"; [1] but this we might regard as a
mere metaphorical expression, still common in poetry.
A passage of the *Aitareya Brahmana,* however,
retains the old conception, in which there was nothing
metaphorical at all. [2] These two worlds, heaven and
earth, were once joined. Subsequently they were
separated (according to one account, by Indra, who
thus plays the part of Cronus and of Tane Mahuta).
"Heaven and earth," says Dr. Muir, "are regarded as
the parents not only of men, but of the gods also, as
appears from the various texts where they are desig-
nated by the epithet Devapatre, 'having gods for their
children '." By men in an early stage of thought this
myth was accepted along with others in which heaven
and earth were regarded as objects created by one of
their own children, as by Indra, [3] who " stretched them
out like a hide," who, like Atlas, "sustains and up-
holds them " ; [4] or, again, Tvashtri, the divine smith,
wrought them by his craft ; or, once more, heaven and
earth sprung from the head and feet of Purusha. In

[1] Muir, v. 22.   [2] iv. 27 ; Haug, ii. 308.
[3] *Rig-Veda,* viii. 6, 5.   [4] *Ibid.,* iii. 32, 8.

short, if any one wished to give an example of that
recklessness of orthodoxy or consistency which is the
mark of early myth, he could find no better example
than the Indian legends of the origin of things.
Perhaps there is not one of the myths current among
the lower races which has not its counterpart in the
Indian Brahmanas.   It has been enough for us to give
a selection of examples.

CHAPTER IX.

GREEK MYTHS OF THE ORIGIN OF THE WORLD AND MAN.

The Greeks practically civilised when we first meet them in Homer—
Their mythology, however, is full of repulsive features—The hypothesis that many of these are savage survivals—Are there other examples
of such survival in Greek life and institutions?—Greek opinion was
constant that the race had been savage—Illustrations of savage survival
from Greek law of homicide, from magic, religion, human sacrifice,
religious art, traces of totemism, and from the mysteries—Conclusion :
that savage survival may also be expected in Greek myths.

THE Greeks, when we first make their acquaintance
in the Homeric poems, were a cultivated people, dwelling, under the government of royal families, in small
city states. This social condition they must have
attained by 1000 B.C., and probably much earlier.
They had already a long settled past behind them, and
had no recollection of any national migration from the
" cradle of the Aryan race ". On the other hand, many
tribes thought themselves earth-born from the soil
of the place where they were settled. The Maori
traditions prove that memories of a national migration
may persist for several hundred years among men
ignorant of writing. Greek legend, among a far more
civilised race, only spoke of occasional foreign settlers
from Sidon, Lydia, or Egypt. The Homeric Greeks
were well acquainted with almost all the arts of life,

though it is not absolutely certain that they could
write, and certainly they were not addicted to reading.
In war they fought from chariots, like the Egyptians
and Assyrians ; they were bold seafarers, being accustomed to harry the shores even of Egypt, and they had
large commercial dealings with the people of Tyre and
Sidon. In the matter of religion they were comparatively free and unrestrained. Their deities, though,
in myth, capricious in character, might be regarded
in many ways as " making for righteousness ". They
protected the stranger and the suppliant ; they sanctioned the oath, they frowned on the use of poisoned
arrows ; marriage and domestic life were guarded by
their good-will ; they dispensed good and evil fortune,
to be accepted with humility and resignation among
mortals.

The patriarchal head of each family performed the
sacrifices for his household, the king for the state, the
ruler of Mycenæ, Agamemnon, for the whole Achæan
host encamped before the walls of Troy. At the same
time, prophets, like Calchas, possessed considerable
influence, due partly to an hereditary gift of second-
sight, as in the case of Theoclymenus,[1] partly to acquired
professional skill in observing omens, partly to the
direct inspiration of the gods. The oracle at Delphi,
or, as it is called by Homer, Pytho, was already famous,
and religion recognised, in various degrees, all the gods
familiar to the later cult of Hellas. In a people so
advanced, so much in contact with foreign races and
foreign ideas, and so wonderfully gifted by nature with
keen intellect and perfect taste, it is natural to expect,

---

[1] *Odyssey*, xx. 354.

if anywhere, a mythology almost free from repulsive elements, and almost purged of all that we regard as survivals from the condition of savagery. But while Greek mythology is richer far than any other in beautiful legend, and is thronged with lovely and majestic forms of gods and goddesses, nymphs and oreads ideally fair, none the less a very large proportion of its legends is practically on a level with the myths of Maoris, Thlinkeets, Cahrocs and Bushmen.

This is the part of Greek mythology which has at all times excited most curiosity, and has been made the subject of many systems of interpretation. The Greeks themselves, from almost the earliest historical ages, were deeply concerned either to veil or explain away the blasphemous horrors of their own "sacred chapters," poetic traditions and temple legends. We endeavour to account for these as relics of an age of barbarism lying very far behind the time of Homer—an age when the ancestors of the Greeks either borrowed, or more probably developed for themselves, the kind of myths by which savage peoples endeavour to explain the nature and origin of the world and all phenomena.

The correctness of this explanation, resting as it does on the belief that the Greeks were at one time in the savage status, might be demonstrated from the fact that not only myths, but Greek life in general, and especially Greek ritual, teemed with surviving examples of institutions and of manners which are found everywhere among the most backward and barbarous races. It is not as if only the myths of Greece retained this rudeness, or as if the Greeks supposed themselves to have been always civilised.

The whole of Greek life yields relics of savagery
when the surface is excavated ever so slightly. Moreover, that the Greeks, as soon as they came to reflect
on these matters at all, believed themselves to have
emerged from a condition of savagery is undeniable.
The poets are entirely at one on this subject with
Moschion, a writer of the school of Euripides. "The
time hath been, yea, it *hath* been," he says, "when
men lived like the beasts, dwelling in mountain caves,
and clefts unvisited of the sun. . . . Then they
broke not the soil with ploughs nor by aid of iron, but
the weaker man was slain to make the supper of the
stronger," and so on.[1] This view of the savage origin
of mankind was also held by Aristotle:[2] "It is probable that the first men, whether they were produced
by the earth (earth-born) or survived from some deluge,
were on a level of ignorance and darkness".[3] This
opinion, consciously held and stated by philosophers
and poets, reveals itself also in the universal popular
Greek traditions that men were originally ignorant of
fire, agriculture, metallurgy and all the other arts and
conveniences of life, till they were instructed by ideal
culture-heroes, like Prometheus, members of a race
divine or half divine. A still more curious Athenian
tradition (preserved by Varro) maintained, not only
that marriage was originally unknown, but that, as
among Australians and some Red Indians, the family
name descended through the mother, and kinship was
reckoned on the female side before the time of Cecrops.[4]

[1] Moschion ; *cf.* Preller, *Ausgewählte Aufsätze*, p. 206.
[2] *Politics*, ii. 8-21 ; Plato, *Laws*, 667-680.
[3] Compare Horace, *Satires*, i. 3, 99 ; Lucretius, v. 923.
[4] Suidas, *s.v.* " Prometheus"; Augustine, *De Civitate Dei*, xviii. 9

While Greek opinion, both popular and philosophical, admitted, or rather asserted, that savagery lay in the background of the historical prospect, Greek institutions retained a thousand birth-marks of savagery It is manifest and undeniable that the Greek criminal law, as far as it effected murder, sprang directly from the old savage blood-feud.[1] The Athenian law was a civilised modification of the savage rule that the kindred of a slain man take up his blood-feud. Where homicide was committed *within* the circle of blood relationship, as by Orestes, Greek religion provided the Erinnyes to punish an offence which had, as it were, no human avenger. The precautions taken by murderers to lay the ghost of the slain man were much like those in favour among the Australians. The Greek cut off the extremities of his victim, the tips of the hands and feet, and disposed them neatly beneath the arm-pits of the slain man.[2] In the same spirit, and for the same purpose, the Australian black cuts off the thumbs of his dead enemy, that the ghost too may be mutilated and prevented from throwing at him with a ghostly spear. We learn also from Apollonius Rhodius and his scholiast that Greek murderers used thrice to suck in and spit out the gore of their victims, perhaps with some idea of thereby partaking of their blood, and so, by becoming members of their kin, putting it beyond the power of the ghosts to avenge themselves. Similar ideas inspire the world-wide savage custom of making an artificial " blood

[1] Duncker, *History of Greece*, Engl. transl., vol. ii. p. 129.

[2] See "Arm-pitting in Ancient Greece," in the *American Journal of Philology*, October, 1885, where a discussion of the familiar texts in Æschylus and Apollonius Rhodius will be found.

brotherhood" by mingling the blood of the contracting parties. As to the ceremonies of cleansing from blood-guiltiness among the Greeks, we may conjecture that these too had their primitive side ; for Orestes, in the *Eumenides*, maintains that he has been purified of his mother's slaughter by sufficient blood of swine. But this point will be illustrated presently, when we touch on the mysteries.

Ritual and myth, as might be expected, retained vast masses of savage rites and superstitious habits and customs. To be "in all things too superstitious," too full of *deisidaimonia*, was even in St. Paul's time the characteristic of the Athenians. Now superstition, or *deisidaimonia*, is defined by Theophrastus,[1] as " cowardice in regard to the supernatural" ($\delta\epsilon\iota\lambda\iota\alpha \pi\rho\grave{o}s \tau\grave{o} \delta\alpha\iota\mu\acute{o}\nu\iota\upsilon\nu$). This "cowardice" has in all ages and countries secured the permanence of ritual and religious traditions. Men have always argued, like one of the persons in M. Renan's play, *Le Prêtre de Némi*, that "l'ordre du monde depend de l'ordre des rites qu'on observe". The familiar endurable sequence of the seasons of spring, and seed-sowing, and harvest depend upon the due performance of immemorial religious acts. "In the mystic deposits," says Dinarchus, "lies the safety of the city."[2] What the "mystic deposits" were nobody knows for certain, but they must have been of very archaic sanctity, and occur among the Arunta and the Pawnees.

Ritual is preserved because it preserves *luck*. Not only among the Romans and the Brahmans, with their endless minute ritual actions, but among such lower

[1] *Characters.*   [2] *Ap.* Hermann, *Lehrbuch*, p. 41 ; *Aglaophamus*, 965.

races as the Kanekas of New Caledonia, the efficacy of religious functions is destroyed by the slightest accidental infraction of established rules.[1] The same timid conservatism presides over myth, and in each locality the mystery-plays, with their accompanying narratives, preserved inviolate the early forms of legend. Myth and ritual do not admit of being argued about. " C'était le rite établi. Ce n'était pas plus absurde qu'autre chose," says the conservative in M. Renan's piece, defending the mode of appointment of

> The priest who slew the slayer,
> And shall himself be slain.

Now, if the rites and myths preserved by the timorousness of this same "cowardice towards the supernatural" were originally evolved in the stage of savagery, savage they would remain, as it is impious and dangerous to reform them till the religion which they serve perishes with them These relics in Greek ritual and faith are very commonly explained as due to Oriental influences, as things borrowed from the dark and bloody superstitions of Asia. But this attempt to save the native Greek character for "blitheness " and humanity must not be pushed too far.[2] It must be remembered that the cruder and wilder sacrifices and legends of Greece were strictly *local ;* that they were attached to these ancient temples, old altars, barbarous *xoana,* or wooden idols, and rough fetish

---

[1] Thus the watchers of the dead in New Caledonia are fed by the sorcerer with a mess at the end of a very long spoon, and should the food miss the mouth, all the ceremonies have to be repeated. This detail is from Mr. J. J. Atkinson.

[2] Claus, *De Antiq. Form. Dianæ,* 6, 7, 16.

stones, in which Pausanias found the most ancient relics of Hellenic theology. This is a proof of their antiquity and a presumption in favour of their freedom from foreign influence. Most of these things were survivals from that dimly remembered prehistoric age in which the Greeks, not yet gathered into city states, lived in villages or kraals, or pueblos, as we should translate κατὰ κώμας, if we were speaking of African or American tribes. In that stage the early Greeks must have lacked both the civic and the national or Panhellenic sentiment; their political unit was the clan, which, again, answered in part to the totem kindred of America, or Africa, or Australia.[1] In this stagnant condition they could not have made acquaintance with the many creeds of Semitic and other alien peoples on the shores of the Levant.[2] It was later, when Greece had developed the city life of the heroic age, that her adventurous sons came into close contact with Egypt and Phœnicia.

In the colonising time, still later—perhaps from 900 B.C. downwards—the Greeks, settled on sites whence they had expelled Sidonians or Sicanians, very naturally continued, with modifications, the worship of such gods as they found already in possession. Like the Romans, the Greeks easily recognised

---

[1] As C. O. Müller judiciously remarks: "The scenes of nine-tenths of the Greek myths are laid in *particular districts of Greece*, and they speak of the primeval inhabitants, of the lineage and adventures of native heroes. They manifest an accurate acquaintance with individual localities, which, at a time when Greece was neither explored by antiquaries, nor did geographical handbooks exist, could be possessed only by the inhabitants of these localities." Müller gives, as examples, myths of bears more or less divine. *Scientific Mythology*, pp. 14, 15.

[2] Compare Claus, *De Dianæ Antiquissima Natura*, p. 3.

their own deities in the analogous members of foreign
polytheistic systems. Thus we can allow for alien
elements in such gods and goddesses as Zeus Asterios,
as Aphrodite of Cyprus or Eryx, or the many-breasted
Ephesian Artemis, whose monstrous form had its exact
analogue among the Aztecs in that many-breasted
goddess of the maguey plant whence beer was made.
To discern and disengage the borrowed factors in the
Hellenic Olympus by analysis of divine names is a
task to which comparative philology may lawfully
devote herself; but we cannot so readily explain by
presumed borrowing from without the rude *xoana* of
the ancient local temples, the wild myths of the local
legends, the *sacra* which were the exclusive property
of old-world families, Butadæ or Eumolpidæ. These
are clearly survivals from a stage of Greek culture
earlier than the city state, earlier than the heroic age
of the roving Greek Vikings, and far earlier than the
Greek colonies. They belong to that conservative
and immobile period when the tribe or clan, settled in
its scattered kraals, lived a life of agriculture, hunting
and cattle-breeding, engaged in no larger or more
adventurous wars than border feuds about women or
cattle. Such wars were on a humbler scale than even
Nestor's old fights with the Epeians; such adventures
did not bring the tribe into contact with alien religions.
If Sidonian merchantmen chanced to establish a factory
near a tribe in this condition, their religion was not
likely to make many proselytes.

These reasons for believing that most of the wilder
element in Greek ritual and myth was native may be
briefly recapitulated, as they are often overlooked.

The more strange and savage features meet us in *local* tales and practices, often in remote upland temples and chapels. There they had survived from the society of the *village* status, before villages were gathered into *cities*, before Greeks had taken to a roving life, or made much acquaintance with distant and maritime peoples.

For these historical reasons, it may be assumed that the *local* religious antiquities of Greece, especially in upland districts like Arcadia and Elis, are as old, and as purely national, as free from foreign influences as any Greek institutions can be. In these rites and myths of true folk-lore and *Volksleben*, developed before Hellas won its way to the pure Hellenic stage, before Egypt and Phœnicia were familiar, should be found that common rude element which Greeks share with the other races of the world, and which was, to some extent, purged away by the genius of Homer and Pindar, *pii vates et Phœbo digna locuti.*

In proof of this local conservatism, some passages collected by K. F. Hermann in his *Lehrbuch der Griechischen Antiquitäten* [1] may be cited. Thus Isocrates writes,[2] " This was all their care, neither to destroy any of the ancestral rites, nor to add aught beyond what was ordained ". Clemens Alexandrinus reports that certain Thessalians worshipped storks, " *in accordance with use and wont* ".[3] Plato lays down the very " law of least change " which has been described. " Whether the legislator is establishing a new state or restoring an old and decayed one, in

---

[1] Zweiter Theil, 1858. [2] *Areop.,* **30.**
[3] Clem. Alex., Oxford, 1715, i. 34.

respect of gods and temples, . . . if he be a man of sense, he will *make no change in anything* which the oracle of Delphi, or Dodona, or Ammon has sanctioned, in whatever manner." In this very passage Plato[1] speaks of rites " derived from Tyrrhenia or Cyprus " as falling within the later period of the Greek *Wanderjähre*. On the high religious value of things antique, Porphyry wrote in a late age, and when the new religion of Christ was victorious, " Comparing the new sacred images with the old, we see that the old are more simply fashioned, yet are held divine, but the new, admired for their elaborate execution, have less persuasion of divinity,"—a remark anticipated by Pausanias, " The statues Dædalus wrought are quainter to the outward view, yet there shows forth in them somewhat supernatural ".[2] So Athenæus[3] reports of a visitor to the shrine of Leto in Delos, that he expected the ancient statue of the mother of Apollo to be something remarkable, but, unlike the pious Porphyry, burst out laughing when he found it a shapeless wooden idol. These idols were dressed out, fed and adorned as if they had life.[4] It is natural that myths dating from an age when Greek gods resembled Polynesian idols should be as rude as Polynesian myths. The tenacity of *local* myth is demonstrated by Pausanias, who declares that even in the highly civilised Attica the Demes retained legends different from those of the central city—the legends, probably, which were current before the villages were "synœcised" into Athens.[5]

---

[1] *Laws*, v. 738.   [2] *De. Abst.*, ii. 18 ; Paus., ii. 4, 5.   [3] xiv. 2.
[4] Hermann, *op. cit.*, p. 94, note 10.   [5] Pausanias, i. 14, 6.

It appears, then, that Greek ritual necessarily preserves matter of the highest antiquity, and that the oldest rites and myths will probably be found, not in the Panhellenic temples, like that in Olympia, not in the *national* poets, like Homer and Sophocles, but in the *local* fanes of early tribal gods, and in the *local* mysteries, and the myths which came late, if they came at all, into literary circulation. This opinion is strengthened and illustrated by that invaluable guide-book of the artistic and religious pilgrim written in the second century after our era by Pausanias. If we follow him, we shall find that many of the ceremonies, stories and idols which he regarded as oldest are analogous to the idols and myths of the contemporary backward races. Let us then, for the sake of illustrating the local and savage survivals in Greek religion, accompany Pausanias in his tour through Hellas.

In Christian countries, especially in modern times, the contents of one church are very like the furniture of another church; the functions in one resemble those in all, though on the Continent some shrines still retain relics and customs of the period when local saints had their peculiar rites. But it was a very different thing in Greece. The pilgrim who arrived at a temple never could guess what oddity or horror in the way of statues, sacrifices, or stories might be prepared for his edification. In the first place, there were *human sacrifices*. These are not familiar to low savages, if known to them at all. Probably they were first offered to barbaric royal ghosts, and thence transferred to gods. In the town of Salamis, in

Cyprus, about the date of Hadrian, the devout might have found the priest slaying a human victim to Zeus,—an interesting custom, instituted, according to Lactantius, by Teucer, and continued till the age of the Roman Empire.[1]

At Alos in Achaia Phthiotis, the stranger *might* have seen an extraordinary spectacle, though we admit that the odds would have been highly against his chance of witnessing the following events. As the stranger approaches the town-hall, he observes an elderly and most respectable citizen strolling in the same direction. The citizen is so lost in thought that apparently he does not notice where he is going. Behind him comes a crowd of excited but silent people, who watch him with intense interest. The citizen reaches the steps of the town-hall, while the excitement of his friends behind increases visibly. Without thinking, the elderly person enters the building. With a wild and un-Aryan howl, the other people of Alos are down on him, pinion him, wreathe him with flowery garlands, and lead him to the temple of Zeus Laphystius, or "The Glutton," where he is solemnly sacrificed on the altar. This was the custom of the good Greeks of Alos whenever

[1] Euseb., *Præp. Ev.*, iv. 17, mentions, among peoples practising human sacrifices, Rhodes, Salamis, Heliopolis, Chios, Tenedos, Lacedæmon, Arcadia and Athens; and, among gods thus honoured, Hera, Athene, Cronus, Ares, Dionysus, Zeus and Apollo. For Dionysus the Cannibal, Plutarch, *Themist.*, 13; Porphyr., *Abst.*, ii. 55. For the sacrifice to Zeus Laphystius, see Grote, i. c. vi., and his array of authorities, especially Herodotus, vii. 197. Clemens Alexandrinus (i. 36) mentions the Messenians, to Zeus; the Taurians, to Artemis, the folk of Pella, to Peleus and Chiron; the Cretans, to Zeus; the Lesbians, to Dionysus. Geusius *de Victimis Humanis* (1699) may be consulted.

a descendant of the house of Athamas entered the
Prytaneion. Of course the family were very careful, as a rule, to keep at a safe distance from the
forbidden place. " What a sacrifice for Greeks ! " as
the author of the *Minos*[1] says in that dialogue which
is incorrectly attributed to Plato. " He cannot get
out except to be sacrificed," says Herodotus, speaking
of the unlucky descendant of Athamas. The custom
appears to have existed as late as the time of the
scholiast on Apollonius Rhodius.[2]

Even in the second century, when Pausanias visited
Arcadia, he found what seem to have been human
sacrifices to Zeus. The passage is so very strange and
romantic that we quote a part of it.[3] " The Lycæan
hill hath other marvels to show, and chiefly this :
thereon there is a grove of Zeus Lycæus, wherein may
men in nowise enter ; but if any transgresses the law
and goes within, he must die within the space of one
year. This tale, moreover, they tell, namely, that
whatsoever man or beast cometh within the grove
casts no shadow, and the hunter pursues not the deer
into that wood, but, waiting till the beast comes forth
again, sees that it has left its shadow behind. And
on the highest crest of the whole mountain there is a
mound of heaped-up earth, the altar of Zeus Lycæus,
and the more part of Peloponnesus can be seen from
that place. And before the altar stand two pillars
facing the rising sun, and thereon golden eagles of yet
more ancient workmanship. And on this altar they
sacrifice to Zeus in a manner that may not be spoken,

[1] 315, c. ; Plato, *Laws*, vi. 782, c.
[2] *Argonautica*, vii. 197. [3] Pausanias, viii. 2.

and little liking had I to make much search into this
matter. *But let it be as it is, and as it hath been
from the beginning.*" The words "as it hath been
from the beginning" are ominous and significant, for
the traditional myths of Arcadia tell of the human
sacrifices of Lycaon, and of men who, tasting the meat
of a mixed sacrifice, put human flesh between their
lips unawares.[1] This aspect of Greek religion, then,
is almost on a level with the mysterious cannibal
horrors of "Voodoo," as practised by the secret societies
of negroes in Hayti. But concerning these things, as
Pausanias might say, it is little pleasure to inquire.

Even where men were not sacrificed to the gods,
the tourist among the temples would learn that these
bloody rites had once been customary, and ceremonies
existed by way of commutation. This is precisely
what we find in Vedic religion, in which the empty
form of sacrificing a man was gone through, and the
origin of the world was traced to the fragments of a
god sacrificed by gods.[2] In Sparta was an altar of
Artemis Orthia, and a wooden image of great rudeness
and antiquity—so rude indeed, that Pausanias, though
accustomed to Greek fetish-stones, thought it must be
of barbaric origin. The story was that certain people
of different towns, when sacrificing at the altar,
were seized with frenzy and slew each other. The
oracle commanded that the altar should be sprinkled
with human blood. Men were therefore chosen by
lot to be sacrificed, till Lycurgus commuted the offering,

[1] Plato, *Rep.*, viii. 565, d.   This rite occurs in some African coronation
ceremonies.

[2] The *Purusha Sukhta*, in *Rig-Veda*, x. 90.

and sprinkled the altar with the blood of boys who
were flogged before the goddess. The priestess holds
the statue of the goddess during the flogging, and if
any of the boys are but lightly scourged, the image
becomes too heavy for her to bear.

The Ionians near Anthea had a temple of Artemis
Triclaria, and to her it had been customary to sacrifice
yearly a youth and maiden of transcendent beauty. In
Pausanias's time the human sacrifice was commuted.
He himself beheld the strange spectacle of living beasts
and birds being driven into the fire to Artemis Laphria,
a Calydonian goddess, and he had seen bears rush back
among the ministrants ; but there was no record that
any one had ever been hurt by these wild beasts.[1]
The bear was a beast closely connected with Artemis.
and there is some reason to suppose that the goddess
had herself been a she-bear or succeeded to the cult of
a she-bear in the morning of time.[2]

It may be believed that where symbolic human
sacrifices are offered, that is, where some other victim
is slain or a dummy of a man is destroyed, and where
legend maintains that the sacrifice was once human,
there men and women were originally the victims.
Greek ritual and Greek myth were full of such tales
and such commutations.[3] In Rome, as is well known,
effigies of men called Argives were sacrificed.[4] As an
example of a beast-victim given in commutation,
Pausanias mentions[5] the case of the folk of Potniæ,
who were compelled once a year to offer to Dionysus

[1] Paus., vii. 18, 19.　　[2] See "Artemis," *postea*.
[3] See Hermann, *Alterthümer.*, ii. 159-161, for abundant examples.
[4] Plutarch, *Quæst. Rom.* 32.　　[5] ix. 8, 1.

a boy in the bloom of youth. But the sacrifice was commuted for a goat.

These commutations are familiar all over the world. Even in Mexico, where human sacrifices and ritual cannibalism were daily events, Quetzalcoatl was credited with commuting human sacrifices for blood drawn from the bodies of the religious. In this one matter even the most conservative creeds and the faiths most opposed to change sometimes say with Tartuffe:—

> Le ciel défend, de vrai, certains contentements,
> Mais on trouve avec lui des accommodements.

Though the fact has been denied (doubtless without reflection), the fact remains that the Greeks offered human sacrifices. Now what does this imply? Must it be taken as a survival from barbarism, as one of the proofs that the Greeks had passed through the barbaric status?

The answer is less obvious than might be supposed. Sacrifice has two origins. First, there are *honorific* sacrifices, in which the ghost or god (or divine beast, if a divine beast be worshipped) is offered the food he is believed to prefer. This does not occur among the lowest savages. To carnivorous totems, Garcilasso says, the Indians of Peru offered themselves. The feeding of sacred mice in the temples of Apollo Smintheus is well known. Secondly, there are expiatory or *piacular* sacrifices, in which the worshipper, as it were, fines himself in a child, an ox, or something else that he treasures. The latter kind of sacrifice (most common in cases of crime done or suspected within the circle of kindred) is not necessarily barbaric, except in its cruelty. An example is the Attic

Thargelia, in which two human scape-goats annu-
ally bore "the sins of the congregation," and were
flogged, driven to the sea with figs tied round their
necks, and burned.[1]

The institution of human sacrifice, then, whether the
offering be regarded as food, or as a gift to the god of
what is dearest to man (as in the case of Jephtha's
daughter), or whether the victim be supposed to carry
on his head the sins of the people, does not necessarily
date from the period of savagery. Indeed, sacrifice
flourishes most, not among savages, but among advancing barbarians. It would probably be impossible to
find any examples of human sacrifices of an expiatory
or piacular character, any sacrifices at all, among
Australians, or Andamanese, or Fuegians. The notion
of presenting food to the supernatural powers, whether
ghosts or gods, is relatively rare among savages.[2]
The terrible Aztec banquets of which the gods were
partakers are the most noted examples of human
sacrifices with a purely cannibal origin. Now there
is good reason to guess that human sacrifices with no
other origin than cannibalism survived even in ancient
Greece. "It may be conjectured," writes Professor
Robertson Smith,[3] "that the human sacrifices offered
to the Wolf Zeus (Lycæus) in Arcadia were originally
cannibal feasts of a Wolf tribe. The first participants
in the rite were, according to later legend, changed
into wolves ; and in later times [4] at least one fragment

---

[1] Compare the Marseilles human sacrifice, *Petron.*, 141 ; and for the
Thargelia, Tsetzes, *Chiliads*, v. 736 ; Hellad. in *Photius*, p. 1590 f. and
Harpoc. *s. v.*

[2] Jevons, *Introduction to the Science of Religion*, pp. 161, 199.

[3] *Encyc. Brit.*, *s. v.* "Sacrifice".   [4] Plato, *Rep.*, viii. 565, D.

of the human flesh was placed among the sacrificial
portions derived from other victims, and the man who
ate it was believed to become a were-wolf." [1]   It is
the almost universal rule with cannibals not to eat
members of their own stock, just as they do not eat
their own totem.   Thus, as Professor Robertson Smith
says, when the human victim is a captive or other
foreigner, the human sacrifice may be regarded as a
survival of cannibalism.   Where, on the other hand,
the victim is a fellow tribesman, the sacrifice is expiatory or piacular.

Among Greek cannibal gods we cannot fail to
reckon the so-called "Cannibal Dionysus," and probably the Zeus of Orchomenos, Zeus Laphystius, who
is explained by Suidas as "the Glutton Zeus".   The
cognate verb ($\lambda\alpha\phi\acute{\nu}\sigma\sigma\epsilon\iota\nu$) means "to eat with mangling
and rending," "to devour gluttonously".   By Zeus
Laphystius, then, men's flesh was gorged in this
distressing fashion.

The evidence of human sacrifice (especially when it
seems not piacular, but a relic of cannibalism) raises
a presumption that Greeks had once been barbarians.
The presumption is confirmed by the evidence of early
Greek religious art.

When his curiosity about human sacrifices was
satisfied, the pilgrim in Greece might turn his attention
to the statues and other representations of the gods.
He would find that the modern statues by famous
artists were beautiful anthropomorphic works in
marble or in gold and ivory.   It is true that the faces
of the ancient gilded Dionysi at Corinth were smudged

[1] Paus., viii. 2.

all over with cinnabar, like fetish-stones in India or
Africa.[1] As a rule, however, the statues of historic
times were beautiful representations of kindly and
gracious beings. The older works were stiff and rigid
images, with the lips screwed into an unmeaning smile.
Older yet were the bronze gods, made before the art
of soldering was invented, and formed of beaten
plates joined by small nails. Still more ancient were
the wooden images, which probably bore but a slight
resemblance to the human frame, and which were
often mere "stocks".[2] Perhaps once a year were
shown the very early gods, the Demeter with the
horse's head, the Artemis with the fish's tails, the
cuckoo Hera, whose image was of pear-wood, the
Zeus with three eyes, the Hermes, made after the
fashion of the pictures on the walls of sacred caves
among the Bushmen. But the oldest gods of all, says
Pausanias repeatedly, were rude stones in the temple
or the temple precinct. In Achæan Pharæ he found
some thirty squared stones, named each after a god.
" Among all the Greeks in the oldest times rude stones
were worshipped in place of statues." The superstitious man in Theophrastus's Characters used to
anoint the sacred stones with oil. The stone which
Cronus swallowed in mistake for Zeus was honoured
at Delphi, and kept warm with wool wrappings.
There was another sacred stone among the Trœzenians,
and the Megarians worshipped as Apollo a stone cut
roughly into a pyramidal form. The Argives had
a big stone called Zeus Kappotas. The Thespians

---

[1] Pausanias, ii. 2.
[2] Clemens Alex., *Protrept.* (Oxford, 1715), p. 41.

worshipped a stone which they called Eros; "their oldest idol is a rude stone".[1] It is well known that the original fetish-stone has been found *in situ* below the feet of the statue of Apollo in Delos. On this showing, then, the religion of very early Greeks in Greece was not unlike that of modern Negroes. The artistic evolution of the gods, a remarkably rapid one after a certain point, could be traced in every temple. It began with the rude stone, and rose to the wooden idol, in which, as we have seen, Pausanias and Porphyry found such sanctity. Next it reached the hammered bronze image, passed through the archaic marbles, and culminated in the finer marbles and the chryselephantine statues of Zeus and Athena. But none of the ancient sacred objects lost their sacredness. The oldest were always the holiest idols; the oldest of all were stumps and stones, like savage fetish-stones.

Another argument in favour of the general thesis that savagery left deep marks on Greek life in general, and on myth in particular, may be derived from survivals of totemism in ritual and legend. The following instances need not necessarily be accepted, but it may be admitted that they are precisely the traces which totemism would leave had it once existed, and then waned away on the advance of civilisation.[2]

---

[1] Gill, *Myths of South Pacific*, p. 60. Compare a god, which proved to be merely pumice-stone, and was regarded as the god of winds and waves, having been drifted to Puka-Puka. Offerings of food were made to it during hurricanes.

[2] The argument to be derived from the character of the Greek γένος as a modified form of the totem-kindred is too long and complex to be put forward here. It is stated in *Custom and Myth*, "The History of the Family," in M'Lennan's *Studies in Early History*, and is assumed, if not proved, in *Ancient Society* by the late Mr. Lewis Morgan.

That Greeks in certain districts regarded with religious reverence certain plants and animals is beyond dispute. That some stocks even traced their lineage to beasts will be shown in the chapter on Greek Divine Myths, and the presumption is that these creatures, though explained as incarnations and disguises of various gods, were once totems *sans phrase*, as will be inferred from various examples. Clemens Alexandrinus, again, after describing the animal-worship of the Egyptians, mentions cases of zoolatry in Greece.[1] The Thessalians revered storks, the Thebans weasels, and the myth ran that the weasel had in some way aided Alcmena when in labour with Heracles. In another form of the myth the weasel was the foster-mother of the hero.[2] Other Thessalians, the Myrmidons, claimed descent from the ant and revered ants. The religious respect paid to mice in the temple of Apollo Smintheus, in the Troad, Rhodes, Gela, Lesbos and Crete is well known, and a local tribe were alluded to as Mice by an oracle. The god himself, like the Japanese harvest-god, was represented in art with a mouse at his foot, and mice, as has been said, were fed at his shrine.[3] The Syrians, says Clemens Alexandrinus, worship doves and fishes, as the Elians worship Zeus.[4] The people of Delphi adored the wolf,[5] and the Samians the sheep. The Athenians had a hero whom they worshipped in the shape of a wolf.[6] A remarkable

---

[1] *Op. cit.*, i. 34.　　　　[2] Scholiast on *Iliad*, xix. 119.

[3] Ælian, *H. A.*, xii. 5 ; Strabo, xiii. 604. Compare "Apollo and the Mouse, *Custom and Myth*, pp. 103-120.

[4] Lucian, *De Deâ Syriâ.*　　　　[5] Ælian, *H. A.*, xii. 40.

[6] Harpocration, δεκάζειν. Compare an address to the wolf-hero, "whc delights in the flight and tears of men," in Aristophanes, *Vespœ*, 389.

testimony is that of the scholiast on Apollonius Rhodius,
ii. 124. "The wolf," he says, "was a beast held in
honour by the Athenians, and whosoever slays a wolf
collects what is needful for its burial." The burial of
sacred animals in Egypt is familiar. An Arab tribe
mourns over and solemnly buries all dead gazelles.[1]
Nay, flies were adored with the sacrifice of an ox near
the temple of Apollo in Leucas.[2] Pausanias (iii. 22) mentions certain colonists who were guided by a hare to a
site where the animal hid in a myrtle-bush. They therefore adore the myrtle, καὶ τὸ δένδρον ἔτι ἐκείνην σέβουσι
τὴν μυρσίνην. In the same way a Carian stock, the
Ioxidæ, revered the asparagus.[3] A remarkable example
of descent mythically claimed from one of the lower
animals is noted by Otfried Müller.[4] Speaking of the
swan of Apollo, he says, " That deity was worshipped,
according to the testimony of the *Iliad*, in the Trojan
island of Tenedos. There, too, was Tennes honoured as
the ἥρως ἐπώνυμος of the island. Now his father was
called Cycnus (the swan) in an oft-told and romantic
legend.[5] . . . The swan, therefore, as father to the
chief hero on the Apolline island, stands in distinct
relation to the god, who is made to come forward still
more prominently from the fact that Apollo himself
is also called father of Tennes. I think we can
scarcely fail to recognise a mythus which was local
at Tenedos. . . . The fact, too, of calling the swan,
instead of Apollo, the father of a hero, demands
altogether a simplicity and boldness of fancy which
are far more ancient than the poems of Homer."

[1] Robertson Smith, *Kinship in Early Arabia*, pp. 195-204.
[2] Ælian, xi. 8.   [3] Plutarch, *Theseus*, 14.
[4] *Proleg.*, Engl. trans., p. 204.   [5] [Canne on Conon, 28.]

Had Müller known that this "simplicity and boldness of fancy" exist to-day, for example, among the
Swan tribe of Australia, he would probably have
recognised in Cycnus a survival from totemism. The
fancy survives again in Virgil's Cupavo, "with swan's
plumes rising from his crest, the mark of his father's
form ".[1] Descent was claimed, not only from a swan
Apollo, but from a dog Apollo.

In connection with the same set of ideas, it is
pointed out that several γένη, or stocks, had eponymous heroes, in whose names the names of the ancestral
beast apparently survived. In Attica the Crioeis have
their hero (Crio, "Ram"), the Butadæ have Butas
("Bullman"), the Ægidæ have Ægeus ("Goat"), and
the Cynadæ, Cynus ("Dog"). Lycus, according to
Harporcation (s. v.) has his statue in the shape of a
wolf in the Lyceum. "The general facts that certain
animals might not be sacrificed to certain gods" (at
Athens the Ægidæ introduced Athena, to whom no
goat might be offered on the Acropolis, while she herself wore the goat skin, ægis), "while, on the other
hand, each deity demanded particular victims, explained by the ancients themselves in certain cases
to be hostile animals, find their natural explanation"
in totemism.[2] Mr. Evelyn Abbott points out, however,
that the names Ægeus, Aegae, Aegina, and others, may
be connected with the goat only by an old *volks-
etymologie*, as on coins of Aegina in Achaea. The real
meaning of the words may be different. Compare

---

[1] *Æneid*, x. 187.

[2] Some apparent survivals of totemism in ritual will be found in the
chapter on Greek gods, especially Zeus, Dionysus, and Apollo.

αἰγιαλός, the sea-shore. Mr. J. G. Frazer does not, at present, regard totemism as proved in the case of Greece.[1]

As final examples of survivals from the age of barbarism in the religion of Greece, certain features in the *Mysteries* may be noted. Plutarch speaks of " the eating of raw flesh, and tearing to pieces of victims, as also fastings and beatings of the breast, and again in many places abusive language at the sacrifices, and other mad doings ". The mysteries of Demeter, as will appear when her legend is criticised, contained one element all unlike these " mad doings " ; and the evidence of Sophocles, Pindar, Plutarch and others demonstrate that religious consolations were somehow conveyed in the Eleusinia. But Greece had many other local mysteries, and in several of these it is undeniable the Greeks acted much as contemporary Australians, Zuñis and Negroes act in their secret initiations which, however, also inculcate moral ideas of considerable excellence. Important as these analogies are, they appear to have escaped the notice of most mythologists. M. Alfred Maury, however, in *Les Religions de la Grèce*, published in 1857, offers several instances of hidden rites, common to Hellas and to barbarism.

There seem in the mysteries of savage races to be two chief purposes. There is the intention of giving to the initiated a certain sacred character, which puts them in close relation with gods or demons, and there is the introduction of the young to complete or advancing

---

[1] See his *Golden Bough*, an alternative explanation of these animals in connection with "The Corn Spirit".

manhood, and to full participation in the savage
Church with its ethical ideas. The latter ceremonies
correspond, in short, to confirmation, and they are
usually of a severe character, being meant to test by
fasting (as Plutarch says) and by torture (as in the
familiar Spartan rite) the courage and constancy of
the young braves. The Greek mysteries best known
to us are the Thesmophoria and the Eleusinia. In
the former the rites (as will appear later) partook of
the nature of savage " medicine " or magic, and were
mainly intended to secure fertility in husbandry and
in the family. In the Eleusinia the purpose was the
purification of the initiated, secured by ablutions and
by standing on the " ram's-skin of Zeus," and after
purifications the *mystæ* engaged in sacred dances, and
were permitted to view a miracle play representing
the sorrows and consolations of Demeter. There was
a higher element, necessarily obscure in nature. The
chief features in the whole were purifications, dancing,
sacrifice and the representation of the miracle play.
It would be tedious to offer an exhaustive account of
savage rites analogous to these mysteries of Hellas.
Let it suffice to display the points where Greek found
itself in harmony with Australian, and American, and
African practice. These points are : (1) mystic dances;
(2) the use of a little instrument, called *turndun* in
Australia, whereby a roaring noise is made, and the
profane are warned off; (3) the habit of daubing
persons about to be initiated with clay or anything
else that is sordid, and of washing this off, apparently
by way of showing that old guilt is removed and a
new life entered upon ; (4) the performances with

serpents may be noticed, while the "mad doings" and
"howlings" mentioned by Plutarch are familiar to
every reader of travels in uncivilised countries; (5)
ethical instruction is communicated.

First, as to the mystic dances, Lucian observes : [1]
"You cannot find a single ancient mystery in which
there is not dancing . . . This much all men know,
that most people say of the revealers of the mysteries
that they ' dance them out ' " (ἐξορχεῖσθαι). Clemens
of Alexandria uses the same term when speaking of
his own "appalling revelations".[2] So closely connected
are mysteries with dancing among savages, that when
Mr. Orpen asked Qing, the Bushman hunter, about
some doctrines in which Qing was not initiated, he
said : "Only the initiated men of that dance know
these things". To "dance" this or that means to
be acquainted with this or that myth, which is represented in a dance or *ballet d'action* [3] (σὺν ῥυθμῷ
καὶ ὀρχήσει μυεῖσθαι). So widely distributed is the
practice, that Acosta, in an interesting passage, mentions it as familiar to the people of Peru before and
after the Spanish conquest. The text is a valuable
instance of survival in religion. When they were
converted to Christianity the Peruvians detected the
analogy between our sacrament and their mysteries,
and they kept up as much as possible of the old rite
in the new ritual. Just as the *mystæ* of Eleusis practised chastity, abstaining from certain food, and above
all from beans, before the great Pagan sacrament, so
did the Indians. "To prepare themselves all the

[1] Περὶ Ὀρχήσεως, chap. xv. 277.   [2] *Ap.* Euseb., *Præp. Ev.*, ii. 3, 6.
[3] *Cape Monthly Magazine*, July, 1874.

people fasted two days, during which they did neyther
company with their wives, nor eate any meate with
salt or garlicke, nor drink any chic. . . . And although the Indians now forbeare to sacrifice beasts
or other things publikely, which cannot be hidden
from the Spaniardes, yet doe they still use many ceremonies that have their beginnings from these feasts
and auntient superstitions, for at this day do they
covertly make their feast of Ytu at the daunces of the
feast of the Sacrament. Another feast falleth almost
at the same time, whereas the Christians observe the
solempnitie of the holy Sacrament, which *doth resemble it in some sort, as in dauncing, singing and
representations."* [1] The holy "daunces" at Seville
are under Papal disapproval, but are to be kept up,
it is said, till the peculiar dresses used in them are
worn out. Acosta's Indians also had "garments which
served only for this feast". It is superfluous to
multiply examples of the dancing, which is an invariable feature of savage as of Greek mysteries.

2. The Greek and savage use of the *turndun*, or
bribbun of Australia in the mysteries is familiar to
students. This fish-shaped flat board of wood is tied
to a string, and whirled round, so as to cause a peculiar
muffled roar. Lobeck quotes from the old scholia on
Clemens Alexandrinus, published by Bastius in annota-
tions on St. Gregory, the following Greek description of
the *turndun*, the "bull-roarer" of English country lads,
the Gaelic *srannam* : [2] "κῶνος ξυλάριον οὗ ἐξῆπται τὸ

---

[1] Acosta, *Historie of the Indies*, book v. chap. xxviii. London, 1604.

[2] Pronounced *strantham*. For this information I am indebted to my
friend Mr. M'Allister, schoolmaster at St. Mary's Loch.

σπαρτίον καὶ ἐν ταῖς τελεταῖς ἐδονεῖτο ἵνα ῥοιζῇ ". " The
conus was a little slab of wood, tied to a string, and
whirled round in the mysteries to make a whirring
noise." As the mystic uses of the *turndun* in Australia, New Zealand, New Mexico and Zululand have
elsewhere been described at some length (*Custom and
Myth*, pp. 28-44), it may be enough to refer the reader
to the passage. Mr. Taylor has since found the instrument used in religious mysteries in West Africa, so
it has now been tracked almost round the world. That
an instrument so rude should be employed by Greek
and Australians on mystic occasions is in itself a remarkable coincidence. Unfortunately, Lobeck, who
published the Greek description of the *turndun*
(*Aglaophamus*, 700), was unacquainted with the
modern ethnological evidence.

3. The custom of plastering the initiated over with
clay or filth was common in Greek as in barbaric
mysteries. Greek examples may be given first.
Demosthenes accuses Æschines of helping his mother
in certain mystic rites, aiding her, especially, by be-
daubing the initiate with clay and bran.[1] Harpocration explains the term used (ἀπομάττων) thus :
" Daubing the clay and bran on the initiate, to explain
which they say that the Titans when they attacked
Dionysus daubed themselves over with chalk, but
afterwards, for ritual purposes, clay was used ". It
may be urged with some force that the mother of
Æschines introduced foreign, novel and possibly
savage rites. But Sophocles, in a fragment of his lost

---

[1] *De Coronâ*, 313.

play, the *Captives*, uses the term in the same ritual sense—

στρατοῦ καθαρτὴς κἀπομαγμάτων ἴδρις.

The idea clearly was that by cleansing away the filth plastered over the body was symbolised the pure and free condition of the initiate. He might now cry in the mystic chant—

ἔφυγον κάκον, εὗρον ἄμεινον.
Worst have I fled, better have I found.

That this was the significance of the daubing with clay in Greek mysteries and the subsequent cleansing seems quite certain. We are led straight to this conclusion by similar rites, in which the purpose of mystically cleansing was openly put forward. Thus Plutarch, in his essay on superstition, represents the guilty man who would be purified actually rolling in clay, confessing his misdeeds, and then sitting at home purified by the cleansing process (περιματ-τόμενος).[1] In another rite, the cleansing of blood-guiltiness, a similar process was practised. Orestes, after killing his mother, complains that the Eumenides do not cease to persecute him, though he has been "purified by blood of swine".[2] Apollonius says that the red hand of the murderer was dipped in the blood of swine and then washed.[3] Athenæus describes a similar unpleasant ceremony.[4] The blood of whelps was apparently used also, men being first daubed

---

[1] So Hermann, *op. cit.*, 133.   [2] *Eumenides*, 273.

[3] *Argonautica*, iv. 693.

[4] ix. 78. Hermann, from whom the latter passages are borrowed, also quotes the evidence of a vase published by Feuerbach, *Lehrbuch*, p. 131, with other authorities.

with it and then washed clean.[1]　The word περιμάτ-
τουσι is again the appropriate ritual term.　Such
rites Plutarch calls ῥυπαραὶ ἀγνεῖαι, "filthy purifications ".[2]　If daubing with dirt is known to have
been a feature of Greek mysteries, it meets us everywhere among savages.　In *O-Kee-Pa*, that curiously
minute account of the Mandan mysteries, Catlin writes
that a portion of the frame of the initiate was "covered
with clay, which the operator took from a wooden
bowl, and with his hand plastered unsparingly over ".
The fifty young men waiting for initiation "were
naked and entirely covered with clay of various
colours ".[3]　The custom is mentioned by Captain John
Smith in Virginia.　Mr. Winwood Reade found it in
Africa, where, as among the Mandans and Spartans,
cruel torture and flogging accompanied the initiation
of young men.[4]　In Australia the evidence for daubing the initiate is very abundant.[5]　In New Mexico,
the Zuñis stole Mr. Cushing's black paint, as considering it even better than clay for religious daubing.[6]

4. Another savage rite, the use of serpents in Greek
mysteries, is attested by Clemens Alexandrinus and
by Demosthenes (*loc. cit.*).　Clemens says the snakes
were caressed in representations of the loves of Zeus
in serpentine form.　The great savage example is
that of " the snake-dance of the Moquis," who handle
rattle-snakes in the mysteries without being harmed.[7]

[1] Plutarch, *Quaest. Rom.*, 68.　　　[2] *De Superstitione*, chap. xii.
[3] *O-Kee-Pa*, London, 1867, p. 21.
[4] *Savage Africa*, case of Mongilomba ; Pausanias, iii. 15.
[5] Brough Smyth, i. 60.　　　[6] *Custom and Myth*, p. 40.
[7] *The Snake-Dance of the Moquis*.　By Captain John G. Bourke,
London, 1884.

The dance is partly totemistic, partly meant, like the
Thesmophoria, to secure the fertility of the lands of
the Moquis of Arizonas.   The *turndum* or ῥόμβος is
employed.   Masks are worn, as in the rites of Demeter
Cidiria in Arcadia.[1]

5. This last point of contact between certain Greek
and certain savage mysteries is highly important.
The argument of Lobeck, in his celebrated work
Aglaophamus, is that the Mysteries were of no great
moment in religion.   Had he known the evidence as
to savage initiations, he would have been confirmed
in his opinion, for many of the singular Greek rites
are clearly survivals from savagery.   But was there
no more truly religious survival ?   Pindar is a very
ancient witness that things of divine import were
revealed.   " Happy is he who having seen these
things goes under the hollow earth.   He knows the
end of life, and the god-given beginning." [2]   Sophocles
" chimes in," as Lobeck says, declaring that the initiate
alone *live* in Hades, while other souls endure all evils.
Crinagoras avers that even in life the initiate live
secure, and in death are the happier.   Isagoras
declares that about the end of life and all eternity
they have sweet hopes.

Splendida testimonia, cries Lobeck.   He tries
to minimise the evidence, remarking that Isocrates
promises the very same rewards to all who live justly
and righteously.   But why not, if to live justly and
righteously was part of the teaching of the mysteries
of Eleusis ?   Cicero's evidence, almost a translation of
the Greek passages already cited, Lobeck dismisses as

---

[1] Pausanias, viii. 16.   [2] Fragm., cxvi., 128 H. p. 265.

purely rhetorical.[1] Lobeck's method is rather cavalier.
Pindar and Sophocles meant something of great
significance.

Now we have acknowledged savage survivals of
ugly rites in the Greek mysteries. But it is only
fair to remember that, in certain of the few savage
mysteries of which we know the secret, righteousness
of life and a knowledge of good are inculcated. This is
the case in Australia, and in Central Africa, where to be
" uninitiated " is equivalent to being selfish.[2] Thus it
seems not improbable that consolatory doctrines were
expounded in the Eleusinia, and that this kind of
sermon or exhortation was no less a survival from
savagery than the daubing with clay, and the ρόμβος,
and other wild rites.

We have now attempted to establish that in Greek
law and ritual many savage customs and usages did
undeniably survive. We have seen that both philosophical and popular opinion in Greece believed in a past
age of savagery. In law, in religion, in religious art,
in custom, in human sacrifice, in relics of totemism,
and in the mysteries, we have seen that the Greeks
retained plenty of the usages now found among the
remotest and most backward races. We have urged
against the suggestion of borrowing from Egypt or
Asia that these survivals are constantly found in *local*
and tribal religion and rituals, and that consequently
they probably date from that remote prehistoric past
when the Greeks lived in village settlements. It may
still doubtless be urged that all these things are

---

[1] *De Legibus* ii. 14 ; *Aglaophamus*, pp. 69-74.
[2] *Making of Religion*, pp. 193-197, 235.

Pelasgic, and were the customs of a race settled in
Hellas before the arrival of the Homeric Achæans,
and Dorians, and Argives, who, on this hypothesis,
adopted and kept up the old savage Pelasgian ways
and superstitions. It is impossible to prove or disprove
this belief, nor does it affect our argument. We allege
that all Greek life below the surface was rich in institutions now found among the most barbaric peoples.
These institutions, whether borrowed or inherited,
would still be part of the legacy left by savages to
cultivated peoples. As this legacy is so large in
custom and ritual, it is not unfair to argue that
portions of it will also be found in myths. It is now
time to discuss Greek myths of the origin of things,
and decide whether they are or are not analogous in
ideas to the myths which spring from the wild and
ignorant fancy of Australians, Cahrocs, Nootkas and
Bushmen.

CHAPTER X.

GREEK COSMOGONIC MYTHS.

Nature of the evidence—Traditions of origin of the world and man—
Homeric, Hesiodic and Orphic myths—Later evidence of historians,
dramatists, commentators—The Homeric story comparatively pure—
The story in Hesiod, and its savage analogues—The explanations of
the myth of Cronus, modern and ancient—The Orphic cosmogony—
Phanes and Prajapati—Greek myths of the origin of man—Their
savage analogues.

THE authorities for Greek cosmogonic myth are extremely various in date, character and value. The
most ancient texts are the *Iliad* and the poems attributed to Hesiod. The *Iliad*, whatever its date, whatever
the place of its composition, was intended to please a
noble class of warriors. The Hesiodic poems, at least the
Theogony, have clearly a didactic aim, and the intention
of presenting a systematic and orderly account of the
divine genealogies. To neither would we willingly
attribute a date much later than the ninth century of
our era, but the question of the dates of all the epic
and Hesiodic poems, and even of their various parts, is
greatly disputed among scholars. Yet it is nowhere
denied that, however late the present form of some of
the poems may be, they contain ideas of extreme
antiquity. Although the Homeric poems are usually
considered, on the whole, more ancient than those

attributed to Hesiod,[1] it is a fact worth remembering that the notions of the origin of things in Hesiod are much more savage and (as we hold) much more archaic than the opinions of Homer.

While Hesiod offers a complete theogony or genealogy of deities and heroes, Homer gives no more than hints and allusions to the stormy past of the gods. It is clear, however, that his conception of that past differed considerably from the traditions of Hesiod. However we explain it, the Homeric mythology (though itself repugnant to the philosophers from Xenophanes downwards) is much more mild, pure and humane than the mythology either of Hesiod or of our other Greek authorities. Some may imagine that Homer retains a clearer and less corrupted memory than Hesiod possessed of an original and authentic " divine tradition ". Others may find in Homer's comparative purity a proof of the later date of his epics in their present form, or may even proclaim that Homer was a kind of Cervantes, who wished to laugh the gods away. There is no conceivable or inconceivable theory about Homer that has not its advocates. For ourselves, we hold that the divine genius of Homer, though working in an age distant rather than "early," selected instinctively the purer mythical materials, and burned away the coarser dross of antique legend, leaving little but the gold which is comparatively refined.

We must remember that it does not follow that

---

[1] Grote assigns his *Theogony* to circ. 750 A.D. The *Theogony* was taught to boys in Greece, much as the Church Catechism and Bible are taught in England; Æschines in *Ctesiph.*, 135, p. 73. Libanius, 400 years after Christ (i. 502-509, iv. 874).

any mythical ideas are later than the age of Homer
because we first meet them in poems of a later date.
We have already seen that though the *Brahmanas* are
much later in date of compilation than the *Veda*, yet
a tradition which we first find in the *Brahmanas* may
be older than the time at which the *Veda* was compiled.   In the same way, as Mr. Max Müller observes,
" we know that certain ideas which we find in later
writers do not occur in Homer.   But it does not
follow at all that such ideas are all of later growth or
possess a secondary character.   One myth may have
belonged to one tribe ; one god may have had his chief
worship in one locality ; and our becoming acquainted
with these through a later poet does not in the least
prove their later origin." [1]

After Homer and Hesiod, our most ancient authorities for Greek cosmogonic myths are probably the
so-called Orphic fragments.   Concerning the dates
and the manner of growth of these poems volumes of
erudition have been compiled.   As Homer is silent
about Orpheus (in spite of the position which the
mythical Thracian bard acquired as the inventor of
letters and magic and the father of the mysteries),
it has been usual to regard the Orphic ideas as of late
introduction.   We may agree with Grote and Lobeck
that these ideas and the ascetic " Orphic mode of
life " first acquired importance in Greece about the
time of Epimenides, or, roughly speaking, between 620
and 500 B.C.[2]   That age certainly witnessed a curious
growth of superstitious fears and of mystic ceremonies

[1] *Hibbert Lectures*, pp. 130, 131.
[2] Lobeck, *Aglaophamus*, i. 317 ; Grote, iii. 86.

intended to mitigate spiritual terrors. Greece was
becoming more intimately acquainted with Egypt and
with Asia, and was comparing her own religion with
the beliefs and rites of other peoples. The times and
the minds of men were being prepared for the clear
philosophies that soon "on Argive heights divinely
sang". Just as, when the old world was about to
accept Christianity, a deluge of Oriental and barbaric
superstitions swept across men's minds, so immediately
before the dawn of Greek philosophy there came an
irruption of mysticism and of spiritual fears. We
may suppose that the Orphic poems were collected,
edited and probably interpolated, in this dark hour of
Greece. "To me," says Lobeck, "it appears that the
verses may be referred to the age of Onomacritus,
an age curious in the writings of ancient poets, and
attracted by the allurements of mystic religions."
The style of the surviving fragments is sufficiently
pure and epic; the strange unheard of myths are
unlike those which the Alexandrian poets drew from
fountains long lost.[1] But how much in the Orphic
myths is imported from Asia or Egypt, how much is
the invention of literary forgers like Onomacritus,
how much should be regarded as the first guesses of
the physical poet-philosophers, and how much is truly
ancient popular legend recast in literary form, it is
impossible with certainty to determine.

We must not regard a myth as necessarily late or
necessarily foreign because we first meet it in an
"Orphic composition". If the myth be one of the
sort which encounter us in every quarter, nay, in

---

[1] *Aglaophamus*, i. 611.

every obscure nook of the globe, we may plausibly
regard it as ancient.   If it bear the distinct marks of
being a Neo-platonic *pastiche*, we may reject it without hesitation.   On the whole, however, our Orphic
authorities can never be quoted with much satisfaction.
The later sources of evidence for Greek myths are not
of great use to the student of cosmogonic legend,
though invaluable when we come to treat of the
established dynasty of gods, the heroes and the
"culture-heroes".   For these the authorities are the
whole range of Greek literature, poets, dramatists,
philosophers, critics, historians and travellers.   We
have also the notes and comments of the scholiasts or
commentators on the poets and dramatists.   Sometimes these annotators only darken counsel by their
guesses.   Sometimes perhaps, especially in the scholia
on the *Iliad* and *Odyssey*, they furnish us with a
precious myth or popular *märchen* not otherwise
recorded.   The regular professional *mythographi*,
again, of whom Apollodorus (150 B.C.) is the type,
compiled manuals explanatory of the myths which
were alluded to by the poets.   The scholiasts and
mythographi often retain myths from lost poems and
lost plays.   Finally, from the travellers and historians
we occasionally glean examples of the tales ("holy
chapters," as Mr. Grote calls them) which were narrated
by priests and temple officials to the pilgrims who
visited the sacred shrines.

These "chapters" are almost invariably puerile,
savage and obscene.   They bear the stamp of extreme
antiquity, because they never, as a rule, passed through
the purifying medium of literature.   There were

many myths too crude and archaic for the purposes of poetry and of the drama. These were handed down from local priest to local priest, with the inviolability of sacred and immutable tradition. We have already given a reason for assigning a high antiquity to the local temple myths. Just as Greeks lived in villages before they gathered into towns, so their gods were gods of villages or tribes before they were national deities. The local myths are those of the archaic village state of " culture," more ancient, more savage, than literary narrative. Very frequently the local legends were subjected to the process of allegorical interpretation, as men became alive to the monstrosity of their unsophisticated meaning. Often they proved too savage for our authorities, who merely remark, " Concerning this a certain holy chapter is told," but decline to record the legend. In the same way missionaries, with mistaken delicacy, often refuse to repeat some savage legend with which they are acquainted.

The latest sort of testimony as to Greek myths must be sought in the writings of the heathen apologists or learned Pagan defenders of Paganism in the first centuries during Christianity, and in the works of their opponents, the fathers of the Church. Though the fathers certainly do not understate the abominations of Paganism, and though the heathen apologists make free use of allegorical (and impossible) interpretations, the evidence of both is often useful and important. The testimony of ancient art, vases, statues, pictures and the descriptions of these where they no longer survive, are also of service and interest.

After this brief examination of the sources of our knowledge of Greek myth, we may approach the Homeric legends of the origin of things and the world's beginning. In Homer these matters are only referred to incidentally. He more than once calls Oceanus (that is, the fabled stream which flows all round the world, here regarded as a *person*) "the origin of the gods," "the origin of all things".[1] That Ocean is considered a person, and that he is not an allegory for water or the aqueous element, appears from the speech of Hera to Aphrodite : "I am going to visit the limits of the bountiful earth, and Oceanus, father of the gods, and mother Tethys, who reared me duly and nurtured me in their halls, when far-seeing Zeus imprisoned Cronus beneath the earth and the unvintaged sea".[2] Homer does not appear to know Uranus as the father of Cronus, and thus the myth of the mutilation of Uranus necessarily does not occur in Homer. Cronus, the head of the dynasty which preceded that of Zeus, is described [3] as the son of Rhea, but nothing

[1] *Iliad*, xiv. 201, 302, 246.

[2] In reading what Homer and Hesiod report about these matters, we must remember that all the forces and phenomena are conceived of by them as *persons*. In this regard the archaic and savage view of all things as personal and human is preserved. "I maintain," says Grote, "moreover, fully the character of these great divine agents as persons, which is the light in which they presented themselves to the Homeric or Hesiodic audience. Uranus, Nyx, Hypnos and Oneiros (heaven, night, sleep and dream) are persons just as much as Zeus or Apollo. To resolve them into mere allegories is unsafe and unprofitable. We then depart from the point of view of the original hearers without acquiring any consistent or philosophical point of view of our own." This holds good though portions of the Hesiodic genealogies are distinctly poetic allegories cast in the mould of the ancient personal theory of things.

[3] *Iliad*, xv. 187.

is said of his father. The passage contains the account
which Poseidon himself chose to give of the war in
heaven : " Three brethren are we, and sons of Cronus
whom Rhea bare—Zeus and myself, and Hades is the
third, the ruler of the folk in the under-world. And
in three lots were all things divided, and each drew a
domain of his own." Here Zeus is the *eldest* son of
Cronus. Though lots are drawn at hazard for the
property of the father (which we know to have been
customary in Homer's time), yet throughout the *Iliad*
Zeus constantly claims the respect and obedience due
to him by right of primogeniture.[1] We shall see that
Hesiod adopts exactly the opposite view. Zeus is the
youngest child of Cronus. His supremacy is an
example of *jüngsten recht*, the wide-spread custom
which makes the youngest child the heir in chief.[2]
But how did the sons of Cronus come to have his
property in their hands to divide ? By right of successful rebellion, when " Zeus imprisoned Cronus
beneath the earth and the unvintaged sea ". With
Cronus in his imprisonment are the Titans. That is
all that Homer cares to tell about the absolute beginning of things and the first dynasty of rulers of
Olympus. His interest is all in the actual reigning
family, that of the Cronidæ, nor is he fond of report-
ing their youthful excesses.

[1] The custom by which sons drew lots for equal shares of their dead
father's property is described in *Odyssey*, xiv. 199-212. Here Odysseus,
giving a false account of himself, says that he was a Cretan, a bastard,
and that his half-brothers, born in wedlock, drew lots for their father's
inheritance, and did not admit him to the drawing, but gave him a small
portion apart.

[2] See Elton, *Origins of English History*, pp. 185-207.

We now turn from Homer's incidental allusions to
the ample and systematic narrative of Hesiod. As
Mr. Grote says, " Men habitually took their information respecting their theogonic antiquities from the
Hesiodic poems" Hesiod was accepted as an authority
both by the pious Pausanias in the second century of
our era—who protested against any attempt to alter
stories about the gods—and by moral reformers like
Plato and Xenophanes, who were revolted by the
ancient legends,[1] and, indeed, denied their truth.
Yet, though Hesiod represents Greek orthodoxy, we
have observed that Homer (whose epics are probably
still more ancient) steadily ignores the more barbarous
portions of Hesiod's narrative. Thus the question
arises : Are the stories of Hesiod's invention, and
later than Homer, or does Homer's genius half-un-
consciously purify materials like those which Hesiod
presents in the crudest form ?   Mr. Grote says : " How
far these stories are the invention of Hesiod himself
it is impossible to determine. They bring us down
to a cast of fancy more coarse and indelicate than the
Homeric, and more nearly resemble some of the holy
chapters (ἱεροὶ λόγοι) of the more recent mysteries,
such, for example, as the tale of Dionysus Zagreus.
There is evidence in the *Theogony* itself that the
author was acquainted with local legends current both
at Krete and at Delphi, for he mentions both the moun-
tain-cave in Krete wherein the newly-born Zeus was
hidden, and the stone near the Delphian temple—the
identical stone which Kronos had swallowed—placed
by Zeus himself as a sign and marvel to mortal men.

[1] *Timæus*, 41; *Republic*, 377

Both these monuments, which the poet expressly refers
to, and had probably seen, imply a whole train of ac-
cessory and explanatory local legends, current probably
among the priests of Krete and Delphi."

All these circumstances appear to be good evidence
of the great antiquity of the legends recorded by
Hesiod. In the first place, arguing merely *a priori*,
it is extremely improbable that in the brief interval
between the date of the comparatively pure and noble
mythology of the *Iliad* and the much ruder *Theogony*
of Hesiod men *invented* stories like the mutilation of
Uranus and the swallowing of his offspring by Cronus.
The former legend is almost exactly parallel, as has
already been shown, to the myth of Papa and Rangi
in New Zealand. The later has its parallels among
the savage Bushmen and Australians. It is highly
improbable that men in an age so civilised as that of
Homer invented myths as hideous as those of the
lowest savages. But if we take these myths to be,
not new inventions, but the sacred stories of local
priesthoods, their antiquity is probably incalculable.
The sacred stories, as we know from Pausanias,
Herodotus and from all the writers who touch on the
subject of the mysteries, were myths communicated
by the priests to the initiated. Plato speaks of such
myths in the *Republic*, 378 : "If there is an absolute
necessity for their mention, a very few might hear
them in a mystery, and then let them sacrifice, not a
common pig, but some huge and unprocurable victim ;
this would have the effect of very greatly diminishing
the number of the hearers". This is an amusing
example of a plan for veiling the horrors of myth.

The pig was the animal usually offered to Demeter, the goddess of the Eleusinian mysteries. Plato proposes to substitute some "unprocurable" beast, perhaps a giraffe or an elephant.

To Hesiod, then, we must turn for what is the earliest complete literary form of the Greek cosmogonic myth. Hesiod begins, like the New Zealanders, with "the august race of gods, by earth and wide heaven begotten".[1] So the New Zealanders, as we have seen, say, "The heaven which is above us, and the earth which is beneath us, are the progenitors of men and the origin of all things". Hesiod[2] somewhat differs from this view by making Chaos absolutely first of all things, followed by "wide-bosomed Earth," Tartarus and Eros (love). Chaos unaided produced Erebus and Night; the children of Night and Erebus are Æther and Day. Earth produced Heaven, who then became her own lover, and to Heaven she bore Oceanus, and the Titans, Cœeus and Crius, Hyperion and Iapetus, Thea and Rhea, Themis, Mnemosyne, Phœbe, Tethys, "and youngest after these was born Cronus of crooked counsel, the most dreadful of her children, who ever detested his puissant sire," Heaven. There were other sons of Earth and Heaven peculiarly hateful to their father,[3] and these Uranus used to hide from the light in a hollow of Gæa. Both they and Gæa resented this treatment, and the Titans, like "the children of Heaven and Earth," in the New Zealand poem, "sought to discern the difference between light and darkness". Gæa (unlike Earth in the New Zealand myth, for there she is purely

<hr />

[1] *Theog.*, 45.   [2] *Ibid.*, 116.   [3] *Ibid.*, 155.

passive), conspired with her children, produced iron, and asked her sons to avenge their wrongs.[1] Fear fell upon all of them save Cronus, who (like Tane Mahuta in the Maori poem) determined to end the embraces of Earth and Heaven. But while the New Zealand, like the Indo-Aryan myth,[2] conceives of Earth and Heaven as two beings who have never previously been sundered at all, Hesiod makes Heaven amorously approach his spouse from a distance. This was the moment for Cronus,[3] who stretched out his hand armed with the sickle of iron, and mutilated Uranus. As in so many savage myths, the blood of the wounded god fallen on the ground produced strange creatures, nymphs of the ash-tree, giants and furies. As in the Maori myth, one of the children of Heaven stood apart and did not consent to the deed. This was Oceanus in Greece,[4] and in New Zealand it was Tawhiri Matea, the wind, " who arose and followed his father, Heaven, and remained with him in the open spaces of the sky ". Uranus now predicted [5] that there would come a day of vengeance for the evil deed of Cronus, and so ends the dynasty of Uranus.

This story was one of the great stumbling-blocks of orthodox Greece. It was the tale that Plato said should be told, if at all, only to a few in a mystery. after the sacrifice of some rare and scarcely obtainable animal. Even among the Maoris, the conduct of the children who severed their father and mother is

---

[1] *Theog.*, 166.

[2] Muir, v. 23, quoting *Aitareya Brahmana*, iv. 27 : " These two worlds were once joined ; subsequently they separated ".

[3] *Theog.*, 175-185.   [4] Apollod., i. 15.   [5] *Theog.*, 209.

regarded as a singular instance of iniquity, and is told
to children as a moral warning, an example to be
condemned.   In Greece, on the other hand, unless we
are to take the *Euthyphro* as wholly ironical, some
of the pious justified their conduct by the example of
Zeus.   Euthyphro quotes this example when he is
about to prosecute his own father, for which act, he
says, " Men are angry with *me ;* so inconsistently do
they talk when I am concerned and when the gods
are concerned ".[1]   But in Greek *the tale has no meaning*.   It has been allegorised in various ways, and
Lafitau fancied that it was a distorted form of the
Biblical account of the origin of sin.   In Maori the
legend is perfectly intelligible.   Heaven and earth
were conceived of (like everything else), as beings with
human parts and passions, linked in an endless
embrace which crushed and darkened their children.
It became necessary to separate them, and this feat
was achieved not without pain.   " Then wailed the
Heaven, and exclaimed the Earth, ' Wherefore this
murder ?   Why this great sin ?   Why separate us ? '
But what cared Tane ?   Upwards he sent one and
downwards the other.   He cruelly severed the sinews
which united Heaven and Earth." [2]   The Greek myth,
too, contemplated earth and heaven as beings cor-
poreally united, and heaven as a malignant power
that concealed his children in darkness.

But while the conception of heaven and earth as
parents of living things remains perfectly intelligible
in one sense, the vivid personification which regarded
them as creatures with human parts and passions had

---

[1] *Euthyphro*, 6.   [2] Taylor, *New Zealand*, 119.

ceased to be intelligible in Greece before the times of the earliest philosophers. The old physical conception of the pair became a metaphor, and the account of their rending asunder by their children lost all significance, and seemed to be an abominable and unintelligible myth. When examined in the light of the New Zealand story, and of the fact that early peoples do regard all phenomena as human beings, with physical attributes like those of men, the legend of Cronus, and Uranus, and Gæa ceases to be a mystery. It is, at bottom, a savage explanation (as in the Samoan story) of the separation of earth and heaven, an explanation which could only have occurred to people in a state of mind which civilisation has forgotten.

The next generation of Hesiodic gods (if gods we are to call the members of this race of non-natural men) was not more fortunate than the first in its family relations.

Cronus wedded his sister, Rhea, and begat Demeter, Hera, Hades, Poseidon, and the youngest, Zeus. "And mighty Cronus swallowed down each of them, each that came to their mother's knees from her holy womb, with this intent that none other of the proud sons of heaven should hold his kingly sway among the immortals. Heaven and Earth had warned him that he too should fall through his children. Wherefore he kept no vain watch, but spied and swallowed down each of his offspring, while grief immitigable took possession of Rhea." [1] Rhea, being about to become the mother of Zeus, took counsel with Uranus and Gæa. By their advice she went to Crete, where Zeus

[1] *Theog.*, 460, 465.

was born, and, in place of the child, she presented to
Cronus a huge stone swathed in swaddling bands.
This he swallowed, and was easy in his mind. Zeus
grew up, and by some means, suggested by Gæa,
compelled Zeus to disgorge all his offspring. " And
he vomited out the stone first, as he had swallowed
it last."[1] The swallowed children emerged alive,
and Zeus fixed the stone at Pytho (Delphi), where
Pausanias[2] had the privilege of seeing it, and where,
as it did not tempt the cupidity of barbarous invaders,
it probably still exists. It was not a large stone,
Pausanias says, and the Delphians used to pour oil
over it, as Jacob did[3] to the stone at Bethel, and on
feast-days they covered it with wraps of wool. The
custom of smearing fetish-stones (which Theophrastus
mentions as one of the practices of the superstitious man)
is clearly a survival from the savage stage of religion.
As a rule, however, among savages, fetish-stones are
daubed with red paint (like the face of the wooden
ancient Dionysi in Greece, and of Tsui Goab among
the Hottentots), not smeared with oil.[4]

The myth of the swallowing and disgorging of his
own children by Cronus was another of the stumbling-
blocks of Greek orthodoxy. The common explanation,
that Time (Κρόνος) does swallow his children, the
days, is not quite satisfactory. Time brings never
the past back again, as Cronus did. Besides, the
myth of the swallowing is not confined to Cronus.

---

[1] *Theog.*, 498.   [2] x. 245.   [3] Gen. xxviii. 18.

[4] Pausanias, ii. 2, 5. " Churinga " in Australia are greased with the
natural moisture of the palm of the hand, and rubbed with red ochre.
--Spencer and Gillen. They are " sacred things," but not exactly fetishes

Modern philology has given, as usual, different analyses
of the meaning of the name of the god. Hermann,
with Preller, derives it from κραίνω, to fulfil. The
harvest-month, says Preller, was named *Cronion* in
Greece, and *Cronia* was the title of the harvest-festival.
The sickle of Cronus is thus brought into connection
with the sickle of the harvester.[1]

The second myth, in which Cronus swallows his
children, has numerous parallels in savage legend.
Bushmen tell of *Kwai Hemm*, the devourer, who
swallows that great god, the mantis insect, and dis-
gorges him alive with all the other persons and animals
whom he has engulphed in the course of a long and
voracious career.[2] The moon in Australia, while he
lived on earth, was very greedy, and swallowed the
eagle-god, whom he had to disgorge. Mr. Im Thurn
found similar tales among the Indians of Guiana. The
swallowing and disgorging of Heracles by the monster
that was to slay Hesione is well known. Scotch
peasants tell of the same feats, but localise the myth
on the banks of the Ken in Galloway. Basutos,
Eskimos, Zulus and European fairy tales all possess
this incident, the swallowing of many persons by a
being from whose maw they return alive and in good
case.

A mythical conception which prevails from Greenland to South Africa, from Delphi to the Solomon
Islands, from Brittany to the shores of Lake Superior,
must have some foundation in the common elements

---

[1] Preller, *Gr. Myth.*, i. 44; Hartung, ii. 48; Porphyry, *Abst.*, ii. 54.
Welcker will not hear of this etymology, *Gr. Gött.*, i. 145, note 9.

[2] Bleek, *Bushman Folk-lore*, pp. 6, 8.

of human nature.[1] Now it seems highly probable that
this curious idea may have been originally invented in
an attempt to explain natural phenomena by a nature-
myth. It has already been shown (chapter v.) that
eclipses are interpreted, even by the peasantry of
advanced races, as the swallowing of the moon by a
beast or a monster. The Piutes account for the dis-
appearance of the stars in the daytime by the hypothesis that the "sun swallows his children". In the
Melanesian myth, dawn is cut out of the body of night
by Qat, armed with a knife of red obsidian. Here are
examples[2] of transparent nature-myths in which this
idea occurs for obvious explanatory purposes, and in
accordance with the laws of the savage imagination.
Thus the conception of the swallowing and disgorging
being may very well have arisen out of a nature-myth.
But why is the notion attached to the legend of
Cronus?

That is precisely the question about which mythologists differ, as has been shown, and perhaps it is
better to offer no explanation. However stories arise
—and this story probably arose from a nature-myth—
it is certain that they wander about the world, that
they change masters, and thus a legend which is told
of a princess with an impossible name in Zululand is
told of the mother of Charlemagne in France. The
tale of the swallowing may have been attributed to
Cronus, as a great truculent deity, though it has no

---

[1] The myth of Cronus and the swallowed children and the stone is
transferred to Gargantua. See Sébillot, *Gargantua dans les Traditions
Populaires.* But it is impossible to be certain that this is not an example
of direct borrowing by Madame De Cerny in her *Saint Suliac,* p. 69.

[2] Compare Tylor, *Prim. Cult.,* i. 338.

particular elemental signification in connection with
his legend.

This peculiarly savage trick of swallowing each
other became an inherited habit in the family of
Cronus. When Zeus reached years of discretion, he
married Metis, and this lady, according to the scholiast
on Hesiod, had the power of transforming herself into
any shape she pleased. When she was about to be a
mother, Zeus induced her to assume the shape of a fly
and instantly swallowed her.[1] In behaving thus, Zeus
acted on the advice of Uranus and Gæa. It was feared
that Metis would produce a child more powerful than
his father. Zeus avoided this peril by swallowing his
wife, and himself gave birth to Athene. The notion
of swallowing a hostile person, who has been changed
by magic into a conveniently small bulk, is very common. It occurs in the story of Taliesin.[2] Caridwen, in
the shape of a hen, swallows Gwion Bach, in the form
of a grain of wheat. In the same manner the princess
in the *Arabian Nights* swallowed the Geni. Here
then we have in the Hesiodic myth an old *märchen*
pressed into the service of the higher mythology.
The apprehension which Zeus (like Herod and King
Arthur) always felt lest an unborn child should over-
throw him, was also familiar to Indra ; but, instead
of swallowing the mother and concealing her in his
own body, like Zeus, Indra entered the mother's body,
and himself was born instead of the dreaded child.[3]
A cow on this occasion was born along with Indra.

---

[1] Hesiod, *Theogonia*, 886. See Scholiast and note in *Aglaophamus*, i.
613. Compare *Puss in Boots* and the Ogre.

[2] *Mabinogion*, p. 473.   [3] *Black Yajur Veda*, quoted by Sayana.

This adventure of the κατάποσις or swallowing of Metis
was explained by the late Platonists as a Platonic
allegory. Probably the people who originated the tale
were not Platonists, any more than Pandarus was an
Aristotelian.

After Homer and Hesiod, the oldest literary authorities for Greek cosmogonic myths are the poems
attributed to Orpheus. About their probable date,
as has been said, little is known. They have reached
us only in fragments, but seem to contain the first
guesses of a philosophy not yet disengaged from
mythical conditions. The poet preserves, indeed,
some extremely rude touches of early imagination,
while at the same time one of the noblest and boldest
expressions of pantheistic thought is attributed to him.
From the same source are drawn ideas as pure as
those of the philosophical Vedic hymn,[1] and as wild
as those of the Vedic *Purusha Sukta*, or legend of
the fashioning of the world out of the mangled limbs
of Purusha. The authors of the Orphic cosmogony
appear to have begun with some remarks on Time
(Κρόνος). "Time was when as yet this world was
not."[2] Time, regarded in the mythical fashion as
a person, generated Chaos and Æther. The Orphic
poet styles Chaos χάσμα πελώριον, "the monstrous
gulph," or "gap". This term curiously reminds one
of Ginnunga-gap in the Scandinavian cosmogonic
legends. "Ginnunga-gap was light as windless air,"
and therein the blast of heat met the cold rime, whence

[1] *Rig-Veda*, x. 90.
[2] Lobeck, *Aglaophamus*, i. 470. See also the quotations from
Proclus.

Ymir was generated, the Purusha of Northern fable.[1]
These ideas correspond well with the Orphic conception
of primitive space.[2]

In process of time Chaos produced an egg, shining
and silver white. It is absurd to inquire, according
to Lobeck, whether the poet borrowed this widely
spread notion of a cosmic egg from Phœnicia, Baby-
lon, Egypt (where the goose-god Seb laid the egg), or
whether the Orphic singer originated so obvious an
idea. *Quærere ludicrum est.* The conception may
have been borrowed, but manifestly it is one of the
earliest hypotheses that occur to the rude imagination.
We have now three primitive generations, time, chaos,
the egg, and in the fourth generation the egg gave
birth to Phanes, the great hero of the Orphic cosmogony.[3] The earliest and rudest thinkers were
puzzled, as many savage cosmogonic myths have
demonstrated, to account for the origin of life. The
myths frequently hit on the theory of a hermaphro-
ditic being, both male and female, who produces
another being out of himself. Prajapati in the Indian
stories, and Hrimthursar in Scandinavian legend—
" one of his feet got a son on the other "—with Lox in
the Algonquin tale are examples of these double-sexed
personages. In the Orphic poem, Phanes is both male
and female. This Phanes held within him " the seed
of all the gods," [4] and his name is confused with the
names of Metis and Ericapæus in a kind of trinity.
All this part of the Orphic doctrine is greatly obscured
by the allegorical and theosophistic interpretations of

---

[1] *Gylfi's Mocking.*   [2] *Aglaophamus*, p. 473.
[3] Clemens Alexan., p. 672.   [4] Damascius, ap. Lobeck, i. 481.

the late Platonists long after our era, who, as usual,
insisted on finding their own trinitarian ideas, *com-
menta frigidissima*, concealed under the mythical
narrative.[1]

Another description by Hieronymus of the first
being, the Orphic Phanes, "as a serpent with bull's
and lion's heads, with a human face in the middle
and wings on the shoulders," is sufficiently rude and
senseless. But these physical attributes could easily
be explained away as types of anything the Platonist
pleased.[2] The Orphic Phanes, too, was almost as
many-headed as a giant in a fairy tale, or as Purusha
in the *Rig-Veda*. He had a ram's head, a bull's head,
a snake's head and a lion's head, and glanced around
with four eyes, presumably human.[3] This remarkable
being was also provided with golden wings. The
nature of the physical arrangements by which Phanes
became capable of originating life in the world is
described in a style so savage and crude that the
reader must be referred to Suidas for the original
text.[4] The tale is worthy of the Swift-like fancy of
the Australian Narrinyeri.

Nothing can be easier or more delusive than to
explain all this wild part of the Orphic cosmogony
as an allegorical veil of any modern ideas we choose
to select. But why the "allegory" should closely
imitate the rough guesses of uncivilised peoples, Ahts,
Diggers, Zuñis, Cahrocs, it is less easy to explain.
We can readily imagine African or American tribes
who were accustomed to revere bulls, rams, snakes,

[1] *Aglaoph.*, i. 483.   [2] Damascius, 381, ap. Lobeck, i. 484.
[3] Hermias in Phædr. ap. Lobeck, i. 493   [4] Suidas *s. v.* Phanes.

and so forth, ascribing the heads of all their various
animal patrons to the deity of their confederation.
We can easily see how such races as practise the
savage rites of puberty should attribute to the first
being the special organs of Phanes. But on the Neo-
Platonic hypothesis that Orpheus was a seer of Neo-
Platonic opinions, we do not see why he should have
veiled his ideas under so savage an allegory. This
part of the Orphic speculation is left in judicious
silence by some modern commentators, such as M.
Darmesteter in *Les Cosmogonies Aryennes.*[1] Indeed,
if we choose to regard Apollonius Rhodius, an Alex-
andrine poet writing in a highly civilised age, as the
representative of Orphicism, it is easy to mask and
pass by the more stern and characteristic fortresses
of the Orphic divine. The theriomorphic Phanes is
a much less " Aryan " and agreeable object than the
glorious golden-winged Eros, the love-god of Apollonius Rhodius and Aristophanes.[2]

On the whole, the Orphic fragments appear to
contain survivals of savage myths of the origin of
things blended with purer speculations. The savage
ideas are finally explained by late philosophers as
allegorical veils and vestments of philosophy; but
the interpretation is arbitrary, and varies with the
taste and fancy of each interpreter. Meanwhile the
coincidence of the wilder elements with the speculations native to races in the lowest grades of civilisation
is undeniable. This opinion is confirmed by the Greek
myths of the origin of Man. These, too, coincide with
the various absurd conjectures of savages.

[1] *Essais Orientaux,* p. 166.   [2] *Argonautica,* 1-12; *Aves,* 693.

In studying the various Greek local legends of the
origin of Man, we encounter the difficulty of separat-
ing them from the myths of heroes, which it will be
more convenient to treat separately. This difficulty
we have already met in our treatment of savage
traditions of the beginnings of the race. Thus we saw
that among the Melanesians, Qat, and among the Ahts,
Quawteaht, were heroic persons, who made men and
most other things. But it was desirable to keep their
performances of this sort separate from their other
feats, their introduction of fire, for example, and of
various arts. In the same way it will be well, in
reviewing Greek legends, to keep Prometheus' share
in the making of men apart from the other stories
of his exploits as a benefactor of the men whom he
made. In Hesiod, Prometheus is the son of the Titan
Iapetus, and perhaps his chief exploit is to play
upon Zeus a trick of which we find the parallel in
various savage myths. It seems, however, from
Ovid [1] and other texts, that Hesiod somewhere spoke
of Prometheus as having made men out of clay, like
Pund-jel in the Australian, Qat in the Melanesian
and Tiki in the Maori myths. The same story is
preserved in Servius's commentary on Virgil.[2] A
different legend is preserved in the *Etymologicum
Magnum* (*voc.* Ikonion). According to this story,
after the deluge of Deucalion, " Zeus bade Prometheus
and Athene make images of men out of clay, and
the winds blew into them the breath of life ". In
confirmation of this legend, Pausanias was shown
in Phocis certain stones of the colour of clay, and

---

[1] *Ovid. Metam.*, i. 82.   [2] *Eclogue*, vi. 42.

" smelling very like human flesh " ; and these, according to the Phocians, were " the remains of the clay from which the whole human race was fashioned by Prometheus ".[1]

Aristophanes, too, in the *Birds* (686) talks of men as πλάσματα πήλου, figures kneaded of clay Thus there are sufficient traces in Greek tradition of the savage myth that man was made of clay by some superior being, like Pund-jel in the quaint Australian story.

We saw that among various rude races other theories of the origin of man were current. Men were thought to have come out of a hole in the ground or a bed of reeds, and sometimes the very scene of their first appearance was still known and pointed out to the curious. This myth was current among races who regarded themselves as the only people whose origin needed explanation. Other stories represented man as the fruit of a tree, or the child of a rock or stone, or as the descendant of one of the lower animals. Examples of these opinions in Greek legend are now to be given. In the first place, we have a fragment of Pindar, in which the poet enumerates several of the centres from which different Greek tribes believed men to have sprung. " Hard it is to find out whether Alalkomeneus, first of men, arose on the marsh of Cephissus, or whether the Curetes of Ida first, a stock divine, arose, or if it was the Phrygian Corybantes that the sun earliest saw—men like trees walking ; " and Pindar mentions Egyptian and Libyan legends of the same description.[2] The Thebans and

---

[1] Pausanias, x. 4, 3.   [2] Preller, *Aus. Auf.*, p. 158.

the Arcadians held themselves to be "earth-born ". "The black earth bore Pelasgus on the high wooded hills," says an ancient line of Asius. The Dryopians were an example of a race of men born from ash-trees. The myth of *gens virum truncis et duro robore nata,* "born of tree-trunk and the heart of oak," had passed into a proverb even in Homer's time.[1] Lucian mentions[2] the Athenian myth "that men grew like cabbages out of the earth ". As to Greek myths of the descent of families from animals, these will be examined in the discussion of the legend of Zeus.

[1] Virgil *Æn.*, viii. 315 ; *Odyssey*, xix. 163 ; *Iliad*, ii. xxii. 120 ; *Juvenal*, vi. 11.   *Cf.* also Bouché Leclerq, *De Origine Generis Humani.*

[2] *Philops.* iii.

CHAPTER XI.

SAVAGE DIVINE MYTHS.

The origin of a belief in GOD beyond the ken of history and of speculation—. Sketch of conjectural theories—Two elements in all beliefs, whether of backward or civilised races—The *Mythical* and the *Religious*—These may be coeval, or either may be older than the other—Difficulty of study—The current anthropological theory—Stated objections to the theory—Gods and spirits—Suggestion that savage religion is borrowed from Europeans—Reply to Mr. Tylor's arguments on this head—The morality of savages.

" THE question of the origin of a belief in Deity does not come within the scope of a strictly historical inquiry. No man can watch the idea of GOD in the making or in the beginning. We are acquainted with no race whose beginning does not lie far back in the unpenetrated past. Even on the hypothesis that the natives of Australia, for example, were discovered in a state of culture more backward than that of other known races, yet the institutions and ideas of the Australians must have required for their development an incalculable series of centuries. The notions of man about the Deity, man's religious sentiments and his mythical narratives, must be taken as we find them. There have been, and are, many theories as to the origin of the conception of a supernatural being or beings, concerned with the fortunes of mankind, and once active in the making of the

earth and its inhabitants. There is the hypothesis
of an original divine tradition, darkened by the smoke
of foolish mortal fancies. There is the hypothesis of
an innate and intuitive *sensus numinis*. There is the
opinion that the notion of Deity was introduced to
man by the very nature of his knowledge and per-
ceptions, which compel him in all things to recognise
a finite and an infinite. There is the hypothesis that
gods were originally ghosts, the magnified shapes of
ancestral spectres. There is the doctrine that man,
seeking in his early speculations for the causes of
things, and conscious of his own powers as an active
cause, projected his own shadow on the mists of the
unknown, and peopled the void with figures of magnified non-natural men, his own parents and protectors,
and the makers of many of the things in the world.

" Since the actual truth cannot be determined by
observation and experiment, the question as to the
first germs of the divine conception must here be left
unanswered. But it is possible to disengage and
examine apart the two chief elements in the earliest
as in the latest ideas of Godhead. Among the lowest
and most backward, as among the most advanced
races, there coexist the *mythical* and the *religious*
elements in belief. The rational factor (or what
approves itself to us as the rational factor) is visible
in religion; the irrational is prominent in myth. The
Australian, the Bushman, the Solomon Islander, in
hours of danger and necessity ' yearns after the gods,'
and has present in his heart the idea of a father and
friend. This is the religious element. The same
man, when he comes to indulge his fancy for fiction,

will degrade this spiritual friend and father to the level
of the beasts, and will make him the hero of comic or
repulsive adventures. This is the mythical or irrational element. Religion, in its moral aspect, always
traces back to the belief in a power that is benign and
works for righteousness. Myth, even in Homer or the
Rig-Veda, perpetually falls back on the old stock of
absurd and immoral divine adventures.[1]

"It would be rash, in the present state of knowledge,
to pronounce that the germ of the serious Homeric
sense of the justice and power of the Divinity is earlier
or later than the germ of the Homeric stories of gods
disguised as animals, or imprisoned by mortals, or
kicked out of Olympus. The rational and irrational
aspects of mythology and religion may be of coeval
antiquity for all that is certainly known, or either of
them, in the dark backward of mortal experience, may
have preceded the other. There is probably no religion nor mythology which does not offer both aspects
to the student. But it is the part of advancing civilisation to adorn and purify the rational element, and to
subordinate and supersede the irrational element, as
far as religious conservatism, ritual and priestly dogma
will permit."

Such were the general remarks with which this
chapter opened in the original edition of the present
work. But reading, reflection and certain additions
to the author's knowledge of facts, have made it seem
advisable to state, more fully and forcibly than before,
that, in his opinion, not only the puzzling element of

[1] M. Knappert here, in a note to the Dutch translation, denies the lowest
mythical element to the Hebrews, as their documents have reached us.

myth, but the purer element of a religious belief sanctioning morality is derived by civilised people from a remote past of savagery. It is also necessary to draw attention to a singular religious phenomena, a break, or "fault," as geologists call it, in the religious strata. While the most backward savages, in certain cases, present the conception of a Being who sanctions ethics, and while that conception recurs at a given stage of civilisation, it appears to fade, or even to disappear in some conditions of barbarism. Among some barbaric peoples, such as the Zulus, and the Red Indians of French Canada when first observed, as among some Polynesians and some tribes of Western and Central Africa little trace of a supreme being is found, except a name, and that name is even occasionally a matter of ridicule. The highest religious conception has been reached, and is generally known, yet the Being conceived of as creative is utterly neglected, while ghosts, or minor gods, are served and adored. To this religious phenomenon (if correctly observed) we must attempt to assign a cause. For this purpose it is necessary to state again what may be called the current or popular anthropological theory of the evolution of Gods.

That theory takes varying shapes. In the philosophy of Mr. Herbert Spencer we find a pure Euhemerism. Gods are but ghosts of dead men, raised to a higher and finally to the highest power. In the somewhat analogous but not identical system of Mr. Tylor, man first attains to the idea of spirit by reflection on various physical, psychological and psychical experiences, such as sleep, dreams, trances, shadows, hallucinations, breath and death, and he gradually extends the conception of soul or ghost till all nature is peopled with spirits. Of these spirits one is finally promoted to supremacy, where the conception of a supreme being occurs. In the lowest faiths there is said, on this theory, to be no connection, or very little connection, between religion and morality. To supply a religious sanction of morals is the work of advancing thought.[1]

This current hypothesis is, confessedly, "animistic," in Mr. Tylor's phrase, or, in Mr. Spencer's terminology, it is "the ghost theory". The human soul, says Mr. Tylor, has been the model on which all man's ideas of spiritual beings, from "the tiniest elf" to "the heavenly Creator and ruler of the world, the Great Spirit," have been framed.[2] Thus it has been necessary for Mr. Tylor and for Mr. Spencer to discover first an origin of man's idea of his own soul, and that supposed origin in psychological, physical and psychical experiences is no doubt adequate. By reflection on these facts, probably, the idea of spirit was reached, though the psychical experiences enumerated by Mr. Tylor may contain points as yet unexplained by Materialism. From these sources are derived all really "animistic" gods, all that from the first partake of the nature of hungry ghosts, placated by sacrifices of food, though in certain cases that hunger may have been transferred, we surmise, by worshippers to gods not *originally* animistic.

In answer to this theory of an animistic or ghostly

---

[1] *Prim. Cult.*, ii. 381. Huxley's *Science and Hebrew Tradition*, pp. 346, 372.

[2] *Prim. Cult.*, ii. 109.

origin of all gods, it must first be observed that all
gods are not necessarily, it would seem, of animistic
origin. Among certain of the lowest savages, although
they believe in ghosts, the animistic conception, the
spiritual idea, is not attached to the relatively supreme
being of their faith. He is merely a powerful *being*,
unborn, and not subject to death. The purely metaphysical question "was he a ghost?" does not seem
always to have been asked. Consequently there is
no logical reason why man's idea of a Maker should
not be prior to man's idea that there are such things
as souls, ghosts and spirits. Therefore the animistic
theory is not necessary as material for the "god-idea".
We cannot, of course, prove that the "god-idea" was
historically prior to the "ghost-idea," for we know no
savages who have a god and yet are ignorant of ghosts.
But we can show that the idea of God may exist,
in germ, without explicitly involving the idea of
spirit. Thus gods *may* be prior in evolution to ghosts,
and therefore the animistic theory of the origin of
gods in ghosts need not necessarily be accepted.

In the first place, the original evolution of a god
out of a ghost need not be conceded, because in perhaps
all known savage theological philosophy the God, the
Maker and Master, is regarded as a being who existed
before death entered the world. Everywhere, practically speaking, death is looked on as a comparatively
late intruder. He came not only after God was
active, but after men and beasts had populated the
world. Scores of myths accounting for this invasion
of death have been collected all over the world.[1]

---

[1] See *Modern Mythology*, "Myths of Origin of Death"

Thus the relatively supreme being, or beings, of
religion are looked on as prior to Death, therefore,
not as ghosts. They are sometimes expressly distinguished as "original gods" from other gods who are
secondary, being souls of chiefs. Thus all Tongan
gods are *Atua*, but all *Atua* are not "original gods".[1]
The word *Atua*, according to Mr. White, is "*A-tu-a*".
"*A*" was the name given to the author of the universe,
and signifies: "Am the unlimited in power," "The
Conception," "the Leader," "the Beyond All". "Tua"
means "Beyond that which is most distant," "Behind
all matter," and "Behind every action". Clearly
these conceptions are not more mythical (indeed A does
not seem to occur in the myths), nor are they more
involved in ghosts, than the unknown absolute of Mr.
Herbert Spencer. Yet the word *Atua* denotes gods
who are recognised as ghosts of chiefs, no less than it
denotes the supreme existence.[2] These ideas are the
metaphysical theology of a race considerably above
the lowest level. They lend no assistance to a theory
that A was, or was evolved out of, a human ghost,
and he is not found in Maori *mythology* as far as our
knowledge goes. But, among the lowest known
savages, the Australians, we read that "the Creator
was a gigantic black, once on earth, now among
the stars". This is in Gippsland; the deities of
the Fuegians and the Blackfoot Indians are also
Beings, anthropomorphic, unborn and undying, like
Mangarrah, the creative being of the Larrakeah

---

[1] *Mariner*, ii. 127.

[2] White, *Ancient History of the Maoris*, vol. i. p. 4; other views in
Gill's *Myths of the Pacific*. I am not committed to Mr. White's opinion.

tribe in Australia. " A very good man called Mangarrah lives in the sky. . . . He made everything"
(blacks excepted). He never dies.[1] The Melanesian
Vui " never were men," were " something different,"
and "were *not* ghosts". It is as a Being, not as a
Spirit, that the Kurnai deity Munganngaur (Our
Father) is described.[2] In short, though Europeans
often speak of these divine beings of low savages as
"spirits," it does not appear that the natives themselves advance here the metaphysical idea of spirit.
These gods are just *beings*, anthropomorphic, or (in
myth and fable), very often bestial, " theriomorphic ".[3]
It is manifest that a divine being envisaged thus need
not have been evolved out of the theory of spirits or
ghosts, and may even have been prior to the rise of
the belief in ghosts.

Again, these powerful, or omnipotent divine beings
are looked on as guardians of morality, punishers of
sin, rewarders of righteousness, both in this world and
in a future life, in places where ghosts, though believed
in, *are not worshipped, nor in receipt of sacrifice*, and
where, great grandfathers being forgotten, ancestral
ghosts can scarcely swell into gods. This occurs among
Andamanese, Fuegians and Australians, therefore,
among non-ghost-worshipping races, ghosts cannot
have developed into deities who are not even necessarily spirits. These gods, again, do not receive sacrifice,
and thus lack the note of descent from hungry food-
craving ghosts. In Australia, indeed, while ghosts
are not known to receive any offerings, " the recent

---

[1] *Journal Anthrop. Inst.*, Nov., 1894, p. 191.

[2] *Ibid.*, 1885, p. 313.

[3] See *Making of Religion*, pp. 201-210, for a more copious statement.

custom of providing food for it "—the dead body of a friend—" is derided by the intelligent old aborigines as ' white fellow's gammon ' ".[1]

The Australians possess no chiefs like " Vich Ian Vohr or Chingachgook " whose ghosts might be said to swell into supreme moral deities. " Headmen " they have, leaders of various degrees of authority, but no Vich Ian Vohr, no semi-sacred representative of the tribe.[2] Nor are the ghosts of the Headmen known to receive any particular posthumous attention or worship. Thus it really seems impossible to show proof that Australian gods grew out of Australian ghosts, a subject to which we shall return.

Some supporters of the current theory therefore fall back on the hypothesis that the Australians are sadly degenerate.[3] Chiefs, it is argued, or kings, they once had, and the gods are surviving ghosts of these wholly forgotten potentates. To this we reply that we know not the very faintest trace of Australian degeneration. Sir John Lubbock and Mr. Tylor have correctly argued that the soil of Australia has not yet yielded so much as a fragment of native pottery, nor any trace of native metal work, not a vestige of stone buildings occurs, nor of any work beyond the present native level of culture, unless we reckon weirs for fish-catching. "The Australian boomerang," writes Mr. Tylor, " has been claimed as derived from some hypothetical high culture, whereas the transition-stages through

[1] Dawson, *Australian Aborigines*, p. 51, 1881.

[2] Howitt, *Organisation of Australian Tribes*, pp. 101-113. " Transactions of Royal Society of Victoria," 1889.

[3] See Prof. Menzie's *History of Religion*, pp. 16, 17, where a singular inconsistency has escaped the author.

which it is connected with the club are to be observed
in its own country, while no civilised race possesses
the weapon." [1]

Therefore the Australian, with his boomerang, represents no degeneration but advance on his ancestors, who
had not yet developed the boomerang out of the club. If
the excessively complex nature of Australian rules of
prohibited degrees be appealed to as proof of degeneration from the stage in which they were evolved, we
reply that civilisation everywhere tends not to com-
plicate but to simplify such rules, as it also notoriously
simplifies the forms of language.

The Australian people, when discovered, were only
emerging from palæolithic culture, while the neighbouring Tasmanians were frankly palæolithic. [2] Far from
degenerating, the Australians show advance when
they supersede their beast or other totem by an
eponymous human hero. [3] The eponymous hero, however, changed with each generation, so that no one
name was fixed as that of tribal father, later perhaps
to become a tribal god. We find several tribes in
which the children now follow the *father's* class, and
thus paternal kin takes the place of the usual early
savage method of reckoning kinship by the mother's
side, elsewhere prevalent in Australia. In one of these
tribes, dwelling between the Glenelg and Mount Napier,
headmanship is hereditary, but nothing is said of any
worship of the ghosts of chiefs. All this social improvement denotes advance on the usual Australian

[1] *Prim. Cult.*, i. 57, 67.
[2] Tylor, preface to Ling Roth's *Aborigines of Tasmania*, pp. v.-viii.
[3] *Kamilaroi and Kurnai*, p. 231.

standard.[1] Of degeneration (except when produced
recently by European vices and diseases) I know no
trace in Australia. Their highest religious conceptions, therefore, are not to be disposed of as survivals
of a religion of the ghosts of such chiefs as the
Australians are not shown ever to have recognised.
The " God idea " in Australia, or among the Andamanese, must have some other source than the Ghost-
Theory. This is all the more obvious because not only
are ghosts not worshipped by the Australians, but also
the divine beings who are alleged to form links between
the ghost and the moral god are absent. There are no
departmental gods, as of war, peace, the chase, love,
and so forth. Sun, sky and earth are equally unworshipped. There is nothing in religion between a
Being, on one hand (with a son or sons), and vague
mischievous spirits, *boilyas* or *mrarts*, and ghosts
(who are not worshipped), on the other hand. The
friends of the idea that the God is an ancient evolution
from the ghost of such a chief as is not proved to have
existed, must apparently believe that the intermediate
stages in religious evolution, departmental gods, nature
gods and gods of polytheism in general once existed
in Australia, and have all been swept away in a deluge
of degeneration. That deluge left in religion a moral,
potently active Father and Judge. Now that conception is considerably above the obsolescent belief in
an otiose god which is usually found among barbaric
races of the type from which the Australians are said
to have degenerated. There is no proof of degeneracy,
and, if degeneration has occurred, why has it left

[1] *Kamilaroi and Kurnai* pp. 277, 278.

just the kind of deity who, in the higher barbaric culture, is not commonly found ? Clearly this
attempt to explain the highest aspect of Australian
religion by an undemonstrated degeneration is an
effort of despair.

While the current theory thus appears to break
down over the deities of certain Australian tribes
and of other low savages to be more particularly
described later, it is not more successful in dealing
with what we have called the "fault" or break in the
religious strata of higher races. The nature of that
"fault" may thus be described : While the deities of
several low savage peoples are religiously regarded
as guardians and judges of conduct both in this life
and in the next, among higher barbarians they are
often little, or not at all, interested in conduct. Again,
while among Australians, and Andamanese, and
Fuegians, there is hardly a verifiable trace, if any trace
there be, of sacrifice to any divine being, among barbarians the gods beneath the very highest are in receipt
even of human sacrifice. Even among barbarians the
highest deity is very rarely worshipped with sacrifice.
Through various degrees he is found to lose all claim
on worship, and even to become a mere name, and
finally a jest and a mockery. Meanwhile ancestral
ghosts, and gods framed on the same lines as ghosts,
receive sacrifice of food and of human victims. Once
more, the high gods of low savages are not localised,
not confined to any temple or region. But the gods
of higher barbarians (the gods beneath the highest),
are localised in this way, as occasionally even the
highest god also is.

All this shows that, among advancing barbarians, the gods, if they started from the estate of gods among savages on the lowest level, become demoralised, limited, conditioned, relegated to an otiose condition, and finally deposed, till progressive civilisation, as in Greece, reinstates or invents purer and more philosophic conceptions, without being able to abolish popular and priestly myth and ritual.

Here, then, is a flaw or break in the strata of religion. What was the cause of this flaw? We answer, the evolution, through ghosts, of "animistic" gods who retained the hunger and selfishness of these ancestral spirits whom the lowest savages are not known to worship.

The moral divine beings of these lowest races, beings (when religiously regarded) unconditioned, in need of no gift that man can give, are not to be won by offerings of food and blood. Of such offerings ghosts, and gods modelled on ghosts, are notoriously in need. Strengthened and propitiated by blood and sacrifice (not offered to the gods of low savages), the animistic deities will become partisans of their adorers, and will either pay no regard to the morals of their worshippers, or will be easily bribed to forgive sins. Here then is, ethically speaking, a flaw in the strata of religion, a flaw found in the creeds of ghost-worshipping barbarians, but not of non-ghost-worshipping savages. A crowd of venal, easy-going, serviceable deities has now been evolved out of ghosts, and Animism is on its way to supplant or overlay a rude early form of theism. Granting the facts, we fail to see how they are explained by the current theory which makes the highest god the latest in evolution from a ghost. That theory wrecks itself again on the circumstance that, whereas the tribal or national highest divine being, as latest in evolution, ought to be the most potent, he is, in fact, among barbaric races, usually the most disregarded. A new idea, of course, is not necessarily a powerful or fashionable idea. It may be regarded as a " fad," or a heresy, or a low form of dissent. But, when universally known to and accepted by a tribe or people, then it must be deemed likely to possess great influence. But that is not the case; and among barbaric tribes the most advanced conception of deity is the least regarded, the most obsolete.

An excellent instance of the difference between the theory here advocated, and that generally held by anthropologists, may be found in Mr. Abercromby's valuable work, *Pre- and Proto-Historic Finns*, i. 150-154. The gods, and other early ideas, says Mr. Abercromby, " could in no sense be considered as supernatural". We shall give examples of gods among the races " nearest the beginning," whose attributes of power and knowledge can not, by us at least, be considered other than " supernatural ". " The gods " (in this hypothesis) " were so human that they could be forced to act in accordance with the wishes of their worshippers, and could likewise be punished." These ideas, to an Australian black, or an Andamanese, would seem dangerously blasphemous. These older gods " resided chiefly in trees, wells, rivers and animals ". But many gods of our lowest known savages live " beyond the sky ". Mr. Abercromby supposes

the sky god to be of later evolution, and to be worshipped after man had exhausted "the helpers that
seemed nearest at hand . . . in the trees and waters
at his very door". Now the Australian black has not
a door, nor has he gods of any service to him in the
"trees and waters," though sprites may lurk in such
places for mischief. But in Mr. Abercromby's view,
some men turned at last to the sky-god, "who in time
would gain a large circle of worshippers". He would
come to be thought omnipotent, omniscient, the
Creator. This notion, says Mr. Abercromby, "must,
if this view is correct, be of late origin". But the
view is not correct. The far-seeing powerful
Maker beyond the sky is found among the very
backward races who have not developed helpers nearer
man, dwelling round what would be his door, if door
he was civilised enough to possess. Such near neighbouring gods, of human needs, capable of being bullied,
or propitiated by sacrifice, are found in races higher
than the lowest, who, for their easily procurable aid,
have allowed the Maker to sink into an otiose god, or
a mere name. Mr. Abercromby unconsciously proves
our case by quoting the example of a Samoyede.
This man knew a Sky-god, Num ; that conception was
familiar to him. He also knew a familiar spirit. On
Mr. Abercromby's theory he should have resorted for
help to the Sky-god, not to the sprite. But he did the
reverse : he said, " I cannot approach Num, he is too
far away ; if I could reach him I should not beseech
thee (the familiar spirit), but should go myself ; but I
cannot ". For this precise reason, people who have
developed the belief in accessible affable spirits go to

them, with a spell to constrain, or a gift to bribe, and
neglect, in some cases almost forget, their Maker. But
He is worshipped by low savages, who do not propitiate ghosts and who have no gods in wells and trees,
close at hand. It seems an obvious inference that the
greater God is the earlier evolved.

These are among the difficulties of the current
anthropological theory. There is, however, a solution
by which the weakness of the divine conception, its
neglected, disused aspect among barbaric races, might
be explained by anthropologists, without regarding it
as an obsolescent form of a very early idea. This
solution is therefore in common use. It is applied to
the deity revealed in the ancient mysteries of the
Australians, and it is employed in American and
African instances.

The custom is to say that the highest divine being
of American or African native peoples has been
borrowed from Europeans, and is, especially, a savage
refraction from the God of missionaries. If this can
be proved, the shadowy, practically powerless "Master
of Life" of certain barbaric peoples, will have degenerated from the Christian conception, because of that
conception he will be only a faint unsuccessful refraction. He has been introduced by Europeans, it is
argued, but is not in harmony with his new environment, and so is "half-remembered and half forgot".

The hypothesis of borrowing admits of only one
answer, but that answer should be conclusive. If we
can discover, say in North America, a single instance
in which the supreme being occurs, while yet he cannot
possibly be accounted for by any traceable or verifiable

foreign influence, then the burden of proof, in other
cases, falls on the opponent. When he urges that
other North American supreme beings were borrowed,
we can reply that our crucial example shows that this
need not be the fact. To prove that it is the fact, in
his instances, is then his business. It is obvious that
for information on this subject we must go to the
reports of the earliest travellers who knew the Red
Indians well. We must try to get at gods behind any
known missionary efforts. Mr. Tylor offers us the
testimony of Heriot, about 1586, that the natives of
Virginia believed in many gods, also in one chief god,
"who first made other principal gods, and then the
sun, moon and stars as petty gods".[1] Whence could
the natives of Virginia have borrowed this notion of a
Creator before 1586? If it is replied, in the usual
way, that they developed him upwards out of sun,
moon and star gods, other principal gods, and finally
reached the idea of the Creator, we answer that the
idea of the Maker is found where these alleged
intermediate stages are *not* found, as in Australia. In
Virginia then, as in Victoria, a Creator may have
been evolved in some other way than that of gradual
ascent from ghosts, and may have been, as in Australia
and elsewhere, prior to verifiable ghost-worship. Again,
in Virginia at our first settlement, the native priests
strenuously resisted the introduction of Christianity.
They were content with their deity, Ahone, " the great
God who governs all the world, and makes the sun to
shine, creating the moon and stars his companions. . . .
The good and peaceable God . . . needs not to be

---

[1] *Prim. Cult.*, ii. 341.

sacrificed unto, for he intendeth all good unto them.'
This good Creator, without sacrifice, among a settled
agricultural barbaric race sacrificing to other gods and
ghosts, manifestly cannot be borrowed from the newly
arrived religion of Christianity, which his priests,
according to the observer, vigorously resisted. Ahone
had a subordinate deity, magisterial in functions,
"looking into all men's actions" and punishing the
same, when evil. To *this* god sacrifices *were* made, and
if his name, *Okeus*, is derived from *Oki* = "spirit,"
he was, of course, an animistic ghost-evolved deity.
Anthropological writers, by an oversight, have dwelt
on Oki, but have not mentioned Ahone.[1] Manifestly
it is not possible to insist that these Virginian high
deities were borrowed, without saying whence and
when they were borrowed by a barbaric race which
was, at the same time, rejecting Christian teaching.

Mr. Tylor writes, with his habitual perspicacity: " It
is the widespread belief in the Great Spirit, whatever
his precise nature and origin, that has long and de-
servedly drawn the attention of European thinkers
to the native religions of the North American tribes".
Now while, in recent times, Christian ideas may undeniably have crystallised round "the Great Spirit,"
it has come to be thought " that *the whole doctrine*
of the Great Spirit was borrowed by the savages from
missionaries and colonists. But this view will not
bear examination," says Mr. Tylor.[2]

Mr. Tylor proceeds to prove this by examples from

---

[1] *History of Travaile into Virginia*, by William Strachey, 1612.
[2] *Prim. Cult.*, ii. pp. 339, 340 (1873). For some reason, Mr. Tylor
modifies this passage in 1891.

Greenland, and the Algonkins. He instances the Massachusett God, Kiehtan, who created the other gods, and receives the just into heaven. This was recorded in 1622, but the belief, says Winslow, our authority, goes back into the unknown past. "They never saw Kiehtan, but *they hold it a great charge and duty that one age teach another.*" How could a deity thus rooted in a traditional past be borrowed from recent English settlers?

In these cases the hypothesis of borrowing breaks down, and still more does it break down over the Algonkin deity Atahocan.

Father Le Jeune, S.J., went first among the Algonkins, a missionary pioneer, in 1633, and suffered unspeakable things in his courageous endeavour to win souls in a most recalcitrant flock. He writes (1633) : "As this savage has given me occasion to speak of their god, I will remark that it is a great error to think that the savages have no knowledge of any deity. I was surprised to hear this in France. I do not know their secrets, but, from the little which I am about to tell, it will be seen that they have such knowledge.

"They say that one exists whom they call Atahocan, who made the whole. Speaking of God in a wigwam one day, they asked me 'what is God?' I told them that it was He who made all things, Heaven and Earth. They then began to cry out to each other, "Atahocan! Atahocan! it is Atahocan!'"

There could be no better evidence that Atahocan was *not* (as is often said) " borrowed from the Jesuits " The Jesuits had only just arrived.

Later (1634) Le Jeune interrogated an old man and
a partly Europeanised sorcerer. They replied that
nothing was certain; that Atahocan was only spoken
of as "of a thing so remote," that assurance was
impossible. "In fact, their word *Nitatohokan* means,
'*I fable, I tell an old story*'."

Thus Atahocan, though at once recognised as identical
with the Creator of the missionary, was so far from
being the latest thing in religious evolution that he
had passed into a proverb for the ancient and the
fabulous. This, of course, is inconsistent with *recent*
borrowing. He was neglected for *Khichikouai*, spirits
which inspire seers, and are of some practical use, re-
ceiving rewards in offerings of grease, says Le Jeune.[1]

The obsolescent Atahocan seems to have had no
moral activity. But, in America, this indolence of
God is not universal. Mr. Parkman indeed writes:
"In the primitive Indian's conception of a God, the idea
of moral good has no part ".[2] But this is definitely
contradicted by Heriot, Strachey, Winslow, already
cited, and by Père Le Jeune. The good attributes
of Kiehtan and Ahone were not borrowed from
Christianity, were matter of Indian belief before the
English arrived. Mr. Parkman writes: "The moment
the Indians began to contemplate the object of his
faith, and sought to clothe it with attributes, it
became finite, and commonly ridiculous ". It did so,
as usual, in *mythology*, but not in *religion*. There
is nothing ridiculous in what is known of Ahone and
Kiehtan. If they had a mythology, and if we knew

---

[1] *Relations*, 1633, 1634.
[2] Parkman, *The Jesuits in North America*, p. lxxviii.

the myths, doubtless they would be ridiculous
enough. The savage mind, turned from belief and
awe into the spinning of yarns, instantly yields to
humorous fancy. As we know, mediæval popular
Christianity, in imagery, *märchen* or tales, and art,
copiously illustrates the same mental phenomenon.
Saints, God, our Lord, and the Virgin, all play
ludicrous and immoral parts in Christian folk-tales.
This is Mythology, and here is, beyond all cavil, a late
corruption of Religion. Here, where we know the
history of a creed, Religion is early, and these myths
are late. Other examples of American divine ideas
might be given, such as the extraordinary hymns
in which the Zuñis address the Eternal, Ahonawilona. But as the Zuñi religion has only been
studied in recent years, the hymns would be
dismissed as " borrowed," though there is nothing
Catholic or Christian about them. We have preferred to select examples where borrowing from
Christianity is out of the question. The current
anthropological theory is thus confronted with
American examples of ideas of the divine which
cannot have been borrowed, while, if the gods are
said to have been evolved out of ghosts, we reply
that, in some cases, they receive no sacrifice, sacrifice
being usually a note of ghostly descent. Again,
similar gods, as we show, exist where ghosts of chiefs
are not worshipped, and as far as evidence goes never
were worshipped, because there is no evidence of the
existence at any time of such chiefs. The American
highest gods may then be equally free from the taint
of ghostly descent.

There is another more or less moral North American
deity whose evolution is rather questionable.   Père
Brébeuf (1636), speaking of the Hurons, says that
"they have recourse to Heaven in almost all their
necessities, . . . and I may say that it is, in fact, God
whom they blindly adore, for they imagine that there
is an Oki, that is, a demon, in heaven, who regulates
the seasons, bridles the winds and the waves of the
sea, and helps them in every need.   They dread his
wrath, and appeal to him as witness to the inviolability of their faith, when they make a promise or
treaty of peace with enemies.   'Heaven hear us to-day'
is their form of adjuration."[1]

A spiritual being, whose home is heaven, who rides
on the winds, whose wrath is dreaded, who sanctions
the oath, is only called "a demon" by the prejudice of
the worthy father who, at the same time, admits that
the savages have a conception of God—and that God,
so conceived, is this demon !

The debatable question is, was the "demon," or the
actual expanse of sky, first in evolution ?   That cannot precisely be settled, but in the analogous Chinese
case of China we find heaven (Tien) and "Shang-ti, the
personal ruling Deity," corresponding to the Huron
"demon".   Shang-ti, the personal deity, occurs most in
the oldest, pre-Confucian sacred documents, and, so far,
appears to be the earlier conception.   The " demon "
in Huron faith may also be earlier than the religious
regard paid to his home, the sky.[2]   The unborrowed

---

[1] *Relations*, 1636, pp. 106, 107.

[2] See Tylor, *Prim. Cult.*, ii. 352, and *Making of Religion*, p. 318 ; also
Menzies, *History of Religion*, pp. 108, 109, and Dr. Legge's Chinese Classics,
in *Sacred Books of the East*, vols. iii., xxvii., xxviii.

antiquity of a belief in a divine being, creative and
sometimes moral, in North America, is thus demonstrated. So far I had written when I accidentally fell
in with Mr. Tylor's essay on "The Limits of Savage
Religion".[1] In that essay, rather to my surprise, Mr.
Tylor argues for the borrowing of "The Great Spirit,"
"The Great Manitou," from the Jesuits. Now, as to
the phrase, "Great Spirit," the Jesuits doubtless caused
its promulgation, and, where their teaching penetrated,
shreds of their doctrine may have adhered to the
Indian conception of that divine being. But Mr.
Tylor in his essay does not allude to the early
evidence, his own, for Oki, Atahocan, Kiehtan, and
Torngursak, all undeniably prior to Jesuit influence,
and found where Jesuits, later, did not go. As
Mr. Tylor offers no reason for disregarding evidence
in 1892 which he had republished in a new edition of
Primitive Culture in 1891, it is impossible to argue
against him in this place. He went on, in the essay
cited (1892) to contend that the Australian god of
the Kamilaroi of Victoria, Baiame, is, in name and
attributes, of missionary introduction. Happily this
hypothesis can be refuted, as we shew in the following
chapter on Australian gods.

It would be easy enough to meet the hypothesis
of borrowing in the case of the many African
tribes who possess something approaching to a
rude monotheistic conception. Among these are
the Dinkas of the Upper Nile, with their neighbours, whose creed Russegger compares to that of
modern Deists in Europe. The Dinka god, Dendid,

[1] *Journ. of Anthrop. Inst.*, vol. **xxi.**, 1892.

is omnipotent, but so benevolent that he is not addressed in prayer, nor propitiated by sacrifice. Compare the supreme being of the Caribs, beneficent, otiose,
unadored.[1] A similar deity, veiled in the instruction
of the as yet unpenetrated Mysteries, exists among the
Yao of Central Africa.[2] Of the negro race, Waitz
says, "even if we do not call them monotheists, we
may still think of them as standing on the boundary
of monotheism despite their innumerable rude superstitions".[3] The Tshi speaking people of the Gold
Coast have their unworshipped Nyankupon, a now
otiose unadored being, with a magisterial deputy,
worshipped with many sacrifices. The case is almost
an exact parallel to that of Ahone and Oki in America.
These were not borrowed, and the author has argued
at length against Major Ellis's theory of the borrowing
from Christians of Nyankupon.[4]

To conclude this chapter, the study of savage and
barbaric religions seems to yield the following facts:—

1. Low savages. No regular chiefs. Great beings,
not in receipt of sacrifice, sanctioning morality.
Ghosts are not worshipped, though believed in.
Polytheism, departmental gods and gods of heaven,
earth, sky and so forth, have not been developed or
are not found.

2. Barbaric races. Aristocratic or monarchic. Ghosts
are worshipped and receive sacrifice. Polytheistic
gods are in renown and receive sacrifice. There is

---

[1] Rochefort, *Les Isles Antilles*, p. 415. Tylor, ii. 337.

[2] Macdonald, *Africana*, 1, 71, 72, 130, 279-301. Scott, *Dictionary of the
Manganja Language, Making of Religion*, pp. 230-238. A contradictory
view in Spencer, *Ecclesiastical Institutions*, p. 681.

[3] *Anthropologie*, ii. 167.   [4] *Making of Religion*, pp. 243-250.

usually a supreme Maker who is, in some cases, moral, in others otiose. In only one or two known cases (as in that of the Polynesian Taaroa) is he in receipt of sacrifice.

3. Barbaric races. (Zulus, monarchic with Unku-lunkulu ; some Algonquins (feebly aristocratic) with Atahocan). Religion is mainly ancestor worship or vague spirit worship; ghosts are propitiated with food. There are traces of an original divine being whose name is becoming obsolescent and a matter of jest.

4. Early civilisations. Monarchic or aristocratic. (Greece, Egypt, India, Peru, Mexico.) Polytheism. One god tends to be supreme. Religiously regarded, gods are moral; in myth are the reverse. Gods are in receipt of sacrifice. Heavenly society is modelled on that of men, monarchic or aristocratic. Philosophic thought tends towards belief in one pure god, who may be named Zeus, in Greece.

5. The religion of Israel. Probably a revival and purification of the old conception of a moral, bene-ficent creator, whose creed had been involved in sacrifice and anthropomorphic myth.

In all the stages thus roughly sketched, myths of the lowest sort prevail, except in the records of the last stage, where the documents have been edited by earnest monotheists.

If this theory be approximately correct, man's earliest religious ideas may very well have consisted, in a sense, of dependence on a supreme moral being who, when attempts were made by savages to describe the *modus* of his working, became involved in the fancies of mythology. How this belief in such a

being arose we have no evidence to prove. We make
no hint at a *sensus numinis*, or direct revelation.

While offering no hypothesis of the origin of belief
in a moral creator we may present a suggestion. Mr.
Darwin says about early man : " The same high mental
faculties which first led man to believe in unseen
spiritual agencies, then in fetichism, polytheism and
ultimately monotheism, would infallibly lead him, so
long as his reasoning powers remained poorly developed, to various strange superstitions and customs ".[1]
Now, accepting Mr. Darwin's theory that early man
had "high mental faculties," the conception of a
Maker of things does not seem beyond his grasp. Man
himself made plenty of things, and could probably
conceive of a being who made the world and the
objects in it. " Certainly there must be some Being
who made all these things. He must be very good
too," said an Eskimo to a missionary.[2] The goodness
is inferred by the Eskimo from his own contentment
with " the things which are made ".[3]

Another example of barbaric man " seeking after
God " may be adduced.

What the Greenlander said is corroborated by what
a Kaffir said. Kaffir religion is mainly animistic,
ancestral spirits receive food and sacrifice—there is
but an evanescent tradition of a " Lord in Heaven".
Thus a very respectable Kaffir said to M. Ar-
brousset, " your tidings (Christianity) are what I
want ; and I was seeking before I knew you. . . .
I asked myself sorrowful questions. 'Who has,

---

[1] Darwin, *Descent of Man,* i. p. 66.
[2] Cranz, i. 199.   [3] Romans, i. 19.

touched the stars with his hands ? . . . Who makes
the waters flow ? . . . Who can have given earth the
wisdom and power to produce corn ?' Then I buried
my face in my hands."

" This," says Sir John Lubbock, " was, however,
an exceptional case. As a general rule savages do not
set themselves to think out such questions." [1]

As a common fact, if savages never ask the question,
at all events, somehow, they have the answer ready
made. " Mangarrah, or Baiame, Puluga, or Dendid,
or Ahone, or Ahonawilona, or Atahocan, or Taaroa,
or Tui Laga, was the maker." Therefore savages
who know that leave the question alone, or add
mythical accretions. But their ancestors must have
asked the question, like the " very respectable Kaffir "
before they answered it.

Having reached the idea of a Creator, it was not
difficult to add that he was " good," or beneficent,
and was deathless.

A notion of a good powerful Maker, not subject to
death because necessarily prior to Death (who only
invaded the world late), seems easier of attainment
than the notion of Spirit which, *ex hypothesi*, demands
much delicate psychological study and hard thought.
The idea of a Good Maker, once reached, becomes,
perhaps, the germ of future theism, but, as Mr. Darwin
says, the human mind was " infallibly led to various
strange superstitions ". As St. Paul says, in perfect
agreement with Mr. Darwin on this point, " they
became vain in their imaginations, and their foolish
heart was darkened ".

---

[1] *Origin of Civilisation*, p. 201.

Among other imaginations (right or wrong) was the belief in spirits, with all that followed in the way of instituting sacrifices, even of human beings, and of dropping morality, about which the ghost of a deceased medicine-man was not likely to be much interested. The supposed nearness to man, and the venal and partial character of worshipped gods and ghost-gods, would inevitably win for them more service and attention than would be paid to a Maker remote, unbought and impartial. Hence the conception of such a Being would tend to obsolescence, as we see that it does, and would be most obscured where ghosts were most propitiated, as among the Zulus. Later philosophy would attach the spiritual conception to the revived or newly discovered idea of the supreme God.

In all this speculation there is nothing mystical; no supernatural or supernormal interference is postulated. Supernormal experiences may have helped to originate or support the belief in spirits, that, however, is another question. But this hypothesis of the origin of belief in a good unceasing Maker of things is, of course, confessedly a conjecture, for which historical evidence cannot be given, in the nature of the case. All our attempts to discover origins far behind history must be conjectural. Their value must be estimated by the extent to which this or that hypothesis colligates the facts. Now our hypothesis does colligate the facts. It shows how belief in a moral supreme being might arise before ghosts were worshipped, and it accounts for the flaw in the religious strata, for the mythical accretions, for the otiose Creator in the background of many barbaric religions, and for the almost universal absence of sacrifice to the God relatively supreme. He was, from his earliest conception, in no need of gifts from men.

On this matter of otiose supreme gods, Professor Menzies writes, " It is very common to find in savage beliefs a vague far-off god, who is at the back of all the others, takes little part in the management of things, and receives little worship. But it is impossible to judge what that being was at an earlier time ; he may have been a nature god, or a spirit who has by degrees grown faint, and come to occupy this position."

Now the position which he occupies is usually, if not universally, that of the Creator. He could not arrive at this rank by " becoming faint," nor could " a nature-god" be the Maker of Nature. The only way by which we can discover " what that being was at an earlier time" is to see what he *is* at an earlier time, that is to say, what the conception of him is, among men in an earlier state of culture. Among them, as we show, he is very much more near, potent and moral, than among races more advanced in social evolution and material culture. We can form no opinion as to the nature of such " vague, far-off gods, at the back of all the others," till we collect and compare examples, and endeavour to ascertain what points they have in common, and in what points they differ from each other. It then becomes plain that they are least far away, and most potent, where there is least ghostly and polytheistic competition, that is, among the most backward races. The more animism the less

theism, is the general rule. Manifestly the current
hypothesis—that all religion is animistic in origin—
does not account for these facts, and is obliged to fly
to an undemonstrated theory of degradation, or to an
undemonstrated theory of borrowing. That our theory
is inconsistent with the general doctrine of evolution
we cannot admit, if we are allowed to agree with Mr.
Darwin's statement about the high mental faculties
which first led man to sympathetic, and then to wild
beliefs. We do not pretend to be more Darwinian than
Mr. Darwin, who compares "these miserable and in-
direct results of our higher faculties" to "the occasional
mistakes of the instincts of the lower animals ".

The opinion here maintained, namely, that a germ
of pure belief may be detected amidst the confusion
of low savage faith, and that in a still earlier stage
it *may* have been less overlaid with fable, is in direct
contradiction to current theories. It is also in contradiction with the opinions entertained by myself before
I made an independent examination of the evidence.
Like others, I was inclined to regard reports of a
moral Creator, who observes conduct, and judges it
even in the next life, as rumours due either to Christian
influence, or to mistake. I well knew, however, and
could, and did, discount the sources of error. I was
on my guard against the twin fallacies of describing
all savage religion as " devil worship," and of expecting to find a primitive " divine tradition ". I was also
on my guard against the modern bias derived from
the " ghost-theory," and Mr. Spencer's works, and I
kept an eye on opportunities of " borrowing ".[1] I had,

―――――――――

[1] *Making of Religion*, p. 187.

in fact, classified all known *idola* in the first edition
of this work, such as the fallacy of leading questions
and the chance of deliberate deception. I sought the
earliest evidence, prior to any missionary teaching, and
the evidence of what the first missionaries found, in
the way of belief, on their arrival. I preferred the
testimony of the best educated observers, and of those
most familiar with native languages. I sought for
evidence in native hymns (Maori, Zuñi, Dinka, Red
Indian) and in native ceremonial and mystery, as
these sources were least likely to be contaminated.

On the other side, I found a vast body of testimony
that savages had no religion at all. But that testimony, *en masse*, was refuted by Roskoff, and also, in
places, by Tylor. When three witnesses were brought
to swear that they saw the Irishman commit a crime,
he offered to bring a dozen witnesses who did *not* see
him. Negative evidence of squatters, sailors and
colonists, who did *not* see any religion among this
or that race, is not worth much against evidence of
trained observers and linguists who *did* find what the
others missed, and who found more the more they
knew the tribe in question. Again, like others, I
thought savages incapable of such relatively pure
ideas as I now believe some of them to possess. But
I could not resist the evidence, and I abandoned my
a priori notions. The evidence forcibly attests grada-
tions in the central belief. It is found in various
shades, from relative potency down to a vanishing
trace, and it is found in significant proportion to the
prevalence of animistic ideas, being weakest where
they are most developed, strongest where they are

least developed. There must be a reason for these phenomena, and that reason, as it seems to me, is the overlaying and supersession of a rudely Theistic by an animistic creed. That one cause would explain, and does colligate, all the facts.

There remains a point on which misconception proves to be possible. It will be shown, contrary to the current hypothesis, that the religion of the lowest races, in its highest form, sanctions morality. That morality, again, in certain instances, demands unselfishness. Of course we are not claiming for that doctrine any supernatural origin. Religion, if it sanctions ethics at all, will sanction those which the conscience accepts, and those ethics, in one way or other, must have been evolved. That the " cosmical " law is "the weakest must go to the wall " is generally conceded. Man, however, is found trying to reverse the law, by equal and friendly dealing (at least within what is vaguely called " the tribe "). His religion, as in Australia, will be shown to insist on this unselfishness. How did he evolve his ethics ?

" Be it little or be it much they get," says Dampier about the Australians in 1688, " every one has his part, as well the young and tender as the old and feeble, who are not able to get abroad as the strong and lusty." This conduct reverses the cosmical process, and notoriously civilised society, Christian society, does not act on these principles. Neither do the savages, who knock the old and feeble on the head, or deliberately leave them to starve, act on these principles, sanctioned by Australian religion, but (according to Mr. Dawson) *not* carried out in Australian practice. " When old people become infirm . . . it is lawful and customary to kill them." [1]

As to the point of unselfishness, evolutionists are apt to account for it by common interest. A tribe in which the strongest monopolise what is best will not survive so well as an unselfish tribe in the struggle for existence. But precisely the opposite is true, aristocracy marks the more successful barbaric races, and an aristocratic slave-holding tribe could have swept Australia as the Zulus swept South Africa. That aristocracy and acquisition of separate property are steps in advance on communistic savagery all history declares. Therefore a tribe which in Australia developed private property, and reduced its neighbours to slavery, would have been better fitted to survive than such a tribe as Dampier describes.

This is so evident that probably, or possibly, the Dampier state of society was not developed in obedience to a recognised tribal interest, but in obedience to an affectionate instinct. "Ils s'entr' aiment les une les autres," says Brébeuf of the Hurons.[2] "I never heard the women complain of being left out of feasts, or that the men ate the best portions . . . every one does his business sweetly, peaceably, without dispute. You never see disputes, quarrels, hatred, or reproach among them." Brébeuf then tells how a young Indian stranger, in a time of want, stole the best part of a moose. "They did not rage or curse, they only bantered him, and yet to take our meat was almost to take our lives." Brébeuf wanted to lecture the lad; his Indian host bade him hold his peace, and the

---

[1] *Australian Aborigines*, p. 62.   [2] *Relations*, 1634, p. 29.

stranger was given hospitality, with his wife and
children. "They are very generous, and make it a
point not to attach themselves to the goods of this
world." "Their greatest reproach is 'that man wants
everything, he is greedy'. They support, with never a
murmur, widows, orphans and old men, yet they kill
hopeless or troublesome invalids, and their whole
conduct to Europeans was the reverse of their
domestic behaviour.

Another example of savage unselfish ethics may be
found in Mr. Mann's account of the Andaman Islanders,
a nomad race, very low in culture. "It is a noteworthy trait, and one which deserves high commenda-
tion, that every care and consideration are paid by all
classes to the very young, the weak, the aged, and the
helpless, and these being made special objects of interest and attention, invariably fare better in regard
to the comforts and necessaries of daily life than any
of the otherwise more fortunate members of the community."[1]

Mr. Huxley, in his celebrated Romanes Lecture on
"Evolution and Morality," laid stress on man's contra-
vention of the cosmic law, "the weakest must go to
the wall". He did not explain the evolution of man's
opposition to this law. The ordinary evolutionist
hypothesis, that the tribe would prosper most whose
members were least self-seeking, is contradicted by all
history. The overbearing, "grabbing," aristocratic,
individualistic, unscrupulous races beat the others out
of the field. Mr. Huxley, indeed, alleged that the
"influence of the cosmic process in the evolution of

society is the greater the more rudimentary its civilisation. Social progress means a checking of the cosmic process at every step and the substitution for it of another, which may be called the ethical process. . . . As civilisation has advanced, so has the extent of this interference increased. . . ."[1] But where, in Europe, is the interference so marked as among the Andamanese? We have still to face the problem of the generosity of low savages.

It is conceivable that the higher ethics of low savages rather reflect their emotional instincts than arise from tribal legislation which is supposed to enable a "tribe" to prosper in the struggle for existence. As Brébeuf and Dampier, among others, prove, savages often set a good example to Christians, and their ethics are, in certain cases, as among the Andamanese and Fuegians, and, probably among the Yao, sanctioned by their religion. But, as Mr. Tylor says, "the better savage social life seems but in unstable equilibrium, liable to be easily upset by a touch of distress, temptation, or violence".[2] Still, religion does its best, in certain cases, to lend equilibrium; though all the world over, religion often fails in practice.

[1] *Ethics of Evolution*, pp. 81-84.   [2] *Prim. Cult.*, i. 51.

END OF VOL. I.